PARANGOLÉ
a journal about
the urbanised planet

PARANGOLÉ is an emerging annual journal that explores ideas on urbanization, design, and architecture with contributions from around the world on topics of mobility, migration, fluidity, multiplicity, reflexivity, uncertainty, immersion, hybridization, diaspora, control, privatization, and heterotopia. The journal title pays homage to the work of Brazilian artist HÉLIO OITICICA and extends the central tenet of 'life as movement' as the body dances with the city.

PARANGOLÉ was created by ALFREDO BRILLEMBOURG/ URBAN-THINK TANK, produced by GRAN HORIZONTE MEDIA and distributed worldwide by HATJE CANTZ VERLAG GMBH. The inaugural issue, MOTHERLAND, is guest-edited by SYNNE BERGBY and IDA ZELINE LIEN (URBAN-A), in collaboration with U-TT TEAM: Associate editor ALEXIS KALAGAS (ETH-Z), designers FACUNDO ARBOIT and IRHANA ŠEHOVIĆ. The journal is available at select bookshops worldwide. For an overview of recent publications by Gran Horizonte Media/ Urban Think Tank, view:
http://u-tt.com/publications/
www.parangoleweb.com

Subscribe now by emailing:
info@parangoleweb.com
urbanthinktank@mac.com

FOR EVERY COPY SOLD OF THIS ISSUE,
WE'RE DONATING TO THE SUSTAINABLE
LIVING URBAN LAB (SLUM LAB)

THIS JOURNAL was made possible through the collaboration with and support of the GLOBAL RESEARCH PROGRAMME ON INEQUALITY (GRIP). The Programme is a collaboration between the University of Bergen (UiB) and the International Science Council (ISC) working to foster co-production of knowledge on the multiple dimensions of inequality.
www.gripinequality.org

Designed by
Córdova Canillas

Copyright © 2021 Gran Horizonte
Media GmbH, Zurich, and authors.

All rights reserved.

Copyright © 2021
Hatje Cantz Verlag, Berlin

MOTHERLAND ISSUE N°1

2010 - 2019
A Decade of Displacement

We are witnessing a changed reality in that forced displacement nowadays is not only vastly more widespread but is simply no longer a short-term and temporary phenomenon.

Filippo Grandi
UN High Commissioner for Refugees

ASYLUM SEEKER: Someone whose request for sanctuary has yet to be processed.

INTERNALLY DISPLACED PERSON (IDP): Any person who have been forced or obliged to flee or to leave their homes or places of habitual residence, in particular as a result of or in order to avoid the effects of armed conflict, situations of generalized violence, violations of human rights or natural or human-made disasters, and who have not crossed an internationally recognized State border.

REFUGEE: any person who owing to well-founded fear of being persecuted for reasons of race, religion, nationality, membership of a particular social group or political opinion, is outside the country of his nationality and is unable or, owing to such fear, is unwilling to avail himself of the protection of that country; or who, not having a nationality and being outside the country of his former habitual residence as a result of such events, is unable or, owing to such fear, is unwilling to return to it.

Figures at a Glance

79.5 MILION
Forcibly displaced people worldwide at the end of 2019

1%

Of the world's population is displaced

80%

Of the world's displaced people are in countries or territories affected by acute food insecurity and malnutrition

73%

Hosted in neighbouring countries

68%

Came from just 5 countries

40%

Of the world's displaced people are children

85%

Hosted in devoloping countries

4.2M

Stateless People

2M

Asylum applications (in 2019)

107,800

Resettled to 26 countries (in 2019)

5.6M

Returnees (in 2019)

Source: UNHCR / displacement data December 2019

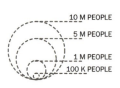

DISPLACEMENT 2019 (UNHCR)

- TOTAL POPULATION OF CONCERN
- IDPs OF CONCERN TO UNHCR, INCL. PEOPLE IN IDP-LIKE SITUATIONS
- ASYLUM-SEEKERS (PENDING CASES)
- TOTAL REFUGEES AND PEOPLE IN REFUGEE-LIKE SITUATIONS

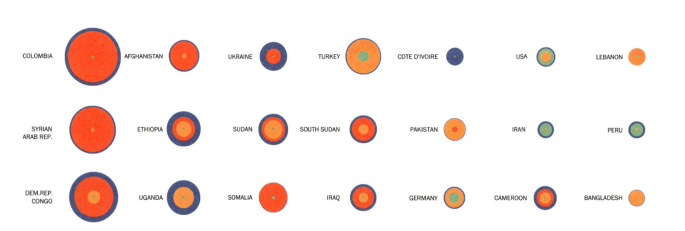

DATA

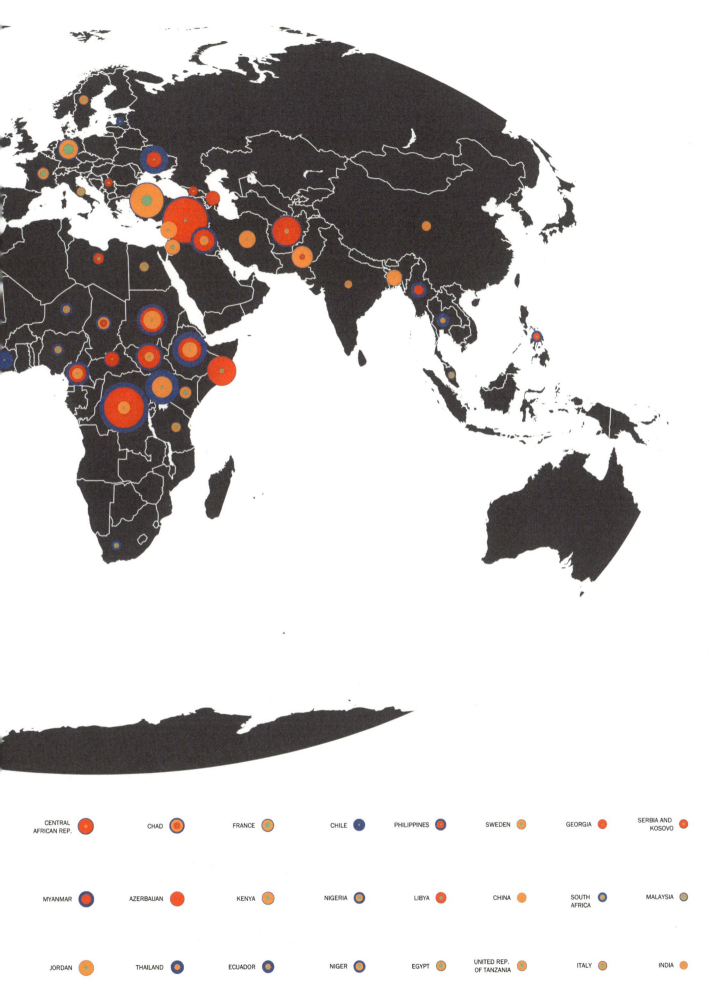

MIGRANTS: To address the lack of a universally accepted definition for "migrant", IOM defines a migrant as a person who moves away from his or her place of usual residence, whether within a country or across an international border, temporarily or permanently, and for a variety of reasons. The term includes a number of well-defined legal categories of people, such as migrant workers; persons whose particular types of movements are legally-defined, such as smuggled migrants; as well as those whose status or means of movement are not specifically defined under international law, such as international students.

271.6 MILLION (MID-2019)

DATA

Venezuela-Colombia border crossing. © George Castellanos (2018)

P. 14
THE "MOTHERLAND" ISSUE

by Alfredo Brillembourg (U-TT)

P. 16
INTRODUCTION

by Ida Zeline Lien and Synne Bergby (Urban-A)

PREAMBLE

P. 24
COVID-19 AND THE CONTAINMENT CRISIS:
IMPLICATIONS FOR AFRICAN URBANISATION,
MOBILITY AND RESILIENCE

by Caroline Wanjiku Kihato and Loren B Landau

P. 28
NEWS FROM CAPE TOWN, SOUTH AFRICA

by Mandisi di Sindo

P. 32
VENEZUELANS ON THE MOVE
FIRST PORT OF CALL: COLOMBIA

by Milena Gomez Kopp

P. 34
A LONG WAY HOME

by Sergey Ponomarev

PART ONE:
FLUID PERMANENCE

P. 52
CONFLICT URBANISM: COLOMBIA

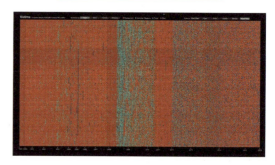

by Juan Francisco Saldarriaga

P. 58
THE COLOMBIAN GOVERNMENT'S RESPONSE
TO IMMIGRATION FROM VENEZUELA

by Wooldy Edson Louidor

P. 62
CAMPS: AN INTERVIEW WITH CHARLIE HAILEY

by Michael Waldrep

P. 68
DEPARTURE CITY: THE DIASPORA AS URBAN DEVELOPER

by Kai Vöckler & Jonas König

P. 76
GOMA, CITY OF REFUGE

by Karen Büscher

P. 82
RETURN, REMAINING AND REMAKING: URBAN SPACE IN POST-CONFLICT TRANSITION

by Naseem Badiey & Christian Doll

P. 86
LETTER FROM MAPUTO: MIGRATION, AMBULATION AND URBAN RECONFIGURATION

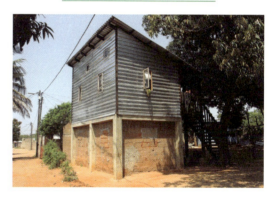

by Bjørn Enge Bertelsen

P. 94
EMERGENCY URBANISM AND ARCHITECTURES OF PRECARITY IN SABRA, BEIRUT

by Are John Knudsen

P. 100
SHATILA: THE ISLAND OF (IN)STABILITY

by Bjørnar Haveland

P. 104
FORCED MIGRATION AND LIVING BETWEEN CITIES:
YOUNG SYRIAN ADULTS IN BEIRUT

by Lucas Oesch

P. 108
THE BATTLE FOR HOME:
AN INTERVIEW WITH MARWA AL-SABOUNI

Interview by Alexis Kalagas

PART TWO:
RESEARCH TO DESIGN

P. 116
HOUSING TOOLBOX FOR TRANSPORTABLE ARCHITECTURE

by Urban- Think Tank

P. 124
SOCIAL FURNITURE

by EOOS

P. 132
BORDER MATERIALITIES

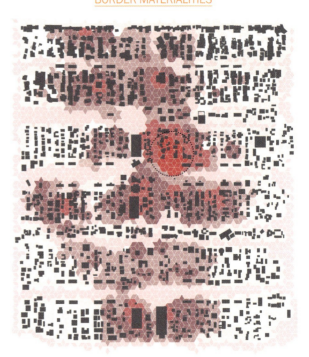

by studio critics Sheffield University,
Nishat Awan and Aya Musmar

P. 140
THE RESTLESS EARTH

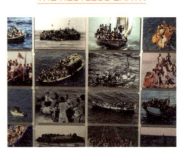

by Fondazione Nicola Trussardi

PART THREE:
STATE CONTROL

P. 138
THE EPHEMERAL THRESHOLDS OF EUROPE

by Irit Katz

P. 156
INTERWOVEN SOVEREIGNTY

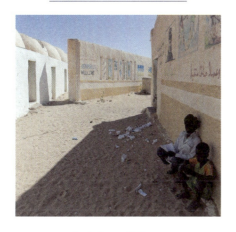

by Manuel Herz

P. 166
THE BORDER FENCES OF CEUTA AND MELILLA

by Xavier Ribas

P. 146
THE NATION AGAINST NATURE: A REPORT FROM SAN DIEGO, TIJUANA

by Teddy Cruz + Fonna Forman

P. 200
STORIES OF DISPLACEMENT FROM ISRAEL AND PALESTINA

by Urban-Think Tank

P. 246
UNDOCUMENTED: THE ARCHITECTURE OF MIGRANT DETENTION

by Tings Chak

"Motherland issue"

Caracas 2003. © Andre Cypriano

We want to understand the conditions of the space of habitation at the heart of the argument for finding a home or adopting a new Motherland.

271.6 migrants
20.4 million refugees
5.6 million Palestine refugees
45.7 million internally displaced people
4.2 million asylum-seekers
3.6 million Venezuelans displaced abroad

IOM (MID-2019) / UNHCR (DECEMBER 2019)

EDITORIAL

THIS first issue of Parangolé titled "Motherland" is concerned with people living in emergency shelters, camps, informal settlements, and those facing future economic hardship, conflict and violence. People on the move are facing specific challenges and vulnerabilities that must be identified and taken into consideration in urban planning and response. We are living in a moment of change, in which we notice the rise of a discussion around design on a local, micro scale and systems-level. This calls for contextualized and adaptive interventions to respond to specific situations. While this journal is being prepared for print, the COVID-19 pandemic engulfs the world, Black Lives Matter protests intensifies, and terrorist attacks continue. With Motherland we bring together researchers and practitioners, aiming to inspire collective efforts in thinking about and interacting with these issues, using a spatial lens.

Editor in Chief
Alfredo Brillembourg (U-TT),
urbanthinktank@mac.com

Alfredo Brillembourg is the founder and editor of Parangolé journal, and co-founder of the interdisciplinary architecture firm Urban-Think Tank (U-TT).

PARANGOLÉ was conceived as a way of initiating an international dialogue between researchers, practitioners, and the readers, where we are committed to present articles that share a critical view of the world. For this edition, Urban- Think Tank (U-TT) has teamed up with Urban-A as guest editors and together we have packed this inaugural issue with reporting from across the world.

In short, this *Motherland* issue aims to understand and engage with displacement and migration in an urban setting using three lenses:

— FOR HUMANITARIANS, *Motherland* demonstrates how overlapping and complex urban conditions create, reinforce or contribute to issues of displacement and migration;
— FOR THEORETICIANS, *Motherland* serves as a critical lens for understanding how complex issues of displacement and migration are impacted by spatial configurations and the notion of "identity of home";
— FOR THE ARCHITECT, *Motherland* shows how underlying and complex realities driving displacement and migration can inform good design solutions.

Flexibility is the common ground for the critical voices that are represented in *Motherland*; a model of organic development that challenges traditional planning. The world is moving toward a more fluid order, despite increasingly stricter measures being enforced by nation states. As a social and political manifestation of that trend, *Motherland* can be seen as a phenomenon of considerable breadth explaining the culture of the built environment. We want to understand the conditions of the space of habitation at the heart of the argument for finding a home or adopting a new *Motherland*.

Finally, this issue aims to establish new arguments and understandings of migration and displacement. Why? Well, for anyone who understands the notion of the "other" and of being uprooted, then you will understand my own Venezuelan condition and that migration is a complex issue, even for those of us who carry almost two decades of living as "the outsider" as a consequence of a world in a messy political and social flux. On the journey through this journal the Venezuelan exodus will resonate with other stories. In the end, it is about living between borders. When I was still based in Caracas, I wrote what we now called the «No Manifesto». I was angry, disappointed, maybe even disillusioned with Venezuela. The political and social conditions in Venezuela were intolerable, and we called for resistance and change through our own actions and by our colleagues. We embraced the notion of the architect-activist, but everywhere we saw obstacles that impeded transformation and progress.

Venezuela is a country with a complicated perspective. Now, conditions in Caracas are worse than ever, as illustrated by the over 10,000,000 percent inflation rate. There are two paths Venezuela can go down: one, an optimistic path of political transition with economic stability; the other, a more realistic path of total collapse and dysfunction. The speed and intensity of Venezuelans' departures to other countries in the region have overflowed the response capacity of states and institutions, as of society in general. We do not have the official numbers of how many Venezuelans cross the border. How many come and go, staying for the time allowed doing some work that provides income to bring to their families or to send money home? How many have crossed the border to settle in destinations that only offer precarious living conditions, with irregular or temporary shelter? There are many difficulties with acquiring reliable data, and it is almost impossible to respond to the requirements of timely and relevant statistics.

I believe that architects and social scientists must engage in the politics of urban space to remain relevant in addressing some of the most pressing global issues of our time. There is a tremendous amount of work to be done and as yet no broad consensus on how to shape the future of displacement and refugees. Even if I have moved, in practice and in principle, from the margins of Caracas to the centre of the world, I take the lessons of Caracas with me; Caracas is everywhere, and we all are global architects.

Introduction

Guest Editors
Ida Zeline Lien and Synne Bergby, Urban-A

Refugees and migrants disembark to the port of Thessaloniki after being transferred from the refugee camp of Moria, Lesvos island 2019 © Ververidis Vasilis / Shutterstock.com

Dear Readers,

IN a time dominated by news on COVID-19, the closure of arrival ports in countries such as Italy and Malta, the burning of Moria Refugee Camp in Lesvos due to imposed quarantines, and strict lockdown measures in the world largest refugee camp in Cox Bazar, are examples of how the crisis is affecting refugees and migrants on the move. While the pandemic makes evident the connectivity and fluidity of the world and our mutual dependencies, we are also being subjected to increased protection measures in the fight against the virus. We are in effect shutting down and shutting out others. Those who are living in precarious or temporary situations are being disproportionally affected and require even greater attention in these uncertain times.

Ida Zeline Lien and Synne Bergby are the founders of Urban-A, a company that brings together an interdisciplinary team of experts within the fields of humanitarian response and urban development.

After the fire in Moria Camp September 2020 © Dråpen i Havet

Economic, political, and security considerations represent often overlapping motivations for leaving home. People are moving in anticipation or because of violence, environmental disasters, economic collapse, frequently due to protracted conflict and instability. The scale and nature of migration and displacement today is growing, taking on an increasingly urban dimension.

In the face of crisis people have relocated, either voluntarily or by force, throughout time. Either to seek refuge or to find a better life away from home. Economic, political, and security considerations represent often overlapping motivations for leaving home. People are moving in anticipation or because of violence, environmental disasters, economic collapse, frequently due to protracted conflict and instability. The scale and nature of migration and displacement today is growing, taking on an increasingly urban dimension. A large share of movement across borders is to neighbouring countries or countries in the same region. Current estimates suggest that there are 272 million international migrants globally, with more people migrating to other countries than ever before. Global displacement is at a record high with more than 41 million internally displaced and close to 26 million refugees.

This inaugural "Motherland" issue of the new Parangolé journal presents research, reporting, photojournalism, and design interventions that identify and explore some of the many forms transitory and permanent conditions of migration and displacement take. The contributions, developed over recent years, serves as points of departure to investigate the complex and interlinked issues linked to migration and displacement.

The journal is divided in two. The articles in Part I discusses the Fluid – Permanence dimension of movement; the various ways migration and displacement take form and contribute to shaping urban landscapes across the world. The articles in Part II discusses State Control; how cross-border movement of people is governed and controlled by authorities. Between Part I and Part II, the From Research to Design section gives examples of how we can engage with some of these issues through evidence-based design.

Preamble

How will COVID-19 change the state of the world? In the opening article of the journal, Caroline Wanjiku Kihato and Loren B. Landau explain how the COVID-19 crisis is intrinsically linked with mobility and governance. The article looks at the consequences of the response measures in Africa and Europe, and how increasingly authoritarian societies are starting to close their borders. Kihato and Landau point to the impossible troika of choices for urban Africans relying on daily wages: violence, virus, or starvation. They argue that while the measures might contribute to flattening the curve in the short-term, attention should be given to the longer-term effects on the most vulnerable, including how the COVID-19 crackdowns will impact community resilience, increase social fragmentation, and further stigmatize poverty. On a local level, Mandisi Disi Sindo gives us an update on how the community's shack theatre is playing a central role in responding to COVID-19 in "News from Cape Town."

Next, Milena Gomez Kopp takes us to Venezuela – a country which is currently experiencing the second largest exodus of migrants and refugees in the world. The situation, which is described as an economic and political crisis, is expected to further deteriorate as a result of the downturn in oil prices, political instability, and COVID-19. To better understand the current situation, Gomez Kopp explains how political and economic factors have shifted the power dynamics between Venezuela and Columbia over the years, and as such have been key drivers of displacement and migration movements between the two countries.

The following photo essay "A Long Way Home" by Sergey Ponomarev, is an excerpt of his personal photobook inspired by the refugees he followed along their journeys to and through Europe. The powerful imageries give us a moment to pause and reflect on the harsh realities faced by many people on the move today.

Part I: Fluid-Permanence

The articles in Part I give us ways to start thinking about and engaging with a range of displacement, migration, and patterns of movement. From different vantage points, the authors show the range and multitude of lived and shared experiences that migration and displacement constitute, providing a more nuanced understanding as a foundation for action. As you read the articles, the spectrum of Fluid – Permanence starts to emerge. Movement may differ in quite a few respects but what unites the experiences of being on the move is the fragility, temporariness, vulnerability, and inclination to constant change. The articles engage with the lived experiences of movement, the result it produces in the places left behind, and the places people pass through and arrive at. The physical expressions span from self-organised to aided organisation of structures and spaces.

Visualisation and analysis of data are powerful tools to uncover dynamics and interlinked factors of displacement. In his article, Juan Francisco Saldarriaga gives us an insight into

Rohingya refugees playing with their kite in Cox Bazar, 2019 © UN Inter Sector Coordination Group CXB

how Columbia University, in collaboration with Universidad de Los Andes, use spatial and temporal patterns of war to inform urban governance. Complimenting this is Wooldy Edson Louidor's account of the complex legal and governance framework for Venezuelan migrants in Colombia, and the consequences for both the migrants and host communities.

How can we think about camps as a physical manifestation of the Fluid – Permanence spectrum of movement? In his interview with Waldrep, Hailey presents the powerful idea that camps accommodate conditions that might otherwise remain without space and indicate change at its earliest stages. This, whether the camp is used as an autonomous settlement in California, or by refugees in Da'daab.

The impact of migration is not, however, only felt in the places where people go to, but also the places that are left behind. In their article, Kai Vöckler and Jonas König gives us a thought-provoking explanation of how forced migration can impact "departure cities", using the case of post-war Prishtina.

The following two articles take us to Goma, DRC, and to Juba, South-Sudan. These two accounts, by Karen Büscher, and Naseem Baidey and Christian Doll respectively, describe how the arrival of large numbers of internally displaced persons (IDPs) and refugees have shaped the growth and urban development patterns in the two cities. In her article on Goma, Büscher suggests how the influx of IDPs as a result of protracted regional violence have generated new forms of urbanism, while Baidey and Doll describe how returnees have been a driving force for the rapid urban transformation of Juba. The authors call attention to the often-invisible ways returning ex-combatants, refugees and internally displaced people have remade urban spaces, and the need to recognise this in any formal urban planning efforts.

Barrio Polana Caniço serves as an interesting example of how youth organise themselves in Teams as an act of resilience in the face rapid urbanisation. The account is from the impoverished neighbourhoods in Maputo, Mozambique. In his article, Bjørn Enge Bertelsen gives us an insider's view of "Teams" and how they defend various egalitarian ideals.

The final four articles in Part I of Motherland take us to the Middle East, with attention to the effects of the conflict in Syria and the protracted displacement from Palestine. In his article, Are John Knudsen describes the living situation in the ramshackle buildings that were once the Gaza-Ramallah Hospital in Beirut. Depicted by Knudsen as a vertical migration history of people escaping conflict, displacement and destitution, these buildings represent emergency urbanism, shaped by generations of displaced persons. Knudsen's article is complimented by Bjørnar Haveland's description and illustration of an imaginary aid project located in Shatila refugee camp in Beirut, which brings into question the roles of western aid, NGOs and researchers. Focusing on the many Syrians who fled their home country, Lucas Oeasch gives an account of the life of some of the Syrian refugees in Beirut. Through a description of the less visible impact of forced migrants on the city, and of the city on forced mi-

Informal Settlements, Kabul, Afghanistan, 2016. © Urban-A / Ida Zeline Lien

grants, the article challenges the predominant but singular attention on the physical expressions of the refugee crisis.

Marwa al-Sabouni offers us an eyewitness account from Syria and describes how the conflict continues to impact everyday life of people who remain in Syria today. Through an in-depth conversation with Alexis Kalagas, Al-Sabouni explains the role of architecture and urban planning in the lead-up and during the war in Syria, arguing that architecture further exacerbated a process of social segregation.

Part II:
From Research to Design

The contributions in Part I demonstrates the fluidity and multiplicity of factors characterising migration and displacement. Given this complexity, how can we start to engage with issues linked to migration and displacement? Is it possible to create evidence-based design and develop physical structures informed by a nuanced understanding of general as well as place-specific factors? The design examples in Motherland suggest that it indeed is. Three design projects are showcased in this section, each providing sensitive and contextualised approaches and solutions that consider the temporality as well as the diverse needs of migrants and displaced persons.

Urban-Think Tank (U-TT) presents four examples of design based on their urban toolbox of "lightweight transportable architecture". Unlike many design projects, these examples highlight the need to shift focus from form-driven to purpose oriented architecture responsive to the spectre and nature of migration and displacement. The projects build upon ideas of modular construction, community capacity building, rapid and incremental upgrading, and quick, prefabricated assembly and disassembly methods, creating something that is temporary in character but with the potential to become permanent. In addition to the Migrant Housing project in Hungary developed to temporarily house migrants arriving to Europe, the examples include flexible market buildings / playgrounds in Barcelona, a homeless shelter in San Francisco, and Social housing in South Africa.

The 'Social Furniture' project, developed by EOOS, show how design can be used to respond to the increased flow of refugees into Europe. The 18 pieces of furniture are guided by a 20-point Social Furniture Manifesto, which should be read as a blueprint for designing furniture with a purpose – beyond furniture as fashion and status items.

Finally, The Border Materialities design studio for the MA in Architectural Design at University of Sheffield gives an insight into cutting-edge learning from engaging with spatial, social, and economic relations within a camp setting. Working on the Za'atri refugee camp in Jordan, near the Syrian border, two groups of students share their work with us, explaining how they apply scenario games and parametric modelling to explore and inform design solutions.

Part III:
State control

Faced with large numbers of refugees, internally displaced

Destroyed buildings after the 4 August 2020 explosion in Beirut © Urban-A/Synne Bergby

persons, and migrants, authorities across the world apply a range of measures to manage and control movement. The articles in the second part of Motherland draw attention to some of the ways in which state control is used to regulate, suppress, divert, redirect, steer or in other ways manage movement flows through physical and spatial measures. Through the readings, an impression of how these physical manifestations of control as oftentimes violent and intrusive structures, emerges. Yet, the articles also describe how these control measures can produce surprising, unexpected and, at times, counterproductive results.

Opening Part II on State control, Irit Katz suggests how makeshift and institutionalised camp spaces represent the shifting forces of migratory movement as they encounter systems and architecture of control. With the recent reporting on the Paris police's brutal removal of migrant camps in mind, Katz provides us with new insight into how one such makeshift camp, the 'Jungle' camp in Calais, was developed and functioned before it was demolished by French authorities.

In his article, Manual Herz takes us to the Sahrawi Arab Democratic Republic in Western Sahara. Using this first-hand account of what a novel type of statehood can look like, Herz calls for a re-examination of how we come to understand and define sovereignty and statehood.

Illustrating the physical expression of state control on landscapes, Xavier Ribas takes us on a photographic journey along the borders of Ceuta and Melilla, two Spanish enclaves on the Northern coast of North Africa, visualizing and contextualising the historical and political ramifications of these architectures of control.

Teddy Cruz and Fonna Forman challenge our thinking around the Mexico-US borderwall construction and its impact. In their article, they argue that Trump's borderwall is an artefact of environmental, social, and economic insecurity, directing attention to the severe environmental consequences of the wall. In response, they propose a reimagination of exclusionary borders, applying the logics of bioregional systems and social ecologies. The Teeter-totter as activism, by Ronald Rael, illustrated on the following page, shows a moment of connection between the two sides of the US-Mexico wall. The stunt went viral as a powerful example of how one can start to disempower the wall as a symbol of violence and oppression.

The last section of State Control consists of two longer contributions. First, Urban-Think Tank (U-TT) takes us to Israel and Palestine, presenting excerpts from a condensed travelogue that documents the histories and lived experiences of people in this region. The stories portray environments and communities clearly marked by the political violence. This requires an alternative strategy for resistance and working towards creating change from the ground-up. Second, the excerpt from Tings Chak's graphic novel takes us to Canada. Through a description of the architecture of migrant detention, Chak gives us a forceful and visual account of lived experiences for those who are in the space between leaving and arriving.

MOTHERLAND (NOUN)   1: A country regarded as a place of origin (as of an idea or a movement).   2: THE country of one's parents or ancestors.   3: A country that is the origin of something.
MOTH• ER• LAND |

23

COVID-19 and the containment crisis: Implications for African urbanisation, mobility and resilience

© Mandisi Disi Sindo

Dr. Caroline Wanjiku Kihato is a Visiting Researcher at The African Centre for Migration & Society (ACMS) at the University of the Witwatersrand, Johannesburg, and a Visiting Fellow at University of Oxford's Department of International Development. Her career has involved both teaching and conducting research in the academic and the non-profit sector in Southern and Eastern Africa, with focus on how marginalised populations access urban markets, and the ways planning and policy regimes support or frustrate these efforts. She explores how these processes intersect with gender, migration and informality, and has a keen interest in developing more inclusive productive spaces for the urban poor in the global south.

Loren B. Landau is a Professor of Migration and Development at the University of Oxford and Research Associate with the African Centre for Migration & Society (ACMS) at the University of the Witwatersrand, Johannesburg. His interdisciplinary scholarship explores mobility, multi-scale governance, and the transformation of socio-political communities across the global south. Along with continued work on xenophobia, inclusion, and representation, he currently oversees a multi-year initiative exploring mobility, temporality, and urban politics in Ghana, Kenya, and South Africa.

HOW is COVID-19 challenging governance in Africa and Europe? With the pandemic and corresponding measures, people's lives have been thrown into turmoil. In their article, Caroline Wanjiku Kihato and Loren B. Landau suggest that the COVID-19 lockdowns and limitations of movement will impact African cities and affect unproportionally the poorest communities, long after the virus is controlled.

by
Caroline Wanjiku Kihato and Loren B Landau

Over the past four years, restricting African mobility has been more important to European and global policy making than at any time since Hannibal crossed the Alps with his war elephants. As the world reels from the impact of the novel corona virus, these restrictions are likely to intensify in both the short and long-term. Through an unfortunate alignment of interests, European destination countries and African states are ever more likely to institute unprecedented lock-downs on local and global movements. To be sure, curbing peoples' mobility is essential in the short-term, especially in dense urban areas where people's circulation can be catastrophic for public health. But authorities are already mobilizing the pandemic to clamp down on people's future movements.

Where migration is inextricable from people's physical survival and livelihoods, doing this undermines the resilience of some of the poorest communities who rely on remittances for necessities: food, shelter, health and education. While few governments were prepared for the pandemic, the violence used to contain populations in some African cities, erodes rather than builds people's trust in their government's ability to address their immediate concerns. It will further undermine future efforts to build productive and inclusive communities. Crisis represents a potential political rupture, and opportunity to realign institutions and relationships. We can collectively lean towards autocracy and coercion or to strengthening collective action and the social contract. Without a substantial shift in current discourse and practice, the latter is far more likely.

Even before the COVID-19-crisis, the European Union was driving Africa's reterritorialization[1]: strengthening border controls[2], limiting movement within and out of the continent, and pressuring states to promote development at 'home'. Out of fear that movements to cities or neighbouring countries might catalyse journeys to Europe, the goal was to supress mobility in all forms: not just international migration, but seasonal labour migration and urbanisation. The idea, as an agreement hashed out at a 2018 EU-Africa summit in Brussels put it, is to generate "substantial socio-economic transformation"[3] so people no longer want to leave for a better life.

In Africa, policy makers have long been ambiguous about African mobility. Leaders tentatively forward plans to facilitate domestic and regional migration and mobility while simultaneously introducing restrictions for foreigners hoping to establish business or residences. In cities, urban planning often continues as if there is not a youthful, continent-wide generation whose movements to, within, and between cities reflects their only real hope of sustaining themselves and their families. Perhaps more accurately, planning continues in ways informed by Malthusian fears[4] of how those young people's presence might undermine political and economic hierarchies. Billions of Euros in aid money intended to control and contain has only heightened a reluctance to accept mobility as natural and essential part of people's lives.

Cities will increasingly be the locus of efforts to police and produce sedentary urban subjects, not only in the short-term but in times long after this crisis. With containment now becoming a public health virtue, the pandemic has given governments extraordinary license to both evict[5], lock-down and control the movement of urban communities. Domestically, the perennial assault on the urban poor is likely to take on new severity. South Africa, ostensibly one of the continent's most progressive states, has already begun implementing plans to 'thin' informal settlement residents in the name of health[6]. Violent stay at home orders[7] in Rwanda[8], South Africa[9], Kenya[10], Ghana[11] and elsewhere have seen state security agents shoot[12] dead and publicly flog people caught in the wrong place. Indeed across Africa, COVID-19 only exposes the frailty of basic infrastructure, public welfare systems and the coercive inclinations of its militaries. Yet the enforcement of curfews and lockdowns disproportionately disadvantages poor communities, where movement is essential to accessing even the most basic services like water and toilets. Many of those living in African cities rely on daily wages. For them, COVID-19 crackdowns present an impossible troika of choices: violence, virus or starvation.

Measures to contain the pandemic also reveal the acute assault on urban residents' economic futures. In a world where economies are spatially concentrated, in regions where families rely on migrant workers, and where individuals' livelihood relies on mobility, curtailing movement becomes a geographic and temporal entrapment. Doing so may flatten the curve but it may undermine communities' long-term resilience, foster social fragmentation, and further stigmatise poverty through a newly reborn 'sanitation syndrome'.[13] Given this context, the pandemic only heightens possibilities of socio-political rupture in the continent's cities.

The European Unions' containment efforts include promoting inclusive and equitable economic growth in Africa through vocational education, improved reproductive health, or enhanced institutional capacity. Part of the strategy entails pumping money and technical aid into the states along Africa's main migrant corridors to create jobs that absorb labour and prevent migration. These interventions could positively affect the region's future, but they are far from sufficient. Sub-Saharan Africa's young and fertile population, which today is about 40 percent larger than Europe's, will be six times[14] the size of Europe's by 2100. Even if fertility rates drop soon, the momentum for population growth will continue as today's children reach adulthood. Generating economic opportunities for them will require unprecedented economic growth[15]: not just in one or two countries for a few years, but across the continent for multiple decades. And this will depend on the ability of some of the world's most persistently stagnant and mismanaged economies to reform themselves. In an era of rising authoritarianism in Africa[16] and elsewhere, the pandemic is a blessing to autocrats. As the continent's experience with Ebola shows[17], combatting the pandemic requires strengthening accountability and building trust between the state and communities. Authoritarianism may work to control people in the short term, but will not produce long-term sustainable results.

The broad efforts to contain Africans are more than simply the exercise of coercive power and exclusion. Such moves are not only about reshaping movement, but also about reshaping futures. Underlying containment campaigns are affronts to African' spatial imaginaries. An effort to convince that Africans have no future elsewhere[18] and that movement would lead to peril[19]. Pressed up against the Mediterranean in late 2019, an African migrant in Tripoli told the BBC that, 'I know if I make it to Europe, I'll be someone tomorrow.' Young Mozambican men in Johannesburg speak about the need to travel and work abroad if they hope to return home and marry.[20] Patterns of movement within the continent – as elsewhere in the world – often build on bequests from previous generations. Indeed, across Southern Africa – as elsewhere on the continent – generations of families have depended on migration. Historically more than half of Lesotho's labour force worked in South Africa[21]. Before Côte d'Ivoire's civil war, Burkina Faso's economy relied heavily on sending workers there[22]. For decades, migration represented the possibility of a step in to the modern[23]. Where post-modern imaginations are infused with an acute awareness and orientation to 'multiple elsewheres,'[24] the freedom to cross boundaries takes on even more significance. Movement for many is not just a means of survival or economic accumulation. It is a rite of passage: a means of claiming a future.

Rationing rights to life and movement are central to practices of contemporary state sovereignty. Surrendering control over these rights to armed forces and police who have often struggled with democratic accountability[25] substantially bolsters long-term threats to individual and collective freedom. These formations will resist a return to constitutionalism and market access. Authoritarian regulations on movements and immobility -- border fences[26], urban expulsions[27], and lockdowns –will likely translate into enduring controls on movements. External support in the form of funds and scientific legitimacy only makes this more likely.

Those trapped by poverty, persecution or these new restrictions may become geographically sedentary, but their position in local and global social and material hierarchies will remain shaped by the circulation of goods, images and ideas. These include sub-Saharan Africa's burgeoning and remarkably youthful population whose prospects for local employment were already deeply constrained[28]. What is certain is that their futures will not look the same. Many across Africa will face heightened vulnerability as grandparents who cared for children are ravaged by disease and remittances dry up. Long-term strategies will be upended, as will pendular mobility and connections between movement, accumulation and status. Families and futures shaped on movement are now far less certain.

Those relying on regular migration across or within borders are not the only ones imperilled. Already the urban and rural poor depend on relatively spontaneous forms of movements and translocality to negotiate the uncertainties associated with Informalisation[29]. Without secure jobs, housing, or services in a single location, people often shift locales and social networks in an effort to avoid becoming marooned in time and space.[30] For the young, an ability to move can represent a chance to escape patriarchal, heteronormative, or generational hierarchies and open opportunities for personal growth and profit.[31] Hundreds of thousands are formally contained in camps from which they are now even less likely to be released into spaces where they can build their own lives.[32] Mobility and translocalism has become a ready way to negotiate these uncertainties: to build connections across space that offers some chance at resilience and possibility amidst precarity.

The 2015 European migration 'crisis' starkly exposed these intersections of mobility and realising futures. The COVID-19 crisis adds the legitimacy of science to these disruptions. The violently enforced stay at home orders will be lifted, but the legacy of heightened mobility restrictions – within and among countries – may not. In the short term, politicians are suppressing critique and coercive institutions are creeping into underground economies for goods, services, and mobility.[33] As the United States' experience[34] in trying to stem the flow of migrants to its Southern border is anything to go on, enhanced border controls have limited effect on the numbers of people moving. Instead, they tend to generate increasingly elaborate mechanisms to subvert such controls. Across the Mediterranean, militarized borders have already set off a kind of arms race between states and smugglers, with increasing collusion between the two. The Libyan slave markets[35] are the most notorious of example, but within Sudan, Niger and elsewhere state and state-like authorities are forming profitable smuggling partnerships. The same will likely to be true at a different scale across African cities.

The uncertainty of whom the plague will strike in the coming months is just one way in which futures are being stolen. The inability to move compromises people's ability to plan, adapt, and ultimately progress. The result will not only be greater material precarity, but also existential uncertainty. Where people stop seeing the possibility of predictable futures or progress, forms of rational decision-making and political engagement will take on new meanings. Many hope for a progressive political turn as the pandemic wanes. This is possible, but people who feel robbed of futures are more likely to acquiesce to authoritarianism or support millenarianism than forge enduring, visionary solidarities.

Without secure jobs, housing, or services in a single location, people often shift locales and social networks in an effort to avoid becoming marooned in time and space. For the young, an ability to move can represent a chance to escape patriarchal, heteronormative, or generational hierarchies and open opportunities for personal growth and profit.

● 1 — Landau, Loren B., 'A Chronotope of Containment Development: Europe's Migrant Crisis and Africa's Reterritorialisation' in Antipode, a Radical Journal of Geography, vol 51, issue 1 (2019) 169 – 186. ● 2 — Andersson, Ruben, 'Illegality, Inc', see http://rubenandersson.com/illegality-inc/ [accessed 08.04.2020]. ● 3 — European Council, European Council meeting (28 June 2018) – Conclusions, CO EUR 9 CONCL 3 (2018). ● 4 — Kimari, W., 'Africa needs to drop the 'youth bulge' discourse' in New Internationalist (2018), https://newint.org/features/2018/01/01/youth-bulge. ● 5 — See https://www.waronwant.org/stop-evictions-shack-dwellers-durban. ● 6 — Wicks, J. and Patrick, A., 'Provinces brace for 'thinning' of settlements in Covid-19 fight' in Sunday Times 5 April 2020. ● 7 — Cara, A. 'Virus prevention measures turn violent in parts of Africa' in AP News 28 March 2020. ● 8 — Butera, S., 'Rwanda Police Shoot 2; Say Officers Attacked on Patrol' in Bloomberg 25 March 2020. ● 9 — Harding, A. 'South Africa's ruthlessly efficient fight against coronavirus', BBC, 3 April 2020. ● 10 — Bearak, M. and Ombuor, R., 'Kenya's coronavirus curfew begins with wave of police crackdowns' in The Washington Post 28 March 2020. ● 11 — Ghanaweb, 'Lockdown: Ghana Police urges public to ignore viral brutality videos', see https://www.ghanaweb.com/GhanaHomePage/NewsArchive/Lockdown-Ghana-Police-urges-public-to-ignore-viral-brutality-videos-910924 [accessed 08.04.2020]. ● 12 — Bearak, M. and Ombuor, R. 'Kenyan police shot dead a teenager on his balcony during a coronavirus curfew crackdown' in The Washington Post 31 March 2020. ● 13 — Swanson, M. W. 1977. 'The Sanitation Syndrome: Bubonic Plague and Urban Native Policy in the Cape Colony, 1900–1909' Journal of African History. 18(3): 387-410. ● 14 — Milanovic, B. 2015. 'Five Reasons Why Migration Into Europe Is A Problem With No Solution', Social Europe, https://www.socialeurope.eu/five-reasons-why-migration-into-europe-is-a-problem-with-no-solution [accessed 08.04.2020}. ● 15 — Clemens, M. and Postel, H. (2018) 'Can Development Assistance Deter Emigration?', summary of the policy paper Deterring Emigration with Foreign Aid: An Overview of Evidence from Low-Income Countries, Center for Global Development. ● 16 — Subramanian, G. 'The Magufuli 'bulldozer' effect' in The Hindu 03 October 2019. ● 17 — Christenseny, D., Dubez, O., Haushofer, J., Siddiqi, B., Voorsk, M. (2020). Building resilient Health Systems: Experimental evidence from Sierra Leone and the 2014 Ebola Outbreak'. ● 18 — Landau, L.B., Freemantle, I. (2019). 'Africa at the gates: Europe's lose-lose migration management plan', AMMODI. ● 19 — IOM, 2019. See https://www.iom.int/news/10000-ghanaian-youth-learn-about-pitfalls-irregular-migration [accessed 08.04.2020]. ● 20 — Madsen, M.L. (2004) 'Living for Home: Policing Immorality among Undocumented Migrants in Johannesburg', African Studies, 63(2):173-192 ● 21 — South African History Online, 'Notes on the migrant labour system in Lesotho'. See. ● 22 — Kress, B. (2006). 'Burkina Faso: Testing the Tradition of Circular Migration', Migration Information Source, migrationpolicy.org. ● 23 — s. ● 24 — Karera, A. (2013). 'Writing Africa into the World and Writing the World from Africa: Mbembe's Politics of Dis-enclosure', Critical Philosophy of Race, Vol. 1, No. 2 (2013), pp. 228-241. ● 25 — Transparency International, see https://www.transparency.org/news/feature/corruption_of_police_in_africa_must_end_now [accessed 08.04.2020]. ● 26 — AlJazeera, 7 April 2020, see https://www.aljazeera.com/news/2020/03/coronavirus-travel-restrictions-border-shutdowns-country-200318091505922.html [accessed 08.04.2020]. ● 27 — Wicks, J., Patrick, A. (2020), 'Provinces brace for 'thinning' of settlements in Covid-19 fight' in Sunday Times 5 April 2020. ● 28 — Landau, L.B., Kihato, C.W. and Postel, H. (2018). 'Europe Is Making Its Migration Problem Worse: The Dangers of Aiding Autocrats' in Foreign Affairs, 5 September 2018. ● 29 — Landau, L.B. (2019). 'Temporality, informality, & translocality in Africa's urban archipelagos', MIASA Working Paper No 2019(4). ● 30 — Simone, A. 2017. 'Living as Logistics: Tenuous Struggles in the Remaking of Urban Collective Life,' In G. Bhan, S. Srinivas and V. Watson (eds.) Routledge Companion to Planning in the Global South. London; New York: Routledge. ● 31 — Lubkemann, S. (2007), Culture in Chaos: An Anthropology of the Social Condition in War, Chicago: University of Chicago Press. ● 32 — Turner, S. (2016) 'Staying Out of Place: The Being and Becoming of Burundian Refugees in the Camp and the City' Conflict and Society, 2(1):37-51. ● 33 — Morais, S. (2020). 'Corruption has crippled SA's capacity to fight coronavirus, lives will be lost - Corruption Watch', in News24, 31 March 2020. ● 34 — Bier, D.J. (2017). 'Why the Wall Won't Work', commentary Cato Institute, first published in the May 2017 issue of Reason. ● 35 — Sherlock, R., Al-Arian, L. (2018). 'Migrants Captured In Libya Say They End Up Sold As Slaves', NPR, 21 March 2018.

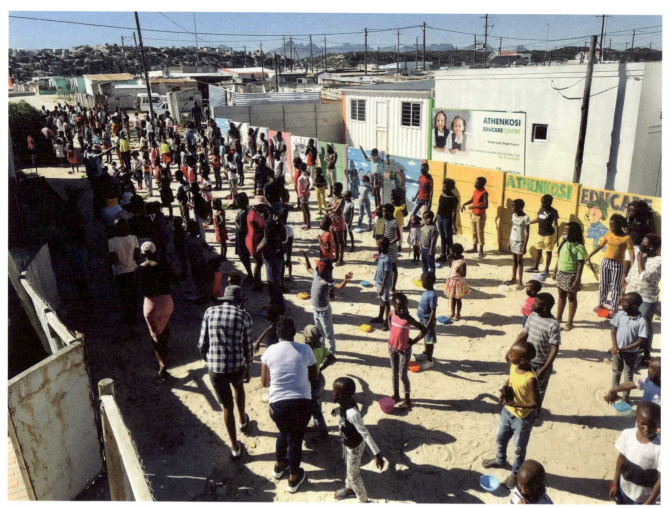

© Mandisi Disi Sindo

News From Capetown South Africa

by
Mandisi di Sindo

KASI RC is a self-funded Shack Theatre based in Khayelitsha. It provides all of its COVID-19 support independent of the government or city municipality.

Follow KASI RC on Twitter & Instagram @kasi_rc.

© Mandisi Disi Sindo

Day 32 of Lockdown

We tried our best to fight CORONA VIRUS with our KASI RC mentees, students and affiliates.

KASI RC HAS:

— a 3 day feeding scheme serving more than 400 people daily @CreativeSoupKitchen

— Given out more than 800 food parcels to needy families around Khaltsha.

— Bought electricity for 168 homes that were in the dark.

— Distributed more than 2000 sanitizers and face masks to underprivileged individuals.

— Converted our theatre into a classroom for those with no data and television to catch up with their studies.

— Created inclusive and diverse works focusing on COVID-19 outbreak and its impact in the townships.

— Mentored our students for theatre shows.

— Handed out 580 bags of oranges to elder people to boost their immune system, donated by Dr Ruben Foundation.

— Had zoom conferences with ENCA, Beautiful News SA, NAF, Heavy Chef, Spiel and more

— Been published on Lead SA, eNCA, The Cape Robyn, Cape Times, Colombia News, US Times, Daily Voice, Corona Monitor etc.

Thank you to our friends, family, business partners, donors, co-workers, competitors and general public for making sure that we do the work that we are doing. Enkosi for supporting our theatre all the way thru!

Greetings from Khayelitsha

4.5 million Venezuelans are displaced abroad according to UNHCR (Global trends 2019)

Venezuela-Colombia border crossing, 2018. © George Castellanos

Venezuelans On the Move
First port of call: Colombia

Milena Gomez Kopp is presently a Visiting Research Scholar at the School of International and Public Affairs (SIPA), Columbia University. She was previously Charge d' Affairs/ Minister Plenipotentiary at the Embassy of Colombia in Turkey, and has been a Professor at the Universidad Externado de Colombia, SIPA, the Colombian Diplomatic Academy and the Middle East Technical University (METU) in Ankara.

Migrant's cheese business start-up in Colombia, 2012. © Milena Gomez Kopp

VENEZUELA is experiencing the second largest exodus of migrants and refugees in the world after Syria. The crisis, fuelled by political instability, economic recession, and most recent the COVID-19 pandemic, is expected to further deteriorate in the time to come. In this article, Milena Gomez Kopp situates the current migration and refugee crisis in a historical context, demonstrating how political and economic factors has shifted the power dynamics and migration patterns between Venezuela and Colombia over the years.

by
Milena Gomez Kopp

The approximately five million Venezuelans, who have left their country in recent years, represent the largest exodus of migrants in the history of the Western Hemisphere. Colombia has enthusiastically welcomed "our brothers and sisters" and, according to the Organization of American States (OAS), it has received the greatest number of Venezuelan migrants and refugees (1.6 million), followed by Peru (900,000), the United States (422,000), Ecuador (400,000) and Chile (400,000). The arrival of this cohort to Colombia also marks the largest presence of immigrants in the country's history and, today, there are more Venezuelans living in Colombia than the population of most of its cities, with the exception of Bogotá, Medellin and Cali.

Ironically, Venezuela has always been a country of immigrants ever since in 1936 it established its first migration policy. As such, in the mid-twentieth century its government allowed the influx of large number of immigrants (mostly from Italy, Spain and Portugal) to settle in the country. Colombian semi-skilled and skilled laborers also benefitted from Venezuela's open-door policy and thousands arrived in the 60's and 70's. Colombians found jobs in the service sector as housekeepers, drivers and gardeners, thanks to a prosperous economy that benefited from the growing petroleum boom. Venezuela became Colombia's rich cousin.

At the beginning of the XXI century, everything changed. One of the wealthiest countries in Latin America, with the world's largest oil reserves, is now faced with a far-flung net out-migration. The exodus of Venezuelans to Colombia began in the beginning of this century when highly educated professionals fled the country, fearing the policies of the government of Hugo Chavez. These "executive emigrants", as the local Venezuelan press called this group of highly skilled professionals, left their country for many reasons, including a difficult job market, insecurity and the deep political polarization that engulfed their nation.

"Executive emigrants" arrived to Colombia in the first wave of Venezuelan migration. They enriched the country with their high purchasing power, skilled labor and investment capital. Former employees of Petroleum of Venezuela (PDVSA), the state-owned oil and natural gas company, for example, provided knowhow to the growing petroleum industry in Colombia and some credit them for spearheading the boom in this sector. Others invested in drug and pharmaceutical companies, restaurants and diverse local businesses. A growing number of the highly educated found jobs in leading universities and many young Venezuelans crossed the border to study in academic institutions all over the country. The first wave of Venezuelan migrants brought prosperity with them. Locals, at this time, were heard joking that the best thing that happened to Colombia was Chavez.

As the situation in Caracas deteriorated, the exodus of Venezuelan citizens continued. By 2014, the economy continued to collapse and the bolivar, the national currency, went into freefall leaving a large percentage of the population without basic necessities. Food and healthcare were scarce for most. As such, thousands took the difficult decision to abandon Venezuela, leaving behind the little they had and traveling with just enough money to get by. These individuals were not fleeing a war, but were leaving a country mired in insecurity and lacking access to services, food and medicine. This second wave of migrants were poor and downtrodden, a stark contrast to those *"compatriotas"* who arrived a decade earlier.

By August 2015, the country reached a turning point when President Nicolas Maduro closed the border between Colombia and Venezuela and, paradoxically, the flows of people to Colombia increased.

Today, Venezuelan migrants and refugees continue to arrive in huge numbers, nearly overwhelming Colombia's capacity to absorb and settle them. The country faces innumerable challenges in this process, but the biggest by far is financial. Although Colombia has received support from foreign governments and international organizations, such as UNHCR and IOM, the country is increasingly overstretched for resources. Fiscal constraints inevitably limit the capacity of the government to continue providing public services to a rapidly growing population in dire need. This crisis has only been able to mobilize a fraction of the international support other groups receive. For example, according to the OAS, Syrian refugees have received $33 billion in donations, South Sudan $9.4 billion and Myanmar $1.2 billion, providing a sharp contrast to the $600 million offered to Venezuelans.

In spite of the various limitations, analysts predict that the number of refugees and migrants arriving from Venezuela will continue to increase dramatically, especially in view of the recent collapse in world oil prices and the pressures caused by the coronavirus pandemic arriving while Venezuelan health services barely function. Before the onset of the pandemic and the dramatic drop in oil prices, the OAS estimated that by the end of this year, the total number of Venezuelan refugees will reach 7 to 7.5 million. But the situation is likely to deteriorate even more. Today, Venezuelans represent the second largest exodus of migrants and refugees in the world, only overshadowed by the Syrians. However, if the numbers continue to grow at the estimated rate, they may become the largest group of refugees globally. The international community must immediately take action by increasing their support to Colombia and other recipient countries to mitigate the plight of desperate Venezuelans, and their overwhelmed hosts. However, in this increasing crazy world, it looks ever so unlikely.

A Long Way Home

Sergey Ponomarev is a freelance photographer, and frequent contributor for NYT. Ponomarev was part of winning team of Pulitzer prize for Breaking News Photography in 2016, was awarded the Robert Capa Gold Medal (shared with Bryan Denton) for his coverage of the Iraq war in 2017 and has won the World Press Photo awards in 2015, 2016, and 2017.

by
Sergey Ponomarev

Curator
Maria Burasovskaya

EXODUS: A Long Way Home is a personal photobook project inspired by the refugees I was privileged to follow and meet during their journeys to and through Europe. It is motivated by a desire to keep telling their stories, even after the cameras and journalists have moved on to the next headline.

At the core of the work is the notion that migration is about much more than the physical movement of people. It is about shifting identities, as nations and peoples shape one other. It is about rebuilding lives and homes from zero. It is motivated by a desire to keep telling this story, even after the cameras and journalists have moved on to the next headline.

"We must go." I heard that phrase repeated hundreds of times, on the pebbled beaches of the Greek islands, at the closed borders in Serbia and Hungary, and in the desperate camps of Idomeni and Athens. During the year that I followed the migrant crisis I saw thousands of traumatised people arrive on the shores of Europe—exhausted, wet and cold. They came from Syria, Iraq, and Afghanistan; from Somalia, Iran, Pakistan, Eritrea, Sudan; and from dozens of other poor and war-torn countries. It was the mantra of the desperate.

I walked with them through fields, rivers and borders. They took only the possessions they could carry on their backs. They walked until their feet were so blistered they could not take another step. Often they didn't know where they were going, or even what country they were in.

The migrant crisis is one of the defining stories of our time. But while the physical exodus of more than one million people from Middle Eastern and African countries to Western and Northern Europe has attracted a huge amount of media attention, much less consideration has been given to what happens next.

While covering the 'Balkan route' for The New York Times, what struck me was how the physical journey was just the first chapter in this story. From the moment these people set foot ashore in Greece their past lives were no more than a memory, their futures were uncertain, and their journey into the unknown had truly begun. Houses, possessions, and loved ones were all left behind. Lives had to be rebuilt from zero.

PREAMBLE

Refugees walk along the rail tracks towards the border with Hungary outside Horgos, Serbia, Thursday September, 10, 2015.

Migrants walk past the temple as they are escorted by Slovenian riot police to the registration camp outside Dobova, Slovenia, Thursday October, 22, 2015.

PREAMBLE

Refugees board the train towards Zagreb at Tovarnik station on the border with Serbia, Croatia, Friday September, 18, 2015.

In Idomeni, Macedonia, Wednesday August, 26, 2015.

Migrants on the run, 2015.

A man tries to save his kid from the police beatings and tear gas after clashes with Hungarian police broke out at the border crossing in Horgos, Serbia, Wednesday September, 16, 2015.

Police on horses escort hundreds of migrants after they crossed from Croatia in Dobova, Slovenia, Tuesday October, 20, 2015.

Migrants stand near the rudimentary map of Europe that is pictured on the wall of a migrant shelter by the Moria processing centre on Lesbos island Greece, Thursday November, 19, 2015.

In Dobova, Slovenia, Saturday October, 24, 2015.

A family of Iranian migrants are surrounded by Greek police as they were blocking the entrance to Macedonia at the Greek-Macedonian border near village of Idomeni, Greece, Thursday December, 3, 2015. Thousands of migrants are stranded on the Greek side after Macedonia blocked access to citizens of countries that are not being fast-tracked for asylum in the European Union. Macedonia now allows only Syrian, Iraq and Afghanistan citizens.

Refugees wait in line for documents at the refugee processing centre in Presevo, Serbia, Thursday August, 27, 2015.

Part One

How can we think about and start to engage with displacement, migration and patterns of movement in a way that captures and responds to the range and multitude of lived and shared experiences?

COLOMBIA'S REPORTED INTERNALLY DISPLACED PEOPLE

Forced Displacement Routes
Registro Único De Víctimas - Red Nacional De Información, Colombia
1900 - 2016

Conflict Urbanism: Colombia
Center for Spatial Research, Columbia University
Masters in Peace Building, Universidad de Los Andes

Conflict Urbanism: Colombia

Juan Francisco Saldarriaga is Senior Data and Design Researcher at the Brown Institute for Media Innovation at Columbia University. An expert in mapping and data visualization, he works at the intersection of design, GIS, journalism, architecture, urbanism, and the humanities.

by
Juan Francisco Saldarriaga

WHAT are the spatial and temporal patterns of the war, and how can spatial data and analysis be used to better understand complex patterns and drivers of forced migration? The Center for Spatial Research at Columbia University, in collaboration with the Universidad de Los Andes, launched the multi-year project "Conflict Urbanism: Colombia" to better understand and answer such questions. In this article, Saldarriaga presents key insights and new findings that have emerged from the spatial mapping and data visualisations for this project, and suggests how the research can inform strategic government intervention in the post-conflict scenario. It is extremely difficult to grasp the full complexity of the Colombian conflict, which has spanned more than 50 years and engulfed the entire country. In a time period of 30 years alone (1985-2016) more than 7 million people were victims of forced displacement in Colombia. The conflict has often spilled over into neighbouring Venezuela, Ecuador, Peru, and Brazil. It has involved multiple actors - from left-wing guerrillas to right-wing paramilitaries - who have battled each other and the state and profited greatly from the illegal drug trade. And it has been shaped and reshaped by a multiplicity of internal and external socioeconomic forces, generating millions of victims of forced displacement, homicide, kidnapping, and sexual violence.

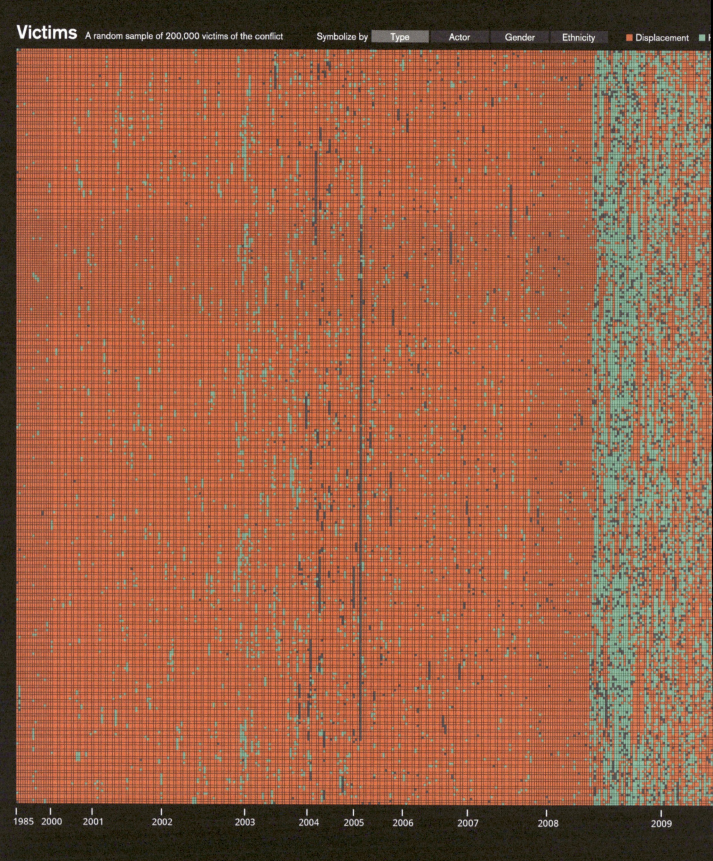

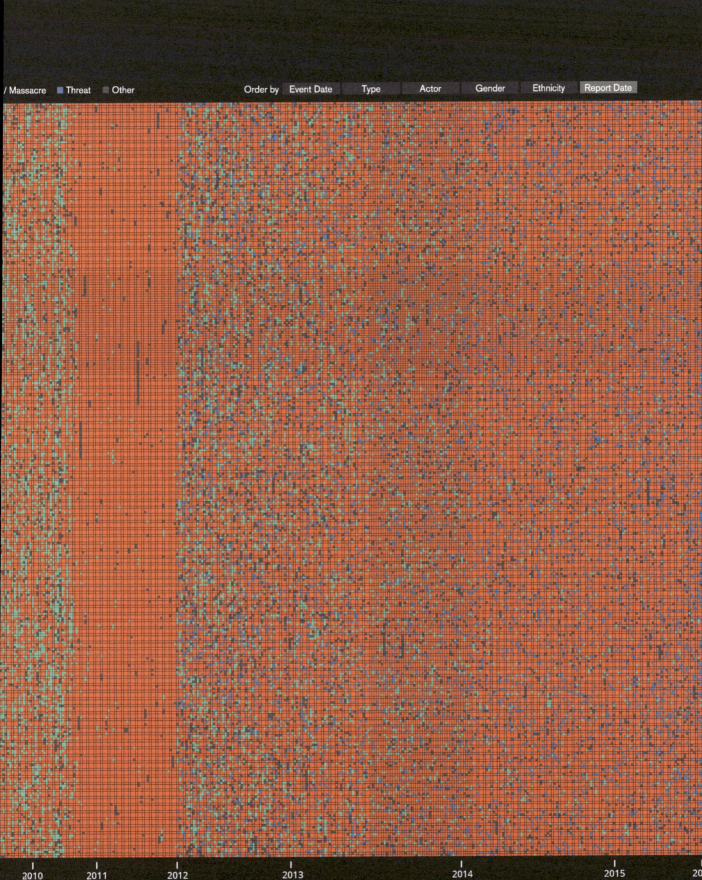

Patterns and ramifications of the Colombian conflict

As forced displacement increases worldwide – due to conflict and climate change – it becomes imperative for city planners, governments, and aid organizations to better understand the regional, national, and supra-national dynamics of this phenomenon, and to use all the available methodological tools to more efficiently allocate resources.

In our research, we apply different methods and metrics to visualize and analyse data on regional dynamics of forced displacement in the Colombian conflict. We find that violence at the origin municipality is the most important driver of displacement. Similarly, destination municipalities with larger social networks of victims of displacement, overall populations, and closer to places of origin attract more displaced people.

Further, our most recent study, to be published in 2020, demonstrates the power of network analysis in understanding displacement patterns. The research reveals a number of key findings: first, even though the reported number of displaced people declined after 2002, forced displacement continued to affect most of the country's municipalities for at least five more years; second, the network of displacement in Colombia is very sparse, with most displaced persons moving from a given municipality to a limited number of other municipalities; third, the metrics identify a number of municipalities as crucial regional nodes based on their central position in the network, compared with other municipalities that have higher numbers of displaced persons. As such, these represent important sites for government intervention in a post-conflict scenario.

Maps as political instruments

The map of internally displaced people in Colombia from 1985 to 2015 is taken from the early phase of the project, where the thickness of the lines represents the number of people who were forcibly displaced, with the thinnest lines representing 50 people and the thickest representing more than 10,000. The colour of the lines indicates the direction of displacement— white the origin, and orange the destination. The map confirms certain well-known facts about the conflict, like the significant number of people that have left small towns for the country's largest cities Bogotá, Medellín, and Cali, or the more than 20,000 people that were displaced after the infamous massacres of Bojayá and La Gabarra. But it also highlights other lesser-known aspects of the war. For example, that medium-sized cities like Florencia, Popayán, Pasto, Santa Marta, and Montería have received more than 600,000 displaced people. It even shows how remote and sparsely populated areas, such as Leticia in the south, or Puerto Inírida in the east, have also been affected. Most importantly though, the map reveals how the conflict has enveloped the whole country in a deep and intricate web of violence and displacement.

To complement our mapping, we created a mosaic of satellite images of some of the most affected municipalities. Captured by the Landsat satellite, and all at the same scale, the images reveal the topographic, morphological, and environmental diversity of the different areas, while highlighting the reach and range of the conflict. In many cases, they make evident the isolation of affected communities. The project's underlying data is drawn from a single dataset assembled by the Colombian government as part of the recent peace process. This data is from 2015, and while the current research under this project has been updated, this is the most recent publicly available data.

The Registro Único de Víctimas includes entries for almost eight million victims, who volunteered information about crimes committed against themselves, or their relatives, in hope of receiving reparations. While the dataset is by far the best source of available information, it remains incomplete and biased. To reveal the inherent gaps, we created an interactive visualization in which each victim is represented as a pixel, and sorted and color-coded based on different attributes. For example, we have color-coded a random sample of 200,000 victims by the type of crime reported—orange for forced displacement, teal for homicides, and blue for threats—and sorted the reports chronologically. Three striking patterns emerge: from mid-2008 to mid-2010, there was a concrete effort to collect reports on homicides and massacres (in teal); from mid- 2010 to 2012, the reports collected were almost exclusively about forced displacement (in orange); finally, from 2012 there was a clear increase in the number of threats reported. What explains these patterns in the collection of the data? Was there a deliberate effort by the government to collect information about specific types of crimes? If so, what were the intentions behind these efforts? And how does this affect the ways in which we analyse and understand the conflict? Ultimately, the patterns reveal more about the collection process than about the actual crimes that were committed, and as such push us to question the dataset itself and treat it with scepticism and care. In Colombia, government agencies have led data collection activities designed to inform policy. Civic groups have driven extensive efforts to document cultural and historical memory with the intention of furthering transitional justice. Our work is situated between these two realms. It introduces spatial memory into the discourse of transitional justice, and provides insights that might inform nuanced policies that are responsive to local needs and cognizant of socio-spatial phenomena. The project uses mapping and data visualization to examine a single massive dataset thoroughly, documenting both its strengths and limitations. It reveals both the intricate paths that people take during conflict, and the complexities of parallel forms of data collection.

BOGOTÁ

From 1985 to 2015, the capital of Colombia received over 540,000 victims of displacement from all over the country; over the last 15 years at an average rate of more than 2,500 people per month.

6,840,116 | Population (2005)
7,290 | Displaced (1985-2015)
536,598 | Arrived (1985-2015)
3,460 | Displaced within (1985-2015)

MEDELLÍN

Colombia's second largest city is not only a major destination for victims of displacement but is also the fifth largest municipality showing displacements.

2,214,494 | Population (2005)
41,118 | Displaced (1985-2015)
373,898 | Arrived (1985-2015)
81,812 | Displaced within (1985-2015)

SANTA MARTA

Located on the Caribbean coast, Santa Marta is half the size of its neighbor Barranquilla but has received almost twice the amount of victims of displacement.

415,270 | Population (2005)
35,085 | Displaced (1985-2015)
143,341 | Arrived (1985-2015)
59,036 | Displaced within (1985-2015)

BUENAVENTURA

Colombia's main port of the Pacific has been the location of 18 massacres by both the FARC and the paramilitaries between 2000 and 2005, and has lost almost a third of its population due to forced displacement.

328,794 | Population (2005)
95,509 | Displaced (1985-2015)
34,393 | Arrived (1985-2015)
152,959 | Displaced within (1985-2015)

FLORENCIA

Located between the mountains and the Amazon jungle, Florencia has almost doubled its population due to the arrival of victims of displacement.

143,871 | Population (2005)
26,683 | Displaced (1985-2015)
109,520 | Arrived (1985-2015)
9,243 | Displaced within (1985-2015)

APARTADÓ

Apartadó has been the center of multiple massacres carried out by the FARC and various paramilitary groups. Unionized banana plantation workers have been specific targets.

131,405 | Population (2005)
50,771 | Displaced (1985-2015)
59,418 | Arrived (1985-2015)
20,960 | Displaced within (1985-2015)

QUIBDÓ

The capital of one of the poorest departments in the country, Quibdó has been a major destination for victims of displacement from nearby communities, including those from Bojayá and Vigía del Fuerte.

112,886 | Population (2005)
19,183 | Displaced (1985-2015)
70,189 | Arrived (1985-2015)
20,960 | Displaced within (1985-2015)

EL CARMEN DE BOLÍVAR

Between 2007 and 2012, more than 25,000 people were victims of displacement in this community. FARC and paramilitary groups have carried out more than 10 massacres in the region.

67,952 | Population (2005)
72,023 | Displaced (1985-2015)
3,415 | Arrived (1985-2015)
52,559 | Displaced within (1985-2015)

TIBÚ

Tibú has been a site of constant conflict between the FARC and paramilitary groups. In 1999, massacres at La Gabarra, caused more than 10,000 displacements, especially towards Cúcuta.

34,773 | Population (2005)
53,422 | Displaced (1985-2015)
15,499 | Arrived (1985-2015)
9,178 | Displaced within (1985-2015)

RIOSUCIO

Riosucio's location on the Atrato River, a strategic corridor for drugs and arms, has made it vulnerable to conflicts between paramilitaries and the FARC. Displaced victims have to travel by boat to Turbo, the nearest city.

28,230 | Population (2005)
74,710 | Displaced (1985-2015)
1,387 | Arrived (1985-2015)
20,369 | Displaced within (1985-2015)

SAMANÁ

Three significant massacres have occurred in Samaná since 1996 by paramilitary forces and the FARC. One of the FARC's tactics consisted of taking over farmlands and turning them into minefields.

25,649 | Population (2005)
26,806 | Displaced (1985-2015)
916 | Arrived (1985-2015)
24,050 | Displaced within (1985-2015)

BOJAYÁ

In May 2002, FARC forces seized Bojayá, destroying a church and killing more than 100 people that had taken refuge there. More than 11,000 people were displaced that month.

9,941 | Population (2005)
29,625 | Displaced (1985-2015)
261 | Arrived (1985-2015)
9,562 | Displaced within (1985-2015)

The Colombian government's response to immigration from Venezuela

Wooldy Edson Louidor is doing his doctorate at the University of Leipzig. He is a lecturer at the Institute for Social and Cultural Studies PENSAR at the Pontifica Universidad Javeriana, Colombia. His research focuses on Colombian, Venezuelan and Haitian migration.[1]

by
Wooldy Edson Louidor

Translation from Spanish
by Vera Hanewinkel

Reporting from the Venezuela-Colombian Border, April 16, 2020

Venezuela-Colombia border crossing, 2018. © George Castellanos

FLUID-PERMANENCE

COLOMBIA is the main target country for Venezuelans trying to escape the crisis in their country. So far, the Colombian governments have responded to this immigration more provisionally than systematically.

Regulations

The Colombian government's response to the significant increase in Venezuelan migration at the common border began on August 13, 2016. The then Columbian President Juan Manuel Santos determined that all Venezuelans wanting to cross the border had to have a "border mobility card" (Tarjeta Migratoria de Tránsito Fronterizo; since February 16, 2017: Tarjeta de Movilidad Fronteriza, TMF).[2] Since the end of 2015, Venezuelans had crossed the border to Colombia in bulk and disorder to buy groceries, medicines and other everyday goods, and then return to their places of residence in Venezuela (commuting migrants). According to the World Bank, "an average of 45,000 people use this card every day to cross the Colombian border."[3]

On August 21, 2015, Nicolás Maduro ordered the Colombian boarder closed. By August 2016, Venezuela had such a shortage of goods that the president had to agree to reopen the border with Colombia as a humanitarian corridor.

However, for Venezuelan migrants who wanted to stay in Colombia (Colombian-based migrants), Santos waited almost two years after the outbreak of the crisis -until July 25, 2017- to introduce the "Special Residence Permit" (Permiso Especial de Permanencia - PEP). This delay was due to the difficult situation in the peace process with the FARC rebel group in Colombia. Venezuela acted as an intermediary in the peace negotiations. Santos had to tackle the issue of Venezuelan migration tactfully in order not to lose his ally Maduro.[4] The negotiations resulted in signing of the peace agreement between the Colombian government and the FARC in September 2016.

Without enough money and without a passport[5] hundreds of thousands of Venezuelan citizens traveled through Colombia to Peru, Ecuador, Chile, Argentina, Brazil and Mexico (transit migrants). For this reason, on December 21, 2018, the Colombian government created through the resolution PIP-TT 3346 the "temporary transit permit"

(Permiso de Tránsito Temporal - PIP-PTT). In December 2018, the IOM and UNHCR forecasted that more than 1.4 million refugees and migrants from Venezuela would cross one or more countries before reaching their final or expected destination country in 2019.[6]

Limits

The Colombian government's response to increased migration has enabled Venezuelans to alleviate their plight in terms of health, education and social security. It also created opportunities for entry in the civil status register[7] and legalization of their stay. But the Colombian government's response has stalled in this emergency mode and is constantly being renewed through resolutions, decrees, and circulars.[8]

The Colombian government has been repeatedly called upon on by the Republican Congress to "adopt a comprehensive humanitarian aid policy".[9] In several judgments, the Constitutional Court also asked to "regulate the residence of Venezuelan migrants on Colombian territory and to protect their fundamental rights to health, education and work".[10]

The Colombian government's provisional decisions had two counterproductive effects: First, they caused government officials who had to implement the government's regulations to override indefinitely the previously applicable regulations and institutional routines in the case of Venezuelan migrants. As such, registry offices, hospitals, and public schools, were made available to Venezuelan's to use in "extraordinary" ways. As such, the Colombian government ordered Venezuelan migrants to have access to state-funded medical "primary care". However, this only applied to people who do not have insurance, who cover the cost of medical care, and who do not have sufficient financial means to pay for this medical service. Normally, only people in mortal danger should benefit from state-funded emergency care. These regulations made the administrative situation in hospitals near the border very difficult, since the staff was confused as to whether the patient even met the criteria for public emergency care.

Second, there were major problems in implementing these decisions both because resources were scarcely made available and because decisions made by the government had little legal force as they were not approved by the legislature. In many cases, they caused tension between the central authorities in Colombia's capital, Bogotá, and authorities and other institutions in the country, which were directly confronted with the extensive Venezuelan migration and in some cases completely overloaded.[11]

The new Colombian president, Iván Duque , who has been in office since August 7, 2018, proposed a "strategy to take migration from Venezuela into account" through the so-called National Council for Economic and Social

(Figure 1) Number and Categories of Venezuelan migrants in Colombia*

Category migrants	Pendulum migrants	Transit migrants	Columbian-based migrants (regular and irregular residence)
Number until August 2019)	3 .3 Milion	Between 350,000-400,000	1,298,300 (thereof 515,286 without a residence permit)
Type of Document to regularize your stay/ start of validity	Border Mobility Card (Tarjeta de Mobilidad Fronteriza-TMF),in use since February 16,2017	Temporary transit permit (Permiso de Transito Temporal-PIP-PTT),in use since December 21,2018.By August 2019,approximately 178,215 people had this temporary residency permit.	Special residence permit (Permiso Especial de Permanencia-PEO),in use since July 25 2017 (89 percent of the 672,947 Venezuelans legally residing in Colombia in July 2019 had this residence permit; the remaining 11 percent kept up with other visas and accreditation legally in the country

*Various sources: UNHCR (2019): Refugiados y Migrantes Venezolanos en Colombia (July), https://acnur.org/5d277c224 (accessed: November 27, 2019). Migración Colombia (2019): Reports Migratorio [Migration Report] (May). Banco Mundial [World Bank] (2018): Migración desde Venezuela a Colombia, impactos y estrategia de respuesta en el corto y mediano plazo. Washington: Banco Mundial (November).

Policy (Consejo Nacional de Política Económica y Social, CONPES)" (Estrategia para la Atención de la Migración desde Venezuela) with effective measures up to 2021. The measures[12] responded to the migration from Venezuela with a new institutional, political, legal and operational framework in the medium term. In dealing with immigration from Venezuela, however, the government tends to forget the situation of other displaced people in the country, which is at least as much in need of regulation as migration from Venezuela: Colombia is the country with the largest number of internally displaced people worldwide (7,816.500 in 2018).[13]

Challenges

The first challenge for Colombia is to establish effective mechanisms to protect both the human rights of Venezuelan migrants and the constitutional rights of internally displaced people and Colombian return migrants, especially victims of the armed conflict in Colombia. The government should abide by the peace agreements to avoid a possible revival of the armed conflict, which would lead to massive uprooting inside and outside Colombia's borders.

The second challenge as the main host country for Venezuelan migrants is to reconcile the response of the Colombian government with other organizations and actors, such as: government agencies dedicated to the promotion, defense and surveillance of human rights, e.g. the Constitutional Court, the Ombudsman and the Ministry of Public Affairs (Ministerio Público) and the Congress of the Republic. Public control bodies such as civil society organizations and human rights defenders working for Venezuelan migrants, have all created hospitality initiatives - from those in remote locations to initiatives in the capital Bogotá - that have been committed to sensitizing, informing and educating the Colombian population of the need to accept Venezuelan migrants, to develop a culture of respect with migrants from Venezuela.

The third challenge is to get the inter-American human rights system more involved - especially the Inter-American Commission on Human Rights (Comisión Interamericana de Derechos Humanos, IACHR). It has advanced legal instruments for dealing with forced migration (e.g. the Cartagena Declaration on Refugees from 1984; Mexico Declaration and Action Plan from 2004 to strengthen the protection of refugees in Latin America; 2014 Declaration and Action Plan from Brazil to strengthen intra-regional cooperation on refugee issues). This would encourage governments and states to provide a common regional response to Venezuelan migration that goes beyond individual government efforts and the efforts of various governments to exchange and coordinate, such as the Quito process.[14]

(Figure 2) Requirements for the special residence permit

> **There are four conditions that any Venezuelan citizen must meet in order to obtain the Special Residence Permit (PEP):**
>
> **1) He/she must be at the time of the publication of this resolution [28 July 2017] in Colombia, 2) entered Colombia with a passport through one of the designated immigration checkpoints, 3) must not have a national or international criminal record, and 4) there must be no valid expulsion or deportation order against him / her . "***

* Resolution 1272 from 2017: http://migracioncolombia.gov.co/index.php/es/documentos/resoluciones/file/185-resolucion-1272-de-2017 (accessed: 24.9.2019).

● 1 — This text is published under the Creative Commons license "CC BY-NC-ND 3.0 DE - Attribution - Non-Commercial - No Editing 3.0 Germany" for bpb.de. ● 2 — https://www.migracioncolombia.gov.co/venezuela/tmf/preguntas-frecuentes-tmf (access: November 27, 2019). ● 3 — Banco Mundial [World Bank] (2018): Migración desde Venezuela a Colombia, impactos y estrategia de respuesta en el corto y mediano plazo. Washington: Banco Mundial (November), p.15 ● 4 — Since February 2019, Maduro's successor Iván Duque has broken off relations with Maduro and recognized Juan Guaidó as the legitimate president of Venezuela. ● 5 — It is very expensive for middle and lower class people to get a passport, also because of the corruption and the high government deficit in Venezuela. It is therefore very difficult for them to get a passport. ● 6 — Plataforma de Coordinación para Refugiados y Migrantes Venezolanos (2019): Plan de Respuesta para Refugiados y Migrantes Venezolanos Enero-Diciembre de 2019, p.14. ● 7 — All Colombians must be registered in the civil status register in order to receive identity documents. Children born in Colombia must also be registered there in order to be recognized as Colombian citizens. However, Venezuelan migrants were initially unable to have their children born in Colombia registered there, which is why they were at risk of becoming stateless, since they were also unable to obtain Venezuelan citizenship. In early August 2019, the Iván Duque government finally granted Colombian citizenship to more than 24,000 Venezuelan children born to Colombia since August 19, 2015 and at risk of statelessness. See Resolution No. 8470 of August 5, 2019 ● 8 — See Wooldy Edson LOUIDOR (2018): La migración forzada venezolana a Colombia (2015-2018): de una revisión documental a los esbozos de un análisis coyuntural y estructural. In: José KOECI ILIN / Joaquín EGUREN (ed.): El éxodo venezolano entre el exilio y la emigración. Lima: Colección OBIMID, pp. 21-46. ● 9 — Law 1873 of December 20, 2017: http://www.secretariasenado.gov.co/senado/basedoc/ley_1873_2017.html (accessed: 12-9-2019). ● 10 — Judgment T-074 of February 25, 2019: https://corte-constitucional.vlex.com.co/vid/769937717 (accessed: September 12, 2019). ● 11 — Wooldy Edson LOUIDOR et al. (2019): Por una frontera garante de los derechos humanos. Colombianos, venezolanos y niños en riesgo de apatridia en el Norte de Santander (2015-2018). Bogotá: Editorial Pontificia Universidad Javeriana. ● 12 — CONPES (2018): Estrategia para la Atención de la migración desde Venezuela (Noviembre). ● 13 — UNHCR (2019): Global Trends 2018. https://www.unhcr.org/statistics/unhcrstats/5d08d7ee7/unhcr-global-trends-2018.html (accessed: 12.9.2019). ● 14 — This is an initiative that 13 Latin American countries took on September 4, 2018 in Quito, capital of Ecuador, to ensure a coordinated response to Venezuelan migration in the region. See the joint declaration by the participating countries at https://www.cancilleria.gob.ec/wp-content/uploads/2018/09/declaracion_quito_reunion_tecnica_regional.pdf (accessed: November 27, 2019).

Camps:
An Interview with Charles Hailey

Charlie Hailey is an architect, writer, and professor in the School of Architecture at the University of Florida. Recently awarded a Guggenheim Fellowship, he is the author of five books, including Camps: A Guide to 21st Century Space and Slab City: Dispatches from the Last Free Place (with Donovan Wiley).

Michael Waldrep, Studio Olafur Eliasson, is a filmmaker, photographer, and researcher focused on architecture and city planning. He was previously a staff member at Urban-Think Tank, where he amongst others contributed to this journal.

Interview by
Michael Waldrep

IN this exclusive interview, Charlie Hailey suggests that camps are unique in registering the struggles, emergencies, and possibilities of global existence. Hailey explores how all camp spaces, whether used for Scout adventures, or to house Guantánamo detainees, are ultimately informed by politics, and can be used to understand the ways in which we perceive and construct built environments. Hailey, the researcher and writer of the book Camps: A Guide to 21st Century Space, spoke with Michael Walddrep to go deeper in understanding these ideas.

Structure built into the spoil bank of the Coachella Canal. © Donovan Wiley

Michael Waldrep: What is the main benefit of cataloguing camps? At first glance, a protest encampment in Texas, a gathering of computer programmers at Foo Camp, and the semi-permanent homes of refugees seem strange bedfellows.

Charlie Hailey: Whether we think of the camp as a type of space, or as a temporally charged situation, it indicates current forces and contemporary circumstances. In each of their permutations, camps accommodate conditions that might otherwise remain without space. And perhaps most importantly they indicate change—whether local or global—at its earliest stages. Documenting the full range of camps offers insight into these prescient spaces, and there are particular overlaps that suggest potentially valuable patterns. For instance, after Hurricane Katrina in 2005, a group of participants from the Burning Man festival reconstituted their theme camp as a relief camp in southern Mississippi. 'Burners Without Borders' continues to this day as an organization combining international disaster relief and community initiatives. This 'meme camp' acts as a bridge between the autonomous camps of Burning Man and camps necessitated by natural disaster. The resulting camp becomes a kind of genetic code for relief efforts.

MW: Your book Camps: A Guide to 21st Century Space, came out in 2009. Have you noticed any new typologies emerge in the period since? While it is clear, for instance, that refugee flows into and across Europe are nothing new, the engagement of the European activist Left in the building of camps in Calais or Lesbos arguably is. Do you see this as a new form of cross-pollination between informal transit camps and activist encampments? Are there others?

CH: You are right—The Jungle's 'Good Chance Theater' is an example where a camp accommodates the performative within situations of necessity and control. It is not unlike the Burners Without Borders relief camps, and I'm not sure the cross-pollination is new, so much as it is more systemic now. The increasing visibility of such camps means that they become references for approaching global displacement generally, and for trying to understand migrant experiences specifically, whether they have a stage or not. The Calais camps also attracted attention from other activist sources like Verso, which donated print media to the camp library 'Jungle Books'. Their agility will allow these resources to follow the camp's dispersed population after the Fall 2016 evictions. This kind of mobilization also increases the possibility for typological hybrids. Looking back, another thing that strikes me is that the publication of Camps came before the emergence of the Occupy Wall Street movement, although some of the classifications I used in the book anticipated Occupy's use of the camp. These protest camps were meme camps in their repeatability, peace camps in their activism,

63

anarchist camps in their process, festival camps in their spirit, and even Forward Operating Site (FOS) camps in their strategic positioning in a theatre of military operations—recalling how Occupy DC placed itself along the lobbyist corridor of K Street NW in Washington. And I cannot help but think about the future role of other quasi-public spaces as sites of resistance now that we are seeing media, tourists, and others camping out in the atrium of Trump Tower in New York, where privately-owned public spaces were originally negotiated with the city to allow for increases in the building's height.

> MW: How crucial is the dimension of control—what you refer to in your book as the divisions between camps of autonomy, control, and necessity? And what are the subsequent impacts on camp architecture and space?

CH: The categories of autonomy, necessity, and control grew out of the diverse objectives I found in the range of camps I looked at. They served as starting points—that is, thresholds into the spaces and processes of camps—and were not intended to impose boundaries or divisions. In many cases, the edges between each category are quite porous, so control is actually present in all three categories. To put it another way, no condition is without conditions. A place like Slab City in Southern California might corroborate, on the surface, its designation as 'the last free place'. But we must ask, free from what? And how free in the end? These are questions to consider in terms of both degree and kind.

> MW: Could you expand on this idea? Is there something special in the case of Slab City in the way it has developed (literally) on the foundations of a military installation? Are there lessons to be learned in the Alejandro Aravena mode of public provision of 'half a house', which is later built out?

CH: Slab City occupies the grounds of a World War II training camp on state-owned land in California's Imperial County. Leftover from the military installation, the eponymous slabs bring order to the harsh and indeterminate desert landscape. Materially, they do offer for building sometimes elaborate, though still ephemeral, shelters. Socially and spatially, they generate differences among those who live there, creating hierarchies of land tenure—those who live on slabs, on graded sand and gravel, or within more marginal, less cultivated desert scrub. 'Freedom' at Slab City resonates with legacies of manifest destiny, but now within an internalized frontier. The slabs carve out spaces of adaptation and resistance, not only from the desert expanse, but also from the promises (some of them failed) of freedom. To that end, the infrastructure of Slab City is not just the physical provision of concrete on sand. It is also more widely drawn. It is the national land ordinance system that allotted section 36 of each township to state boards of education as "free public space for common schools". Most other states sold off these land holdings years ago, but California's section 36 land has remained. It is the underlayment of soils that are not quite viable for the agricultural production that occurs a few miles west in Imperial Valley's industrial agriculture system. It is the availability of pallets and cardboard material leftover from the burgeoning solar farm developments on nearby land. Alongside many others, these sometimes invisible systems of land use, topography, and economic flows make up the matrix of the camp. With such systems at work, we see translations between camping types, and Slab City's autonomous settlement grows within the military camp's legacies and residues of control. In an inverse but related adaptation, the British Royal Navy converted Sir William Butlin's holiday camps into highly controlled training camps during World War II. When the war ended, holiday goers and tourists returned. Only camps accommodate such space.

> MW: The artist-managers of Burning Man have little in common with refugee camp administrators, except perhaps that neither are usually trained architects. What can architectural training bring to bear in the design of camps?

CH: That is a great question, and one that comes up a lot. We often hear that architects are great problem solvers, but I think architects are actually particularly skilled at framing problems. And, in a broad range of situations, that is a specific area where we as architects can contribute to the discussion of camps. Problem setting requires one to be attuned to complex systems and relations—between scalar shifts, within communication systems, among resources and distribution, and with infrastructure and dwelling. Architects can bring ideas for connecting logistics with experience. Ostensibly, architects know how to build buildings, but in camps it is the relations between things that make the place. I have always been interested in things in the making. I also remain concerned with the tension between detail and territory. Camps are inherently about relations between things, and between people and things, setting in motion dynamic interactions. For example, this might be the anchorage of a tent peg relative to the soil conditions of the overall site and wind speeds. Or it could be the availability of wood for cooking fires in a refugee camp. In some cases, refugees living in camps must travel as far as a 30-kilometer round trip to collect firewood in a rapidly degrading and dangerous landscape. The planning of camps must take into account the context of camps, their total environment, as well as the entire range of scales.

> MW: What can architects and designers take from Camps? If there are lessons to be learned from a comparison of the diverse range of camp typologies, are there lessons that can be applied to more permanent forms of architecture?

CH: The Dutch Situationist, Constant Nieuwenhuys, once said that a camping area is a form, however primitive, of a city. Although not yet cities, camps should be considered nascent urban forms. They are settlements that have been decreed temporary, but made permanent by

Shelter build from a caravan at Slab City. © Donovan Wiley

Shelter build of pallets and palm fronds in Slab City. © Donovan Wiley

Camp Dunlap Guard House at Slab City entrance. © Donovan Wiley

necessity. Camps make present future trajectories of migration, trace invisible flows of capital, make room for aspirations of shifting demographics, and demonstrate essential definitions of dwelling itself. As camps anticipate change, their adaptability is agility in movement and ideology. Camps accommodate the nomadic, while also embracing foundational and elemental aspects of shelter.

> MW: In your research, what are the major differences that you have noted between cities that began as camps and those that were the product of urban design?

CH: This reminds me of two different examples. The passage from camp to city is sometimes a process of accretion and crystallization of the temporary—much of which might be user-created and vernacular in origin—into something more permanent. I am thinking of Michel Butor's reading of Mediterranean development, particularly Istanbul, where fabric canopies became more solid roofs, and horizontal density grew vertically. The planning of camps begins quite differently. When I talked with the architect involved in designing Hagadera refugee camp at Dadaab in north-eastern Kenya, he was surprised to see that the camp's layout—conceived in 1992—was very much the same more than 20 years later. He also noted how the urgency of the camp's formation did not allow for site-specific design. In 1992, with the rapid increase of displaced populations from Somalia, there was only one month from schematic development until the arrival of refugees. An imposed infrastructure was filled and plugged into.

> MW: Do you believe that the relevance of the research presented in Camps has grown in the face of increased migration and the heightened international focus on a so-called refugee crisis?

CH: In my first book, I proposed camps as a field of study, and camps continue to be witnesses to conflicted histories and complicated aspirations. Over the past six or seven years, the number of forcibly displaced persons has increased by 20 million. Despite growing numbers and increasing displacement, camps are still considered temporary. In his book City of Thorns, Ben Rawlence talks about the construction of Dadaab's new camp, Ifo 22 . When they toured the site late in 2010, as it was still being developed. However, Kenyan officials stopped the construction of shelters made from Interlocking Stabilised Soil Block (ISSB) because they were considered too permanent, too much like houses. It is critical to think about camps not as ends in themselves, but as a part of an extended field that includes existing urban environments, longer-term communities, and sustained livelihood. Since 2009, in other circumstances, camps have also continued to offer sites for inquiry as well as resistance. Occupy Wall Street was a target criticism for its lack of clear objectives, but I have argued that the camps the movement spawned were the goal all

Housing for asylum seekers – Basislager, Zürich. © Alfredo Brillembourg

along. They offered visualizations of a message, also serving as scenes of disclosure to reveal a process of achieving democratic consensus. And the offshoot Occupy Our Homes successfully drew attention to the foreclosure crisis in the United States, which might have otherwise remained an abstraction to those who were not affected across the country. In thousands of yards, these camps made visible the mechanism that caused the problem, occupying the broken relation itself - the space that should belong to the homeowner, but was instead the space of the bank. They occupied the vacuum left by eviction.

> MW: Are there particular challenges that arise at the stage at which camps, especially those you term 'Necessity Camps', concretize into more permanent settlements?

CH: I think the relativism of those terms does not really apply to camps. Instead, we find each within the other — paradoxical situations like chronic mobility and transient fixity. In practice, camps of necessity endure. The Kenyan government has announced plans to close the five refugee camps that comprise Dadaab, but the complex was established in 1991, and its camps accommodate a generation that has really only known this one environment. After Hurricane Charley, the post-disaster camp dubbed 'FEMA City' stayed in place for nearly three years. That is, twice the amount of time FEMA allots for emergency shelter. In this case, ironies of mobility and intransience are also at play. It is illegal to tow a FEMA-issued trailer. Camps must respond to displacement with longer-term visions. I agree with Alejandro Aravena's argument that tents in refugee camps are "money that melts"[3] He suggests that more durable solutions, like incremental housing, are "payments in advance". Camps should not be protracted, but instead be proactive in their duration.

● 1 — Hailey used the term 'Meme camp' in Camps to describe ethically thematized disaster relief camp" that becomes a kind of "genetic code" for the development of future disaster relief efforts. ● 2 — See Ben Rawlence, City of Thorns: Nine Lives in the World's Largest Refugee Camp (2016). ● 3 — See Jessica Mairs, 'Refugee Camps are a Waste of Money, Says Alejandro Aravena' Dezeen (30 November 2015)

FLUID-PERMANENCE

Kosovo informal apartment additions to old buildings. © Daniel Schwartz

WHAT is the impact of forced migration on the places that are left behind? After NATO-led troops brought an end to the war in Kosovo in 1999, the capital, Prishtina, experienced an immediate and extended building boom, financed in large part by a flow of remittances from dispersed members of the diaspora. In this article, Kai Vöckler and Jonas König explore how the complex dynamics of forced migration can reverberate in an urban context beyond the physical movement of people.

by
Kai Vöckler & Jonas König

Departure city: the diaspora as urban developer

© Daniel Schwartz

Kai Vöckler is a Professor at the Offenbach University of Art and Design and a founding member of Archis Interventions, the not-for-profit branch of Archis. He has worked on urban development projects in Germany and Southeast Europe.

Jonas König is a lecturer in urban and regional economics at Technical University Berlin. He has also taught at the HafenCity University Hamburg (HCU), in the Digital Media program of Leuphana University Lüneburg and at Istanbul Technical University.

Since 2015, railway stations have become iconic places in the public mind as a result of the stream of migrants seeking to enter the European Union. From Keleti Pályaudvar in Budapest, where thousands of refugees were stuck for a forced stopover, to München Hauptbahnhof, where locals gathered to applaud and welcome the same group of people on their onward journey. Even if symbols by definition abridge—and often oversimplify—reality, it is still remarkable that this list does not include one station representing a point of decampment. The beginning of a migrant's journey can appear clandestine. Departures take place in silence, while the places of arrival have become subjects of a vibrant debate.

Doug Saunders has made a seminal contribution to urban studies with his research on the 'arrival city', suggesting that migration is at the heart of contemporary urban development and a primary factor reshaping urban space[1]. Despite challenges, an influx of people is associated with several positive effects, so long as cities are willing to integrate new inhabitants. In turn, cities can offer a broad array of opportunities for newcomers. Though research and policy efforts are crucial as migration numbers increase - and with approximately 272 million people already living outside their countries of birth - they only deal with one side of the story[2]. Migration is both arrival and departure. There is no immigration without emigration, and each typically coexists within one city. At least in the long run, it is timing that determines which dominates.

Prishtina, the capital of Kosovo, can be understood as a departure city. Its recent development has been shaped by emigration. While Prishtina grew rapidly in the immediate aftermath of the Kosovo War, it has since become a hub for a massive outflow of people[3]. Estimates suggest that at least one-third of Kosovars live abroad[4]. In effect, the Aeroporti Ndërkombëtar and Stacioni i Autobusve are the focal points in the urban fabric. While the two facilities have been - or will become - the starting points for many Kosovars on their outward journey, the traces and consequences of emigration are visible throughout the city. Places like Prishtina are counterparts to the metropolitan areas that attract migration. They are by-products of increasing human mobility. But the impact of emigration is not a simple story of decline or shrinking cities. The reality is far more complex.

Migration and Urban Development

Emigration means more than a person's sudden absence in a given location. In order to properly understand Prishtina as a departure city, it is important to recall three central characteristics of migration processe[5]. Firstly, migration only rarely results in a permanent shift of a person's place of residence from A to B. More frequently, the change in locations is temporary. Relocation to another country or city only lasts for a certain period of time, or happens during a specific phase in one's life. Even in cases of long-term or permanent emigration, there may be stretches in which someone returns to his or her old home, be it voluntarily or involuntarily (due to the expiry of a residence permit for instance).

Secondly, migration does not necessarily follow a straight route to the desired destination. Rather than immediately preceding from A to B, the path is more likely to involve bypasses, circuitous loops, and wrong directions. Migration is tied up with multiple diversions and stages. Fleeting in nature, their dynamics vary. Probably even more than movement itself, delays and waiting determine the rhythm of migration flows, and spells of immobility precede each new departure. One must wait until sufficient funds are at hand, and until the necessary visas and permissions have been granted. Thus, migration does not begin with actual departure. It has already begun in the first stages of planning and preparation, indicating a readiness to emigrate.

Thirdly, migration is a genuinely relational phenomenon. It forges a complex set of relations between people and places, which begin to emerge as soon as the move to another territory becomes an option, and do not sever upon arrival. During preparations for departure, cognitive ties arise. The target location begins to occupy space in the emigrant's mind. Meanwhile, social networks gain in significance. Contacts are established and reinforced with those who have already emigrated, or those also about to leave. Once in the new place, networks are maintained with those left behind, whether business partners, friends, or family. And as these trans-spatial patterns emerge - often with personal deprivation - political interdependencies shift too. The target country's immigration policies, for example, play an important role locally in cities of origin.

It is these temporal, non-directional, and relational characteristics that introduce a greater level of complexity. At least two aspects of migration impact indirectly on urban space. Firstly, both the preparation for, and return from, emigration require a specific formal and informal infrastructure[6]. Cities providing this tend to become hubs within broader migration flows. People move to such places to prepare for the next stage of their journey, or return temporarily for visits or to wait for the renewal of official paperwork. Like in a station, departure and arrival movements flow into one another. The city can be a starting point or stopover, as well as the ultimate goal; the desired place of return, or at least a site where emigrants leave ephemeral traces. And like in a station, waiting tends to be the dominant practice—the departure city as waiting room.

Secondly, emigration forge networks and generates relational spaces. Equally, it alters the position of cities in transnational networks. While some elements of these

Prishtina's construction boom triggered the emergence of a local construction industry. © Jonas Koenig

networks remain invisible in the urban fabric, only changing the perception and symbolic representation of places, others materialize and directly impact on the cityscape. From an empirical perspective, this seems to hold true specifically for financial flows from the diaspora. Remittances, which are commonly invested in the real estate sector, can become a dominant factor in the urban development of the cities where recipients reside. International diasporas - as the case of Prishtina illustrates in relation to the broader global network of Kosovars - haunt the cities of their departure.

Turbo-Urbanism: Post-Conflict Prishtina

Prishtina, like the entire Balkan region, has long been shaped by migration flows[7]. Throughout the 1960s and 70s, for instance, Kosovo (as an autonomous province of Serbia within the Federal Republic of Yugoslavia) was an important place of origin for guest workers employed in Germany, Austria, and Switzerland. During the 1990s, the number of refugees rose due to increasing tensions between the Albanian parts of the Kosovar population and the Serbian central government, which escalated into a war between Serbian military forces and the Kosovo Liberation Army (UÇK) in 1998. After the controversial intervention of NATO ended the conflict, Prishtina witnessed a tremendous shift and acceleration in urban development—a form of 'turbo-urbanism' characteristic of post-conflict situations and involving different migration movements.

With the war over, Prishtina became a magnet for three groups of people pouring into the city: migrants from rural areas, who hoped for better prospects for the future and perceived Prishtina as a stopover on their path abroad; refugees, whose asylum had been revoked and had to return to their country of origin; and employees of international organizations, who came to Kosovo to form a provisional international administration or work in non-governmental initiatives. Taken together, this multifarious inflow greatly increased the number of inhabitants. While reliable figures are unavailable, the population of Prishtina approximately doubled within a few years, triggering a high demand for housing and an unprecedented construction frenzy. It is estimated that over 70 percent of the city structure was (over)built during this phase[8].

Given the weakness, or lack, of institutional oversight, much construction occurred in unclear legal circumstances and informally. Prishtina sprawled erratically when peripheral farmland was transformed into building lots. Families erected dwellings for their own use, often comprising several identical buildings that were shared

© Daniel Schwartz

among brothers and their households. Meanwhile, the single-story houses of the historic centre were replaced with office blocks, shops, and mixed-use developments featuring the blue glass facades found all over Southeast Europe. Even buildings protected by preservation laws disappeared overnight. Extensions - often equivalent to entire new dwellings - mushroomed on top of apartment complexes from the Yugoslav era[9]. Together, these emerging structures fed into an apparently chaotic mosaic of uncontrolled urbanism, with a high-density centre, unclear city borders, and severe problems caused by private developers neglecting infrastructure and public space.

Much of this activity was not only informal in terms of regulatory and ownership issues, but also the construction process, with little input from architects. Occasionally, a civil engineer was consulted. Smaller developments were self-initiated and erected in family-based networks, utilizing materials found at do-it-yourself (DIY) warehouses. Project initiators introduced designs based on their experiences as emigrant workers on construction sites in Western Europe. Larger residential and commercial projects were developed through coalitions between landowners and construction companies, based on bartering and profit-sharing. Given the volatile post-conflict environment and unsteady construction process, designs tended to be highly flexible. The demands of potential buyers and the availability of funds drove perpetual adaptations.

Waiting Room Prishtina:
Remittances and Real Estate

Prishtina's post-conflict building boom can largely be explained by a sharp surge in demand. Money flowing into the country via international institutions also contributed. The real estate market offered high profits, with most parts of society benefiting[10]. But more recently, the boom has slowed and formalized. Notwithstanding a stagnant economy, very high levels of unemployment, and widespread emigration, Prishtina is still sprawling, the densification of the city centre continues, and more and more high-rise structures and large multifunctional complexes are at least projected. According to a recent survey, 55 percent of Kosovars below the age of 30 wish to leave[11]. Many have already done so, be it temporarily or permanently, legally or illegally. It is this swirling group of people that holds the key to understanding much of the ongoing construction in Prishtina.

Although (temporarily) working abroad and sending money back home to the extended family has a long tradition in the region, remittances from the diaspora became crucial

© Jonas Koenig

during and after the conflict. Exact figures are elusive, but it has been estimated that in 2002 remittances represented about 50 percent of household income[12]. While this figure has decreased, now amounting to 16 percent of GDP, remittances still play a crucial role in keeping everyday life running for many families[13]. Increasingly, they are also invested, primarily in the real estate sector. Many members of the diaspora deploy financial resources to acquire housing, whether in representative villas that have mushroomed in recent years, or single apartments or basic dwellings built independently during visits. Diaspora capital also funds smaller commercial projects, or is pooled to finance large-scale developments.

What makes both forms of resource allocation interesting is that they tend to be more an investment in symbolic and relational capital than a vehicle to obtain short-term financial profit. Creating housing space after the post-conflict surge, for instance, hardly responds to an urgent need. Once built, few of the homes are actually used. Standing empty for much of the year, they wait for the summer holidays or their owners' potential final return.

Instead, these buildings substantiate familial and social relations and allow members of the diaspora to be present symbolically in Prishtina's urban space. The structures exist due to desire, not demand. Building them invokes the past and anticipates a future yet to come. In the context of this specific temporality, any urgency to complete projects is lost, contributing to a makeshift urbanism.

This also holds true—at least to some extent—for commercial investments. Like the oversized villas and residential developments that have been erected by segments of the diaspora and their extended families, some commercial buildings seem to be more a physical expression of power and success than the answer to a vibrant and ongoing demand for office and retail space. Often, the publication of drafts and plans, and the commencement of construction works, appears to have a greater value than actually completing a project. And given that projects tend to be financed by cash and not bank loans, there are no interest payments that would insert greater discipline into the process. As a result, some of the large-scale developments emerging in Prishtina are like guests that arrived too early to a party[14].

The Past and the Future

As the case of Prishtina illustrates, remittances from the diaspora can be considered as a structuring element in departure cities. They are one of the ways in which emigration impacts on urban development, and as such, these flows of money and resources are now a typical feature of urbanism in the (European) periphery. For instance, remittances represent 26.2 percent of the GDP of Moldova and

© Jonas Koenig

around 15 percent in Armenia and Bosnia & Herzegovina, where 44.5 percent of the population lives abroad[15]. At the same time, remittances are more than a basic form of financial investment, and should not be viewed as a fundamentally economic phenomenon. They are deeply intertwined with social, political, and symbolic relations. It is this complexity, and its materialization in space, which opens up additional questions.

Like migration processes in general, remittances connect spaces and forge trans-local interactions. But they also reconfigure the temporalities of cities. In Prishtina, this has led to a 'hauntological' present of the past, and a chasm between the future and daily reality, which is shaped by a specific rhythm of waiting and lag. Architectonically, the temporality of the departure city results in provisional and highly adaptable building processes. Aesthetically, 'turbo-style' architecture recombines futuristic and anachronistic elements, as well as globalized symbols and a specific self-built culture informed by building materials from international suppliers[16]. Looking to the future, a number of challenges remain.

In what way should the diaspora, as a class of (temporarily) absent inhabitants but influential actors, be involved? How could its activities be coordinated? How can authorities encourage more productive engagement, rather than excessive investment in the built environment that is high on symbolism, but offers little practical utility? Kosovo has already established an Agency of Diaspora, though it focuses on cultural and economic issues, not questions of social and urban development. Given the structural openness of cities, municipal cooperation between the urban centres of the diaspora and their counterparts in Kosovo might be more suitable for coping with the challenges that arise from a group of people that somehow inhabit two cities simultaneously[17]. Whether the place of arrival or departure, both should be more than just stations.

● 1 — Doug Saunders, *Arrival City: How the Largest Migration in History is Reshaping Our World* (2001). ● 2 — UN Department of Economic and Social Affairs (DESA), 2019. ● 3 — Kai Vöckler, Prishtina is Everywhere–Turbo Urbanism: The Aftermath of a Crisis (2008). ● 4 — See International Organization for Migration, 'Kosovar Diaspora' (2016) accessed at http://kosovo.iom.int/kosovo-diaspora-0. ● 5 — Jonas König, 'Pristina: Departure City?' (2016) 62 dérive 4 [in German]. ● 6 — Regina Bittner et al (eds), *Transit Spaces* (2006). ● 7 — Ulf Brunnbauer, Globalizing Southeastern Europe: Emigrants, America, and the State Since the Late Nineteenth Century (2016). ● 8 — Vöckler (2008). ● 9 — Sven Quadflieg & Gregor Theune (eds), Nadogradnje: Urban Self-Regulation in Post-Yugoslav Cities (2016). ● 10 — This does not hold true for most ethnic minorities—for instance, Kosovo-Serbs and Roma. ● 11 — Dane Taleski & Bert Hoppe, Youth in South East Europe: Lost in Transition (2015). ● 12 — Economic Strategy and Project Identification Group, Towards a Kosovo Development Plan: The State of the Kosovo Economy and Possible Ways Forward (ESPIG Policy Paper No. 1, 2004). ● 13 — World Bank Group, Migration and Remittances Factbook 2016 (3rd ed, 2016). ● 14 — Simon Battisti, 'Kulla e Pambaruar' 35 Log 100. ● 15 — World Bank Group (2016). ● 16 — Srjdan Jovanovic Weiss, Almost Architecture (2006). ● 17 — Gerd Held, Territorium und Großstadt: Die Räumliche Differenzierung der Moderne (2005).

Department of Urbanism. © Karen Büscher

Goma, city of refuge

Karen Büscher is an Assistant Professor at Ghent University. Her research focus is on the relationship between violent conflict and urbanization in Eastern D.R. Congo, looking at issues such as urban governance in civil war, humanitarian urbanism, urban impacts of forced displacement and rural-urban transformation.

by
Karen Büscher

SITUATED at the heart of the Great Lakes, Goma straddles the border between the Democratic Republic of Congo and Rwanda. The city has been profoundly shaped since the early-1990s by the complex dynamics of protracted regional violence, which has produced repeated waves of internally displaced persons. Drawn to Goma by the promise of security and livelihood opportunities, Karen Büscher suggests how these arrivals have generated new forms of urbanism.

© Karen Büscher

Perceptions of Goma, in the conflict-afflicted North Kivu region of the Democratic Republic of Congo, have been shaped by stereotypes. It's seen as a rebel heartland, a commercial centre of the war economy, and a zone of sexual violence and ongoing humanitarian crisis. After more than 25 years of civil war, Goma has transformed from a dormant town into a regional hotspot, attracting businessmen, international development organizations, volunteers, and investors, as well as countless people fleeing violence in the rural hinterlands.

During the several episodes of armed confrontation in Goma's rural hinterlands of Masisi and Rutshuru, the city witnessed a massive influx of internally displaced people. In a general context of war and violence, it was possible to attain a minimum level of physical security in Goma due to the relative concentration of Congolese security forces, the presence of provincial administration, the international aid community, and peacekeeping troops[1]. Hence its image as a *ville de refuge or ville d'asile*, a status that emerged and re-emerged throughout the city's recent history and expresses both hospitality and suffering. Where at present there is a relative stability in the area around Goma and internally displaced people (IDPs) camps after the last 'crisis' have been closed down in 2015, the arrival and integration of IDPs - commonly referred to as *déplacées* - has undoubtedly left its traces on the urban socio-spatial landscape.

In line with the general trend in sub-Saharan Africa of fast urban growth, Goma's urban peripheries have been expanding and urbanizing in a rapid and haphazard way.

FLUID-PERMANENCE

The arrival of IDPs over the past decades in these peri-urban areas lacking basic infrastructure like water and electricity has added to existing pressures. Over time, some of the temporary IDP settlements have transformed into permanent neighbourhoods, generating unforeseen new urbanisms characterised by vulnerability, instability and contestation.

Peri-urban neighbourhoods like *Mugunga* and Lac Vert reveal much about the production of locality, and the day-to-day transformation of the city, through a complex intertwining of forced displacement and urbanization[2]. Informal and bottom-up urbanisation is magnified through strategies employed by 'newcomers' to order their lives, secure their livelihoods, and integrate into socioeconomic networks. Today, the IDP camps in Goma which emerged after the last major wave of violence in the territories of Masisi and Rutshuru have been closed down, but low-level conflict continues to push people into the urban centre. These then 'self-settle', often in the peripheral districts with or without the help of relatives.

In 2018, the Democratic Republic of Congo had the largest displaced population in Africa with more than 4,49 million IDPs[3]. The long history of forced displacement in North Kivu has had a profound impact. By mid-1994, there were approximately 500,000 IDPs in Eastern Congo. In 2003, after five years of war, this number peaked at 3.4[4] million. Between 2007 and 2014, fighting between the military and armed groups led to fluctuating IDP flows, and recent intensified violence in and around Beni brings the balance to approximately 1.6 internally displaced today[5]. The socio-spatial reconfiguring effect of the war has resulted in a population that is increasingly mobile and increasingly urban[6]. In search of security, IDPs tend to flee to locations that provide a minimum connection to state security services and infrastructure. Besides protection, urbanized environments also offer livelihood opportunities for people disconnected from their land. The informal peri-urbanisation of larger cities like Goma are not the unique outcome of this conflict-induced spatial transformation. Another documented phenomenon is the emergence of boomtowns around protracted IDP camps in rural areas of the Kivu provinces[7].

The Safe City

In 2014, IDPs accounted for 11 percent of Goma's entire population[8]. Yet, since usually only a minority of IDPs stays in camps while the majority self-settles in the city, and many IDPs do not register with authorities, it remains difficult to establish a complete picture. Protracted displacement due to ongoing instability also complicates the return of IDPs to their home areas. A large number have been forced to move several times. For thousands of déplacées in Goma it is not their first stay. At times they have sheltered in a camp, in other periods with family or friends[9]. This dynamic has resulted in a situation of continuous, cyclical mobility, where people oscillate back and forth between the city and their village depending on safety conditions.

Self-settled IDPs in Goma often rely on relatives, but strangers can also play this role. Ethnicity frequently shapes patterns of urban self-settlement. Fear of discrimination and exposure to insecurity encourages IDPs to stay with members of the same ethnic community, where the level of solidarity experienced should not be underestimated[10]. Yet, in terms of access to resources, livelihoods, services and basic rights, IDPs are often confronted with discrimination. After having found physical security in the city, IDPs often face socio-economic as well as political insecurity. Additionally, they are often the victim of accusation and feel insecure due to stereotypes, such as being victims of insecurity but also being alleged to be involved in insecurity. For example, a group of former IDPs in the neighbourhood of Mugunga explained how they are sometimes "seen as terrorists, because they originate from those zones where the rebels operate"[11].

Accidental Urbanity

Against a backdrop of protracted displacement, IDPs in Goma live in limbo[12]. Initially, it's an in-between life - between 'home' and the city, between rural and urban surroundings. The 'accidental' urbanity produced in this context strikes a balance between safety and contingency, and is shaped by the tension between temporality and permanency. It's clear that many IDPs in Goma perceive their urban life as transitory; being in the city rather than of the city. The city can be seen as the locus, rather than focus, of their lives. But in a situation where after almost three decades of war displacement has become a permanent state of being for thousands of people, any sense of temporariness is nuanced. While Goma appears as a place of transition, where urban integration can only be achieved to a certain degree, the city can also represent a zone of opportunity. Long-term displacement may lead to long-term engagement, creating permanent forms of urbanization. At the same time, this urbanity is clearly shaped by high levels of instability and precarity.

For many IDPs that remain in Goma for a substantial period, the urban setting ultimately offers options to construct a 'new' identity and identify with a new life. The city, with its extended educational facilities, healthcare, infrastructure, transport, markets, and culture, can provide an appealing environment to broaden one's horizons. Especially among the young, the city and urban culture have become new points of reference in their self-identity, and Goma a second home: a place of invention, interaction, struggle, and expectation. In contrast to camp environments, where IDPs rely on humanitarian assistance and survive in effective isolation from the surrounding area and community, those in the city are forced to actively interact with their urban setting. As one woman explained:

> *"Last year, I stayed in the Mugunga III camp. They gave us food, but it wasn't enough. After some time my son found out that we could stay here [Ndosho] with the family of my brother-in-law. It's better to stay with people you know. But to have food every day, it's difficult, because my brother-in-law has many people to feed already. So we try our best to find some-thing ourselves... Sometimes I wash clothes for my neighbours. But it's hard".*

Patchwork Livelihoods

A key feature of the coping economy is its almost complete immersion in the cash economy. Subsistence production is scarce. Housing, food, healthcare, and transport require ready currency. Déplacées often end up with low-paid and irregular work as petty traders, brewers, or transporters, or perform physically intensive labour. They exist on the edges of the urban labour market, which is delimited by sharp social divisions. At the same time, these marginal activities constitute the cornerstone of the local economy in Goma, on which 90 percent of the urban population relies. Because of their lack of integration in social and ethnic recruiting networks, IDPs are left in the weakest position. But like the majority of Goméens, they are compelled to combine multiple forms of informal activities to survive.

© Karen Büscher

To 'regulate' IDP employment, local authorities in several districts have introduced systems of jetons [tokens], distributed by the local chef du quartier. Jetons are handed out to not only control labour arrangements, but also differentiate between 'locals' and IDPs. On the one hand, these small pieces of cardboard offer a certain power and legitimacy to those who dispense them. On the other, they legalize or confirm the status of the person who receives them. The system reinforces the control of authorities over mobility and integration, echoing the role played by humanitarian agencies in camps. IDPs see the system as a discriminatory strategy enacted by local inhabitants to protect their own job market. It tends to reinforce—and even institutionalize—the 'temporality' of the experience of displacement.

Where possible, IDPs fall back on small-scale agriculture, leading to an increasing 'rurbanisation' of the urban periphery. This phenomenon refers the encroachment of rural livelihoods and socio-spatial characteristics on urban environments[13]. Districts like Mugunga and Lac Vert have become spaces of peri-urban cultivation, where urban and rural features mingle, and it is sometimes difficult to distinguish between being in a city or village. Subsistence cultivation is theoretically possible in the vast, open peripheral zones. These spaces are almost always someone's property, however, and IDPs often resort to illegal occupation, fuelling additional tensions with local communities.

Another consequence is a huge decrease in agricultural production in the hinterland. Combined with high

FLUID-PERMANENCE

demand generated by the growing urban population, this has led to spectacular price inflation for staple foods.

The arrival and integration of thousands of IDPs has placed considerable social, economic, and spatial pressures on Goma and its inhabitants. Existing urban governance structures have been unable to cope with the influx of déplacées in a context where the majority of the population lives in poverty. According to many Goméens, conflict-related displacement has resulted in a general 'degradation' of social life. Residents point to phenomena such as maybobo [street children], prostitution, sexual abuse, and banditisme as direct consequences of the presence of IDPs in the city. But despite these negative impacts and new patterns of conflict and competition, some benefits have accrued. Most visibly, the emergence of Goma as the regional capital of the 'humanitarian industry' has led to the indirect creation of economic opportunities[14].

Reconfiguring Space, Culture, and Identity

Across the central urban districts of Goma, the continuing arrival of large numbers of IDPs has led to a state of overpopulation. In the absence of any formal program of spatial interventions to deal with such developments, the result has been the deterioration of overwhelmed urban infrastructure. In parallel, the ongoing division of existing land parcels has sharply reduced living space for local inhabitants. These central districts are now characterized by the smallest plots, and the largest concentration of households per plot, in the entire city. In addition, because the hosting capacities of the communities in question have been far exceeded, there is a serious lack of medical and educational services. The situation has become critical.

For those residing in peripheral districts, which suffer from a lack of infrastructure, the impact is even more tangible. Due to the high levels of corruption of government departments responsible for the allocation of plots, newcomers have started building in a chaotic fashion, including in the middle of roads, or on land designated for public space. The way in which IDPs have used and occupied territory in these districts is a clear reflection of the relationship between conflict and processes of urbanization. The link between war-related rural-to-urban displacement and spatial transformation is in some cases straightforward. Mugunga, for instance, urbanised in the mid-1990s after the presence of the Rwandan post-genocide refugee camps. Afterwards, it hosted several IDP camps of which some lasted for almost ten years. The concentrated and protracted presence of IDPs resulted in a fast growth of its physical infrastructure. For example: in 2005, the Mugunga neighbourhood counted 2373 buildings, in 2010 these had increased to 9924 and in 2014 to 15275[15].

The changing use and function of the urban landscape is characterized by the 'accidental' character of IDP interaction with urban space, expressing an uneasy straddling of the line between 'making place' and settling down[16]. These peri-urban districts are examples of an initially provisional makeshift urbanity, where people rent or construct illegally and can be removed from their 'homes' at any time. The fact that after having resided for more than 20 years in a district one is still perceived as 'displaced' points to the inability of déplacées to claim urban space as their own. Settling in Goma is often a question of specific rights and land titles. Temporary leasing contracts or informal dwelling arrangements do not furnish any legal rights.

The presence of IDPs and dynamics of rurbanisation reinforce the caractère villageois of the periphery or the urban 'margins'. While Goma's central districts are seen as developed, évolué, and modern, the periphery is viewed as a place of backwardness, poverty, and ignorance. These are geographies of not only spatial, but also psychological, transition. As Trefon has rightly expressed, the areas at the edge of the city form "fascinating spaces of imbalance, where ordinary people have imagined new constructions of space and time"[17]. The dual tracks of physical urbanization are also reflected in processes of symbolic socio-spatial categorization and identification. When identity is constructed around urbanity, one's level of urbanity is often spatially confirmed. Most IDPs remain stuck in provisional urban lives and identities, neither urban nor rural.

However, as a crucial aspect of urbanity, the spatial quality of urban environments always forms the basis for the construction of new identities. The perception of oneself as 'urban' is strongly connected to notions of modernity and globalism. In the case of younger déplacées in Goma especially, individuals emphasize their urban identity, and often position themselves in contrast to the 'older generations'. Their aspirations to engage in an 'urban lifestyle' are expressed through a rejection of 'traditional' rural life, as well as through the appropriation of 'modern' urban culture, including language, music, and fashion. As a result, in some cases 'displaced' identities imply more than a sense of loss. To a certain extent, IDPs in Goma are able to transcend the generalized state of fragmentation and disruption.

The image of Goma as a city of refuge represents a double-sided picture - the city as a safe haven, and the city as a site producing new forms of insecurity and instability. Processes of socioeconomic and spatial integration of IDPs in the city offer a useful starting point to understand the transformation of urban economies, politics, landscapes, and identities in a context of war and violence. Forced displacement is a direct consequence of war. Besides focusing on how this displacement is produced, we should pay attention to what displacement in itself produces in the urban sphere. Historical social and economic aspects of particular urban localities strongly influence the experience of IDPs. But in turn, through their participation in local networks and their manipulation of urban landscapes, they also create and recreate the city.

● 1 — Karen Büscher 'Violent conflict and urbanization in Eastern D.R. Congo: The city as a safe haven' in: Mary Kaldor & Saskia Sassen (eds) Cities at War; Global Insecurity and Urban Resistance (2020), Columbia University Press (160-183). ● 2 — Lisa Pech, Karen Büscher & Tobia Lakes, 'Intraurban development in a city under protracted armed conflict : Patterns and actors in Goma, DR Congo', Political Geography (2018) 66 : 98 – 112 ; Maarten Hendriks & Karen Büscher, Insecurity in Goma : Experiences, Actors and Responses, Londdon & Nairobi : Rift Valley Institute, 2019. ● 3 — https://reliefweb.int/report/democratic-republic-congo/democratic-republic-congo-internally-displaced-persons-and-4. ● 4 — Human Rights Watch, Always on the Run: The Vicious Cycle of Displacement in Eastern Congo (2010) 19. ● 5 — See http://reliefweb. int/map/democratic-republic-congo/democratic-republic-congo-internally-displaced-persons-and-returnees. ● 6 — Karen Büscher, 'Reading Urban Landscapes of War and Peace: the Case of Goma, DRC' in Annika Björkdahl (ed), Spatialising Peace and Conflict: Mapping the Production of Place, Sites, and Scales of Violence (2016). ● 7 — Büscher Karen & Mathys, Gillian, 'War, ddisplacement and rural-urban transformation : Kivu's Boomtowns, Eastern D.R. Congo', European Journal of Development Research 31(1, 2019 ; Büscher, Karen, 'Urbanisation and the political geographies of violent struggle foor power and control : mining boomtowns in eastern Congo', International Development Policy, 2019. ● 8 — Norwegian Refugee Council, 'Living Conditions of Displaced Persons and Host Communities in Urban Goma', Goma : 2014, p 9. ● 9 — Karen Büscher 'Violent conflict and urbanization in Eastern D.R. Congo: The city as a safe haven' in: Mary Kaldor & Saskia Sassen (eds) Cities at War; Global Insecurity and Urban Resistance (2020), Columbia University Press (160-183). ● 10 — See Mercy Corps, Assessing the Humanitarian Response to Chronic Crisis in North Kivu (2014). ● 11 — Usalama Project III mental mapping exercise with IDPs, Goma, 11 April 2019. ● 12 — Awa M Abdi, 'In Limbo: Dependency, Insecurity, and Identity Amongst Somali Refugees in Dadaab Camps' (2005) 22 Refuge 7; Alison Mountz et al, 'Lives in Limbo: Temporary Protected Status and Immigrant Identities' (2002) 2 Global Networks 335. ● 13 — See Théodore Trefon, 'Hinges and Fringes: Conceptualizing the Peri-Urban in Central Africa' in Francesca Locatelli & Paul Nugent (eds), African Cities: Competing Claims on Urban Spaces (2009). ● 14 — See Karen Büscher & Koen Vlassenroot, 'Humanitarian Presence and Urban Development: New Opportunities and Contrasts in Goma, DRC (2010) 34 Disasters 256. ● 15 — Lisa Pech, Karen Büscher & Tobia Lakes, 'Intraurban development in a city under protracted armed conflict : Patterns and actors in Goma, DR Congo', Political Geography (2018) 66 : 98 – 112. ● 16 — See Bram J Jansen, The Accidental City (2011). ● 17 — Trefon (2009).

RETURN, REMAINING AND REMAKING:
Urban space in post-conflict transition

Naseem Badiey is a storyteller working in multiple mediums. As a political sociologist, Badiey has wide experience from research projects in post-conflict settings, and is currently working at the Alameda County Probation Department.

Christan Doll is a postdoctoral teaching scholar at the department of sociology and anthropology at North Carolina State University. His research bridges work on sovereignty, on the state as a cultural order and hegemonic effect, on urban space, on interventional development and humanitarian governance, and on hope and futurity in the face of precarity.

by
Naseem Badiey & Christian Doll

View of Juba from Jebel Kujur, 2008. © Naseem Badiey

IN July 2011, Juba became the world's newest national capital. After decades of conflict, the city was suddenly a magnet for a massive returning wave of ex-combatants, refugees, and internally displaced people. Exploring the effects of this rapid transformation, Naseem Badiey and Christian Doll suggest that planning efforts in post-conflict situations must take into account the invisible ways that returnees remake urban space.

FLUID-PERMANENCE

In January 2009, authorities began to demolish informal settlements throughout Juba, South Sudan. By May, the demolitions had left over 30,000 people homeless, eliciting condemnation from international agencies[1]. Most of these inhabitants had arrived only a few years earlier. They included ex-combatants, internally displaced persons (IDPs), refugees returning from neighbouring countries, and members of the diaspora. Each with different experiences of war, the groups reflected the diversity of the new state. In turn, the demolitions reflected how urban planning initiatives were ignoring the complexity of land rights amid an influx of returnees. With prices soaring, issues of reconciliation and integration to contend with, and competing claims on the crowded city, returnees were caught in the middle of an impasse.

When a 2005 peace agreement ended Sudan's long civil war—six years before a referendum gave the southern region its independence, and eight years before the new Republic of South Sudan descended into its own civil conflict—Juba was designated as the capital. The former garrison town changed enormously in the ensuing years, due largely to the massive in-migration of returnees, who had been scattered across the region and globe. At the time of the agreement, approximately 686,000 Sudanese refugees were living in neighbouring states, and two million southerners were displaced in camps around Khartoum. Also converging on Juba in 2006 were members of the diaspora, ex-combatants looking to settle in the city, foreigners pursuing business ventures, and a burgeoning aid community engaged in 'post-conflict reconstruction'. This sudden influx spurred heavy competition over land.

While many South Sudanese held customary land rights in their areas of origin, to new arrivals Juba represented economic and political opportunities. It symbolized the possibilities of a new, developed, and peaceful South Sudan, offering access to education, employment, and social services, and a space to reconnect to existing social networks and build new ones. Upon arrival, however, returnees faced the paradox of extremely high land prices and limited housing development. Few affordable housing options existed. Plots on the private market were selling for more than $15,000, making them inaccessible to 99 percent of the population[2]. Well-connected residents with local government ties could acquire plots through official allocations. Aid workers and foreigners could afford tent hotels charging exorbitant prices of up to $200 a night. But for most, formal housing remained out of reach.

Taking matters into their own hands, newcomers established homes on vacant plots in peripheral settlements—areas once off-limits due to land mines and heavy fighting. They dug boreholes, cleared roads, and built permanent structures, asserting their right as citizens to live in the capital. By creating new neighbourhoods, returnees reshaped Juba's urban layout and reconfigured its shifting geography. The seeds of a new nation were sown. By 2008, the town was transformed. Informal settlements marked by ad hoc divisions and construction stretched in every direction. Impromptu structures had sprung up in almost every vacant plot, and more lavish housing, built by titleholders, was overfilled as extended families congregated on these properties. Main roads that had once been pedestrian thoroughfares were now filled with cars and motorcycles. The war-ravaged colonial town was becoming a bustling city.

Local residents reacted defensively, fearing displacement by official plans that catered to the demographic changes, as well as the rapidly increasing cost of living. The informal settlements, and land claims that accompanied them, challenged visions of Equatorian privilege, and raised the question of what constituted lawful residence[3]. Local elites characterized the settlers as 'land grabbers' that were 'robbing' rightful owners[4]. Land disputes increased during the immediate transition period, reflecting struggles over who enjoyed legitimate residence, and which institutions had the authority to decide. While returnees were animated by their hope in a prosperous and peaceful future, long-time inhabitants were anxious about the nature of change and the place of South Sudan's diverse communities in the new state. Insecurity and competition over land and residency exacerbated existing tensions rooted in historic rivalries and wartime experiences.

The state's role in managing the transformation was unclear. In the chaotic post-conflict period, the functioning of all levels of the decentralized government was still being debated. Jurisdiction over land was a point of contention between members of two competing authorities: the government of South Sudan, and the (then) Central Equatoria State government. Leaders from the Sudan People's Liberation Army (SPLA) envisioned a multi-ethnic capital, from which a new state and national identity would emerge. But the rapid demographic change, and accompanying competition over land, exposed unresolved layers of authority in the newly autonomous region. As legislators debated regulatory approaches, international planners and with governmental interlocutors were drawing up plans to remake the town. While they envisaged riverfront walkways and neatly gridded neighbourhoods that crossed existing settlements and ethnic enclaves, locals and returnees were imagining, and enacting, different urban futures.

The official planning process was fuelled by optimism that change could only be positive, and 'development' would naturally be constructive, not destructive. Like many top-down efforts, the various initiatives simplified reality by bringing the city into a singular logic under which all elements - especially people and settlements - aligned to hegemonic goals. Juba, like other post-war contexts, carried the weight of a multiplicity of expectations from new inhabitants, who tied their own notions of citizenship to the city. These dramatic changes formed the backdrop to a series of land disputes that erupted throughout the town, some threatening to escalate into violence. One large neighbourhood that became a site of contestation spurred by self-resettlement and investment was Gudele, a sprawling peri-urban settlement on the northwest margins of Juba. The following vignettes, drawn from interviews conducted in mid-2008, offer a closer look at the challenges.

Squatting, Settling, and Investing

"I bought a small plot in Gudele", William, a long-time Juba resident, told me (Naseem). When he showed me the tin-roofed structure he had built, I was impressed by its size. I asked William if he had moved his extended family there from the small mud hut on a church compound in Kator, where they were squatting in cramped quarters. He shook his head. "It is for income". The idea was that newcomers—rich newcomers like aid workers and researchers like me—would stay and pay rent.

A couple of miles away, nuns from the small Sisters of the Sacred Heart congregation worked to remove a large community of self-settled returnees from a tract of land they owned in Block 9. The settlement was unique in its multi-ethnic composition, a microcosm of the type of national unity the new government wanted to build to overcome decades of ethnic violence and political rivalry over territory.

The nuns' claim to the land rested in part on the fact

Juba, 2006. © Naseem Badiey

Gudele compound under construction, 2015. © Christian Doll

they had remained during the decades of violent civil war, playing a political role few others could, such as informing human rights organizations of the names of missing individuals, as well as abuses committed by the government. One of the nuns, Sister Melanie, explained:

> "During the war we could have evacuated and gone to Uganda, or gone to stay with our sisters in Khartoum, but we said, 'no, we cannot go'. We are for the people, we have to suffer with them. In fact, those who are treating us like this are people who were not with us here... some were in Uganda, some were in Khartoum. When we were suffering here, they were not around. They don't know what happened here."

In order to position their interests against disadvantaged groups while retaining their moral authority as a religious charitable organization, the nuns defined their 'community' as those who had been 'in-side' Juba during the war years. They distinguished those who had been 'outside' as opportunists, who did not appreciate their years of work and generosity, and were instead coming to 'grab land'. The nuns emphasized the illegitimacy of the occupants, pointing out that they did not have legal documents, and were not needy. According to Sister Melanie, "those people act as if they have a right to live there. Some of them, at least three-quarters, are working class. And the others build houses there and rent them—they're not living there".

Despite his entrepreneurial activities in Gudele as an aspiring landlord, William, who was a close friend and fellow congregant to the nuns, was not included in the group of people they were disparaging because he was not an 'outsider'. That is, he was not a returnee. The Gudele settlers were in the disadvantaged position typical of most returnees. Separated from their communities, without ancestral claims to land in Juba, lacking the funds to acquire land through the private market, and unable to rely on political connections, their only recourse was to physically link themselves to the land through occupation and construction, in the hopes that they would eventually be issued leases for the plots on which they had built.

Originally from the nearby village of Lanya, Sarah was one of the settlers in Block 9. A young woman in her thirties, she had lived in Juba as a child. After years as a refugee in Uganda and Kenya, she returned in 2006 intending to become a resident. When she heard of the settlement in Gudele, it was a simple process of finding a small area, registering with the elected 'Block Chief', and paying a modest fee. Sarah argued that going to her home areas, where she enjoyed customary land rights, was not a viable option, because her livelihood depended on access to employment and social services in Juba. "Most people, they can't go to their villages... I work in Juba, how do they expect me to come from Lanya and work in Juba? That is the reason why I should be here in Juba". Had formal channels of land acquisition been available, Sarah argued, returnees would have taken that route.

As it was, the local government-controlled land allocations, and the private land market was unaffordable. Jane, another young settler in Block 9, pointed out, "if you want to rent a house [in Juba], they charge you six months' rent in advance! Where will you get that money? If they come to demolish us we have nowhere to go". The returnees who had settled in Gudele articulated a universalist discourse of Southern Sudanese identity, citizenship, and human rights, in which the state did not privilege ethnicity or community membership, but was responsible for promoting certain rights—to housing and access to employment opportunities and services. As Jane maintained, they had the right to be in Juba, as citizens would in any other capital, because their government was there, and because there should not be a distinction between locals and 'outsiders'.

> *"The message we got is that*
> *you come and stay in somebody's place,*
> *and you don't have rights. I was living in Uganda*
> *as a refugee, but at home I don't expect my people to*
> *treat me the same way, because this is where I have*
> *rights. This is where I feel I'm at home. This is*
> *where I feel I'm the citizen of this place.*
> *If I'm a citizen of this land, I should*
> *be respected more."*

Need was pitted against legal claims, and both were justified as 'rightful residents'. The question of where returnees should stay was linked to ideas of territorial identity, a mechanism that predated conflict in South Sudan, but that in the post-war period served as a strategy to protect against rapid demographic change, and to preserve the political autonomy of local communities vis-à-vis the new Sudan People's Liberation Movement (SPLM)-led government, whose authority was still contested in some parts of the fledgling state.

Aftermath

In the newly independent South Sudan, claims to space - whether based in indigenous rights, land ownership, occupation, or citizenship - have continued to proliferate. In 2015, Taban, a member of the Juba City Council, noted that most authorities still considered Gudele an unmanageable and ungovernable space, where policing, let alone the formalization of land ownership, was a challenge. Conflict among government leaders in South Sudan, which began in December of 2013, played out especially violently in Gudele. Nuer[5] citizens were targeted under the assumption that they were allied with the emerging rebellion, leading many to flee to the hastily established UN Protection of Civilian camps set up just outside of Gudele.

While some people regularly commuted from the camp to school or work in other parts of the city, others felt newly alienated to the city in the ever-changing political context. In February 2015, a university student named Paul lamented how the tightly knit, diverse community in Gudele had been disrupted. He had been staying on his uncle's plot for the past two years, and enjoyed the convenience with which he could reach school and other parts of town. He felt ties with those who had settled in neighbouring plots before and after he arrived. He was sad to have seen one of his neighbours, a Nuer, leave amid the nightly gunfire in early 2014, but took solace in his ability to escort this friend to transport out of Juba. As a Dinka, he could assuage the concerns of any authorities that questioned him.

Such disruption, then, had not wholly dampened the new linkages and opportunities returnees had built. Michael, a Zande man who acquired a plot in Gudele in 2006 after coming to Juba for school, explained in May 2015 that the greatest challenge for Gudele settlers upgrading their dwellings from grass and mud to concrete and metal was the fluctuation in the prices of these imported materials. But they managed to do so, and many, like Michael, could build more than structures from the stability of their Gudele plots. Michael had a stable NGO job, a truck and two cars he hired out, and a small concrete block-making business, all run out of his small plot, which also housed his brother and two Ugandans who worked for him.

Any urban planning effort in post-conflict environments must take into account the manner in which returnees and other non-elites - like Michael and Paul - are remaking space and building communities in ways invisible to top-down planning. Memories of war, expectations, notions of citizenship and ownership, and the conflicts and creations that emerge from them, are just as much a part of the making of cities like Juba as the legal documentation and government designs that tend to be focused on.

● 1 — IRIN, 'Sudan: Thousands Homeless as Shelters Demolished in Juba', 26 May 2009, available at: http://www.unhcr.org/refworld/docid/4a1f8c731a.html [accessed 24 November 2009]. ● 2 — Author interview. ● 3 — In Juba, this term principally refers to the indigenous ethnic groups of Central Equatoria State. ● 4 — Drawn from author interviews with a Bari Catholic priest (August 2008), the Paramount Chief of Juba (September 2008), and the Juba County Commissioner (July 2008). ● 5 — Nuer and Dinka are South Sudan's two predominant and most populous tribes and ethnic rivals.

Letter from Maputo: Migration, Ambulation and Urban Reconfiguration

Bjørn Enge Bertelsen is professor of Social Anthropology at University of Bergen (UiB) and the executive director of Global Research Programme on Inequality (GRIP).

by
Bjørn Enge Bertelsen

GRIP is a collaboration between UiB and International Science Council (ISC) working to foster co-designed processes of knowledge creation to understand the multiple dimensions of rising inequalities.

Maputo, 2019. © Isabelle Hugøy

IN bairros across Maputo, the implementation of "notions of resilience" in urban governance necessitates a rethinking of groups called *teams*. Given Bairro Polana Caniço's high-density nature and its noncadastrialized physical layout, it is unsurprisingly seen as spatialized in a very concrete urban sense. As Bjørn Enge Bertelsen points out in his essay, various egalitarian ideals, including the freedom to roam, are exuberantly engaged by *teams* in street-level attempts to bring an impoverished neighbourhood of African urbanity more on par with life in the Global North.

FLUID-PERMANENCE

ON a late afternoon in January 2019, I was in Bairro Polana Caniço, Maputo, and got into a white, old and half-derelict Toyota with "Tiago" who was a member of a so-called team—an informally organized group of youth common in poor areas of the city. Contemporary Mozambican rap group "Los Promessores" with the song "Falsas Promessas" ("False Promises") was blaring through oversized loudspeakers lodged in the back-window. As usual, we drove around slowly, meandering our way on the sandy roads between predominantly poor households. Stopping for a refuel of beer sold from a makeshift kiosk, Tiago recounted to me his frustration with the influx of wealthy people to the area:

> *"The rich can go screw themselves! They are part of the system of the rich, of development, of resilience. They think they are the only ones that can have a life, that can become big. To them we are lesser humans (humanos menores) with no worth. But we refuse to accept this! And with teams we create, live, expand, dream!"*

As Tiago emotionally expresses, utopian visions are intrinsic to everyday life, also in places such as Maputo. Moreover, at the current moment, the urban world is increasingly emerging as human being's imaginal and spatial terrain par excellence as a site of collective protest or as the context for experimenting with relationalities and modalities of life: Wedged between imagination and description, being and becoming, the urban affords both repressive and egalitarian and emancipatory possibilities.

Maputo: Multiforms Migrations and Movements

Tiago's outlook is characteristic of the global south's urban revolution and how migration and movement are central to postcolonial political groups like Tiago in the face of urban reconfiguration. Mozambique, moreover, is of course founded on a variety of often coerced patterns of migration and movement—from the colonial era to the present. Central here is the colonial division of the country using the Zambezi River as a boundary where African subjects north of the river were part of forced labor and migratory regimes in the large-scale concession companies. Africans south of the river were part of long-term, recurrent and in part forced labor migration, mainly to the mines around Johannesburg. Following the 1975 independence, various forms of migration between Johannesburg and Maputo—including mine work, trade and smuggling—continued to shape imaginaries and practices among all socio-economic strata of Maputo. Moreover, given the scale of circulation of people and goods—licit as well as illicit—between Johannesburg and Maputo, the cities may be seen as twining each other and to comprise a singular migratory complex. The erratic influxes of migrants, a minority of which are asylum seekers, continue to shape urban orders in Mozambique—including Zimbabweans in the central city of Chimoio, Malawians in Tete and Somalis, Nigerians, Congolese and others in major cities like Maputo, Beira and Nampula. Contemporary internal migration in Mozambique is also hugely important, making cities function as repositories of migrants, comprising both rurbanization of the (nominal) urban as well as extensive and complex connectivities between urban and rural spaces of, for instance, Maputo.

87

Maputo, 2016. © Bjørn Enge Bertelsen

Tiago's life story does reflect such multiform contemporary histories of migration: Hailing from a family with ties to both an area close by Nampula and the Northern Cabo Delgado province, he speaks not only Portuguese but also the Mozambican languages of his father and mother. Crucially, also, his story underlines a significant feature of (post)colonial life: Movement, even if merely ambulatory or cyclical, even if merely being between the twin cities of Maputo and Matola, indicate possibilities—economic, political as well as experiential.

In the following, I contextualize Tiago's movements further—particularly in relation to the growing presence of so-called teams—such as Tiago's—that roam Maputo's bairros—its poor areas. Teams can be defined as groups of young men (and some women) who cruise the spaces of the bairros, often in cars. As will be clear, the flickering urban governance through teams seems to salvage a temporal dimension from the Mozambican Afro-socialist project of the early independence period (1975-1986): A refusal to accept a confinement to present imposing limits for human expansion. Such a reading is also in keeping with developments Simone reminds us about: "[w]hat is created does not so much ground or orient [inhabitants], but constitutes a politics of making home on the run, a form of fugitive graces, where particular operational entities […] come to the fore through practices of care". While the teams do reflect "making home on the run", their roving and rowdy mobile presence also indexes a distinct life-affirming utopic register amidst the ruins of urban reconfiguration.

Mobility and Urban Reconfiguration in Maputo

Global multitudes are flocking to and generating new urban configurations—multiplex and hyperdiverse theatres teeming with life and intense experimentation with its material, symbolic and social form. Postcolonial urban formations are particularly rife with dynamics of spatial and political interrelatedness and diverse temporalities, and, additionally, often in Africa exhibit elements of "rogue urbanism". Yet, in Africa and elsewhere, we also see contours of cities oriented towards disciplining and controlling urban subjects and to preclude the emergence of alternative potential trajectories of development, enrichment, emancipation. Such a neoliberal prefiguration, what Stein has termed the "rise of the real estate state", also entails urban reconfiguration around producing an ecological order of insisting on the present—a particular present. Such insistence on the "now" eclipses an imagined future (in the form of development or revolution) which is called off as always already collapsed and crisis-ridden and to be replaced by resilient orders.

But, crucially, the new megapolises do not merely stabilize and sedentarize populations spatially as well as politically. Rather than only being tractor beams of human and fiscal capital, the constantly mutating urban orders harbor histories of displacement and migration: In the Mozambican context, this also means cities are becoming places of refuge, however impermanent, of those fleeing internal and external wars. For Maputo, this has implied that bairros

Maputo, 2019. © Isabelle Hugøy

are comprised of refugees and migrants from the country's north and its contemporary Al Shabaab conflict, the country's center where military instability waxes and wanes and, even, a host of refugees from Somalia as well as Nigeria. Many of these migrants retain complex relations to the places from whence they hailed, commonly also returning to these areas. This in turn is transforming the bairros of Maputo. Thus, wandering through Bairro Mafalala in Maputo, one would for example encounter several mosques resulting from the influx of migrants from the Comoros and, more recently, migrants from other African countries.

Adding, thereby, to the long-established patterns of forced and voluntary migration to and from South Africa and elsewhere, the city may be seen as a locus for the very possibility of movement—rather than as a spatial container of stable urban life. More than just underlining the important point made by Simone about people comprising the infrastructure of the postcolonial or African city, the case of Maputo, its history and the teams undergird how migration, displacement and ambulation are key to the horizon of poor Mozambicans like Tiago.

Teams, movement and the reshaping of Bairro Polana Caniço

Bairro Polana Caniço is not merely being challenged from its spatial margins in a cadastral sense—a form of gentrification eating away at a poor area from the sides. Concretely, this has meant that the eastern sections of Bairro Polana Caniço (i.e. north of the main artery Avenida Julius Nyerere) have gentrified heavily while the remaining non-fully gentrified spaces of the area are being shot through and perforated by fortified enclaved apartment buildings.

Perhaps contra-intuitively, in conversations with professionals affiliated with the Maputo municipality, as well as the personnel of development agencies and international NGOs, such perforation is regarded as beneficial. A common argument is that these enclaves produce a more "robust", "resilient" and "sustainable" city. In the words of a development worker affiliated with a large international NGO in September 2017:

"Bairro Polana Caniço is becoming stronger and more resilient with people with wealth coming in. With some houses becoming better, the whole bairro becomes upgraded. For the poor this is good. They learn from the rich to take care of themselves, to take responsibility for their own spaces. They [the poor] can no longer wait on NGOs or the Municipality—they have to learn to create strong and smart communities themselves and they have to learn to negotiate directly with businessmen and entrepreneurs. Frelimo [the government] cannot help them anymore. Only in this way can Maputo become resilient and smart."

As evident from this quote, in this "sprouting" of gentrification there is a powerful idea that the poor can successfully (and should) negotiate directly with capitalist developers (or their seedy agents) to sell their plots of land. In Maputo alone, 80 gated communities have sprung up in the last few years—some also, spectacularly, in quite

Maputo, 2019. © Isabelle Hugøy

destitute, high-density areas such as Bairro Polana Caniço. These enclaves function as virtual corporate city-states and, thereby, torpedo the fictions of a singular urban space and the centric city inhabited by urban citizens equipped with rights. However, they also establish relations—often exploitative—with their poorer neighbors, enlisting many of these in extremely poorly paid jobs as security guards for men or as empregadas (domestic workers) for women. Security, then, emerges as a symbolic form of violence through producing and marketing an objectified form of relationality coated in the discourse of resilience governance and future-oriented urbanism. The symbolic violence of securitization thereby entails a naturalization of a regime of fluid and predatory governance—dynamics central to resilience-oriented urbanization.

Unsurprisingly, the sense of benefit coming from the incursion of the wealthy, the perforation of the bairro and its (alleged) production of resilience—as expressed by the NGO worker above—was not readily shared by residents in Bairro Polana Caniço. Critical comments often revolved around disappointment that the state had abandoned them to speculators, agents and urban developers, that many of the wealthy saw them as servants and that their possibilities for developing their houses, plots and, thus, their lives were curtailed. Such change is often coached in terms of flexibility and of sharing spaces and resources—an appeal to marginalized urban poor who have previously barely had access to any notable resources or service provision. These now experience being instructed by development workers or by real estate agents to simultaneously service the rich and their own spaces.

This aggressive re-purposing of Maputo's urban poor does not unfold without opposition, as in the recurring violent protest that took place across Maputo in the shape of a series of crippling uprisings. However, while the specter of large-scale protests remain—its emancipatory potential, for instance, being suspended in time in WhatsApp messages recalling those heady events—there are other forces that may be described as comprising counter-movements: namely what in Maputo are called teams.

Such teams are characterized by a strong, audible, and visible presence in urban areas: Defiantly cruising the bairros in their cars, often pooling money to have acquired the vehicle and sometimes also sleeping in them. As Tiago expressed in the opening quote, they commonly refuse to be co-opted by shifting politics of violent appropriation by aggressive buyers of land or be immobilized by predatory forces of policing. Instead, the youths assertively and sometimes aggressively auto-generate presences and subjectivities that are tangible, noisy, and sometimes upsetting of the general order.

Sporting names like Team Suicido (Team Suicide), Team Guerrerro (Team Guerrilla), Team Arma do Crime (Team Weapon of Crime) or Team All Eyes on Me, they demand attention and are oriented toward provoking. A posture of antagonism and opposition that seeks to thwart the machinations of urban politics and reconfigurations, was effectively communicated in January 2016 by a 19-year old

Maputo, 2019. © Bjørn Enge Bertelsen

member of Team Bolada 1 Million—the term bolada meaning a negotiation that is dirty or illegal and which would very often involve a form of sham. The young man, whom I will name Paulo, replied to my question of why there were now, seemingly, so many teams around in Maputo—team names being written on walls and cars everywhere:

> "People are fed up! Poor are being pushed around – like before, like always. But now there is change; the poor is now useful as a poor person. He is now useful as a guard [guarda] to secure the rich while protecting the big chiefs. They say it is good that he is poor as he is not using resources, as not being bad to nature. This is a lie – it is an enormous sham [É mentira, isso – uma bolada big]! We do not accept it. We do not want to not have anything—to not be human, to be subhuman working for the big chiefs – to be a slave of nature. This has no value. For this we drive around, for this we do not care about rules, about the party [The ruling Frelimo party], about politics. They want to take away our life. For this we have to make our life ourselves."

Several others I talked to and hung around with, also made similar comments against what they saw as the instrumental use of the poor within a politics of poverty that was now, all agreed, couched within a discourse of an environmentally sound system of urban development. As Paulo's defiance exemplify, the teams comprise a particular form of counter-movement, albeit one that is irreducible to a conventional politics of resistance to marginalization—or as a response to what Sassen has identified as a global antagonistic process of an "expulsion of the poor".

Working with teams in, especially, Bairro Polana Caniço, it seems clear that these are often organized around a loosely defined area, a zona, which may be expanded, reduced or transferred all according to the dynamic and shifting notions of space. The tags that established teams (as well as those aspiring to become one) inscribe onto walls must be seen as experimentation with a politics of visibility—rather than the demarcation of something akin to gang territory. Typically centered on young men with limited or no connections to sources of salaried income (except for boladas), zonas and tags are not as important as the drawing on existing utopic political imaginaries as a form of enactment of a future that many express. In doing so, they also draw on Maputo and Mozambique's long history of complex forms of migration and the cities as repositories of refugees—especially by co-opting notions of circulation and migration being wellsprings for wealth and well-being, as many of those going back and forth to Johannesburg suggest.

There is also some research to suggest that similar forms of gangs or looser groups of (especially) young men have roamed the bairros earlier. For instance, David Morton writes that during the late colonial era in the 1950s and 1960s, young African men in Bairro Chamanculo on Sun days meandered their way through the bairro: "The adolescent servants dressed themselves up in their most stylish clothes and formed temporary gangs of

Maputo, 2019. © Isabelle Hugøy

convenience, roaming suburban lanes in search of other gangs to fight or innocents to rough up." Elderly interlocutors from Bairro Polana Caniço tell similar stories of fights and animosity between rival groups.

However, what is particular about teams—in contrast to the gangs of the old—is that their practices comprise a particular postcolonial form of life-affirming politics that reflects and redirects both the possibilities and temporalities of the Mozambican Afro-socialist period and contemporary forms of mobility and ambulation. Mobilizing aspects of Mozambican utopian politics' past—aspects that are readily available in both popular discourse and memory—teams comprise a multiplex and critical subversive engagement with urban spaces and its production of the poor as flexible operators of an emergent urban regime of resilience, adaptation and self-reliance. In the face of current urban reconfiguration, teams re-direct an imaginary of unhindered migration to achieve a sense of purpose.

Conclusion: Teams and Countering Resilience

As should be clear from both Tiao and Paulo, teams reflect a composite experience of resilience governance organized around a re-territorialization of urban domains by gentrifying structures that encapsulate and, crucially, re-purpose rather than eradicate the poor. Such dynamics reveal an ideological plain where sociality, corporality and reproduction become subjected to modes of governance where life is downscaled to maintenance work (self-service provision) or to uphold hierarchical structures (e.g. becoming security guards servicing the buildings of the rich in the bairros). In practice in Maputo, resilience governance, then, entails a re-reterritorialization of vistas for human being and her urban life: Sought eradicated are Socialist utopic ideals of the egalitarian kind, including rights, equal pay for equal work, freedom to roam (as space has become increasingly privatized to the point of doing away with urban commons), or notions of an expansive (national or urban) society where life will continue to sprout, to grow, to expand and, thereby, bring an impoverished world of African urbanity more on par with life in the global north.

In Maputo—subject to intense, changing and experimental modes of capitalist extraction and dominance—the urban poor may be read as prime exemplars of the non-egalitarian, lesser human: They are self-governing in the sense of constantly being recreated as repositories of resilience, auto-repair and adaptability (to ecological change and capitalist change—the two forces oftentimes merging into one composite form of rupturing event). Further, they are, seemingly, cut off from what was before often referred to as the state: Formations of order-inducing governance that from a unitary and centric point of view surveilled and intervened in generative as well as rupturing ways into the domain of the social. The demise of the (also the fiction of) a unitary postcolonial state does not, of course, mean that sovereignty, governance and its violence has, somehow, been vacated from

Maputo, 2016. © Bjørn Enge Bertelsen

the flow and unfolding of life. Rather, it should be taken to mean that urban formations, and especially in the south, are now in this post-polis age more susceptible to (and the result of) experimental forms of assemblages.

In the account of resilience governance and teams in Maputo, the urban is understood as a particular site for utopic emancipation that is, nonetheless and necessarily, unfinished, fleeting and, in essence both a non-place and non-placeable. Moreover, what seems to emerge from Polana Caniço is that the politics of resilience, adaptation, and environmentalism as it unfolds, entails urban reconfigurations that both have sacrificial as well as utopian elements—beyond the politics of bios and polis inherent to it.

Nonetheless, the mere existence and proliferation of teams also show us another possibility—another way life unfolds and ambulates in the urban anthropocene: Often drawing implicitly or explicitly on particular Afro-socialist utopic registers, these resist to be docilified or to have their existences circumscribed by labour relations that are exploitative. Put differently, rejecting to being confined to lesser and lesser human spaces—in the sense of being allocated increasingly fewer possibilities, resources, domains—the teams respond by expanding and inflating life: Celebrating exuberance, excess and trangression, they embody mobile, non-destituent forms of life that are irreducible to capitalist forms of exploitation, to predatory state violence and, indeed, to be uncapturable by vistas of embracing destituent power as a way of politically being in the world.

● 1 — See also Morten Nielsen and Paul Jenkins, "Insurgent aspirations? Weak middle-class utopias in Maputo, Mozambique". Critical African Studies, 2020. 1-21. DOI: 10.1080/21681392.2020.1743190. ● 2 — AbdouMaliq Simone, Improvised Lives. Rhythms of Endurance in the Global South. Cambridge: Polity Press. 2019. ● 3 — Zachary K. Guthrie, Bound for Work. Labor, Mobility, and Colonial Rule in Central Mozambique, 1940-1965. Charelottesville, VA: University of Virginia Press, 2018. ● 4 — Barbara Heer, Cities of Entanglements. Social Life in Johannesburg and Maputo through Ethnographic Comparison. Bielefeld: transcript Verlag, 2019. ● 5 — Inge Tvedten, "It's all about money": urban–rural spaces and relations in Maputo, Mozambique. Canadian Journal of African Studies / Revue canadienne des études africaines 52 (1):37-52, 2018. ● 6 — AbdouMaliq Simone, Improvised Lives, p.28. ● 7 — Edgar Pieterse and AbdouMaliq Simone, eds. 2013. Rogue urbanism: emergent African cities. Auckland Park and Cape Town: Jacana Media and African Centre for Cities. ● 8 — Samuel Stein, Capital City. Gentrification and the Real Estate State. London: Verso Books. 2019. ● 9 — Bjørn Enge Bertelsen. Violent Becomings: State Formation, Sociality, and Power in Mozambique. New York: Berghahn Books, 2016. ● 10 — Morten Nielsen, Jason Sumich, and Bjørn Enge Bertelsen, "Enclaving: Spatial detachment as an aesthetics of imagination in an urban sub-Saharan African context." Urban Studies:1-21, 2020. https://doi.org/10.1177/0042098020916095. ● 11 — Morten Nielsen and Paul Jenkins, "Insurgent aspirations? Weak middle-class utopias in Maputo, Mozambique". Critical African Studies, 2020. 1-21. DOI: 10.1080/21681392.2020.1743190 ● 12 — Bjørn Enge Bertelsen, "Effervescence and Ephemerality: Popular Urban Uprisings in Mozambique". Ethnos 81 (1): 25-52, 2016. ● 13 — Luís de Brito et al. Revoltas Da Fome: Protestos Populares Em Moçambique. Maputo: IESE. 2015. ● 14 — Saskia Sassen, Expulsions. Brutality and Complexity in the Global Economy. Cambridge, MA: Harvard University Press, 2014. ● 15 — David Morton, Age of Concrete: Housing and the Shape of Aspiration in the Capital of Mozambique. Athens, OH: Ohio University Press. 2019, p.71-72. ● 16 — See also Christian Groes-Green, "Orgies of the moment. Bataille's anthropology of transgression and the defiance of danger in post-socialist Mozambique". Anthropological Theory 10 (4): 385-407, 2010.

Emergency Urbanism and Architectures of Precarity in Sabra, Beirut.

Are John Knudsen is Research Professor (Phd Anthropology) at the Chr. Michelsen Institute (CMI), Bergen, Norway. He specializes on micro conflict, displacement, camp-based and urban refugees in the Middle East, in particular Lebanon, and has published books, chapters and journal articles on these topics.

by
Are John Knudsen

SINCE the mid-1980s, generations of displaced people have sought refuge in the ramshackle buildings that were once the Gaza-Ramallah Hospital, a multi-story hospital complex built by the Palestinian Liberation Organization (PLO). Damaged during the civil war, today the buildings blend in with the run-down Sabra-Shatila neighbourhood in Beirut's "misery belt." The multi-story buildings are examples of emergency urbanism whereby displaced people seek refuge in cities, and their story can be read as a vertical migration history of people escaping conflict, displacement, and destitution. In this article Are John Knudsen examines the buildings as archives of spatial and political histories, providing a genealogy of displacement and emplacement that can inform the study of emergency urbanism and point to solutions in cities for refugees lacking access to affordable housing.

FLUID-PERMANENCE

Gaza hospital, c. 1980, undated picture © courtesy of the PLO

The hospital complex comprised four buildings with specialized wards and local staff working alongside foreign doctors and nurses as volunteers during the civil war (1975–90). The main hospital building's sophisticated construction included floors dedicated to obstetrics and gynaecology as well an underground operation theatre.

Introduction

In the late 1970s the Gaza-Ramallah Hospital ("Gaza buildings") in Beirut was the Palestinian Liberation Organization's (PLO) prestige project and premier installation. Built in 1978 and opened a year later, the hospital was from 1982 run by the Palestinian Red Crescent Society. Damaged during the civil war (1975–90), the buildings started to fill up with Palestinian refugees fleeing ruined camps and neighbourhoods and have since remained emergency shelters for the homeless and destitute. Today nothing about these decaying buildings gives away the former role and grandeur of the Gaza hospital complex. The Gaza hospital epitomised the heyday and decline of the PLO's power in Lebanon and is an example of emergency urbanism whereby displaced people seek refuge in cities.

The Gaza buildings' history is an especially interesting one due to the way it caters to both the wartime and post-war displaced and due to the ways the buildings' form and function have changed to accommodate them. This means not only analysing the buildings as symbols or markers of historical epochs or periods, but as archives of spatial and political histories. The multi-story buildings can be read as a vertical migration history where generations of refugees and migrants have escaped conflict, displacement, and destitution. Examining the buildings' transformation provides a genealogy of displacement and emplacement that can inform the study of emergency urbanism and can help identify solutions in cities for refugees lacking access to affordable housing.

The buildings differ both in their size, internal management and clientele (Figure 1). In 2007, about 275 families lived in the four buildings; ten years later the number had almost doubled (505 families), the majority Syrians (44%), followed by Palestinians (32 %), Bangladeshi (8%), other, mainly Africans and Asians (6,5%), Palestinians from Syria (5%), and impoverished Lebanese (4%) . The boom in the unregulated property market after the 2011 Syrian refugee crisis increased the demand for private accommodation and inflated rents. In the Gaza buildings, Syrian lodgers were accommodated by adding new basement and roof top flats and subdividing and subletting two and three-room flats. Additionally, many of the original Palestinian owners have sublet their properties to incoming Syrians and either moved to Shatila or Sunni-majority suburbs nearby. In this way the buildings have also

Beirut © Bjørnar Haveland

changed character, they are no longer Palestinian, but rather increasingly multi-ethnic, with some buildings having a majority of Syrians.

In the Middle East and North Africa region, 80–90 per cent of the refugees live in towns and cities, mainly in substandard accommodation alongside other urban poor. However, there are no effective policies in place for refugees in urban areas, and the capacity to cater for refugees is often weak or lacking. In Lebanon, the large majority of the about one million Syrian refugees live under threat of eviction in overcrowded residential buildings and apartments. Since the Syrian revolt in 2011, the Sabra-Shatila area experienced a rapid influx of refugees from Syria. The Gaza buildings' tenants epitomise this process of urban encampment, and despite emergency rehabilitation of the buildings (Figure 2), this cannot offset the structural problems, such as lack of ventilation, and dampness that cause chronic health problems for residents.

Housing informality

Throughout the Middle East, housing informality and emergency urbanism co-exist amidst a rampant neo-liberalism. The historical transformation of urban Beirut is likewise reflected in the Gaza buildings' change from hospital to squatted war relic with vertical stratification and clientele typical of the periods of civil war and post-civil war displacement (Figure 3). These histories of change could therefore be considered examples of urban architectures of displacement and the creation of emergency shelter. Emergency urbanism is an avenue for urban survival for many, and a route to prosperity for the few who have been able to take advantage of the economic opportunities offered by informality, new displacement crises, and foreign migrants. The provision of adequate, low-cost housing would reduce both income differentials and profit margins and safeguard the rights to housing for the urban displaced.

Beirut © Bjørnar Haveland

The obvious need for such a change also points towards the need to reshape the policy debate on refugees from service provision and temporary shelter towards affordable housing and tenure security in urban areas. Most of the world's refugees live in cities and urban areas, and even more so in the Middle East where outdated policies, lack of money and political will engender emergency urbanism and destitution for the urban poor and displaced alike. This article has been a contribution towards understanding the causes and consequences of emergency urbanism by attending to the archival qualities of buildings and shelters. Analysing the buildings as archives of spatial and political histories can inform the study of emergency urbanism and further the shift towards inclusive cities, a new urban agenda, and the provision of adequate housing for refugees and urban poor alike.

Gaza buildings (G 1–4), aerial view (Google map, overlaid by new floor plans)
@ Image courtesy of Bjørnar Haveland

Figure 1: About 300 meters north of the Shatila refugee camp, along the west main Sabra road, the Gaza hospital complex originally comprised a nursing school, administration block, hospital, and maternity unit, locally referred to as Gaza 1–4 (Figure 2). The Gaza buildings' borderline location is at the juncture between the Hizbollah-controlled banlieues (Southern Suburbs) and metropolitan Beirut, which is at the same time a transition zone between Sunni- and Shia majority communities that divides the city and forms part of a contested frontier zone. Located near the major highway connecting Beirut with the South and surrounded by low-income neighbourhoods at the edge of the city's so-called "misery belt," the Gaza buildings lie within a legal, administrative and geographical twilight zone.

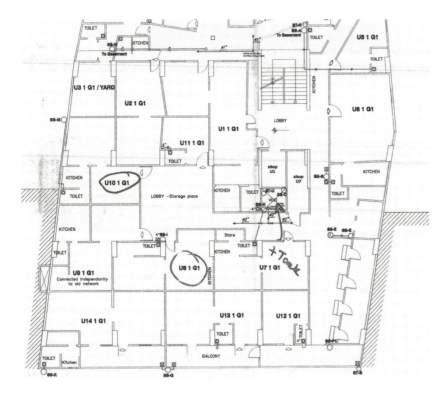

G1 building, 1st floor rehabilitation plan @ document courtesy of the NRC

Figure 2: From 2007 to 2009, the Norwegian Refugee Council (NRC) with funding from the European Agency for Humanitarian Action (ECHO) completed an emergency rehabilitation of the Gaza 1 and 3 buildings (Figure 3). The new plumbing, toilets, and sewage facilities as well as access to piped water could not, however, offset the structural problems, lack of ventilation, and dampness that cause chronic health problems for residents.

FLUID-PERMANENCE

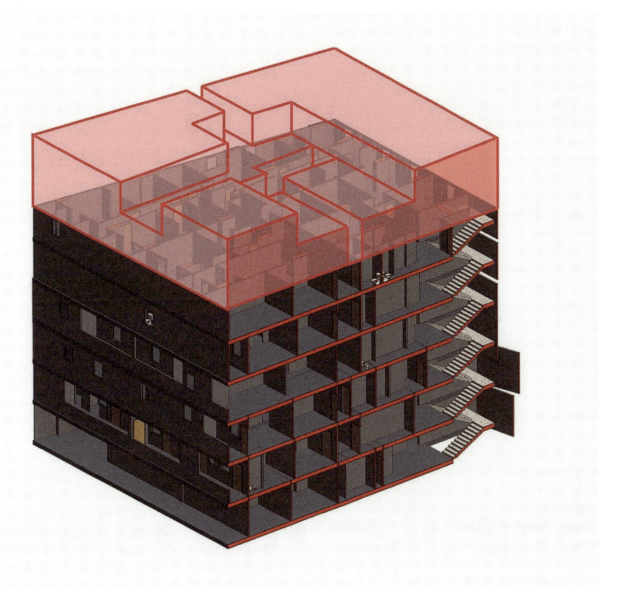

Gaza 1, floor plan (1-6), with outline of new top floors (7-8).
@ 3D image courtesy of Bjørnar Haveland

Figure 3: The first refugees moved in during 1985 when the damaged and looted buildings were still burnt-out shells, and within one year those buildings had been filled with Palestinian squatters. Despite the structural problems, overcrowding and dampness, needy families are drawn to the Gaza buildings in search for affordable housing, in-kind support, and as a last resort in the struggle for urban survival. Filled almost beyond capacity, the lodgers have exploited every nook and cranny of the dilapidated buildings – corridors, elevator shafts, roofs and basements – to extend living and storage space. Moving though the congested floors in the Gaza buildings resembles a vertical migration history, with residents escaping repeated conflict, displacement and destitution emblematic of Lebanon's chequered civil war and post-civil war period.

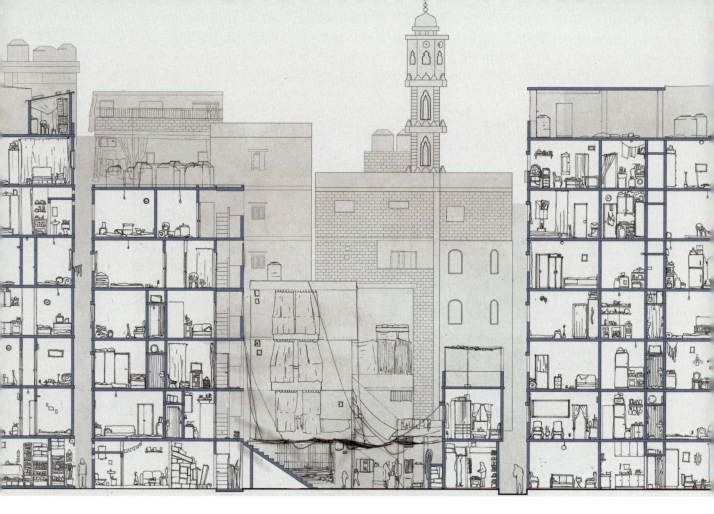

Shatila: The island of (in)stability

by
Bjørnar Haveland

THE Shatila refugee camp was established in 1949 for Palestinian refugees fleeing Palestine during the Nakba. The camp is located in Beirut next to the Sabra neighbourhood (of the Gaza buildings discussed in the foregoing article). Shatila was severely devastated during the 1982 Israeli invasion of Lebanon, and repeatedly targeted during the Lebanese civil war. On 16 -18 September 1982, between 700 and 3500 residents were massacred in the camp and the Sabra neighborhood – predominantly Palestinian residents.

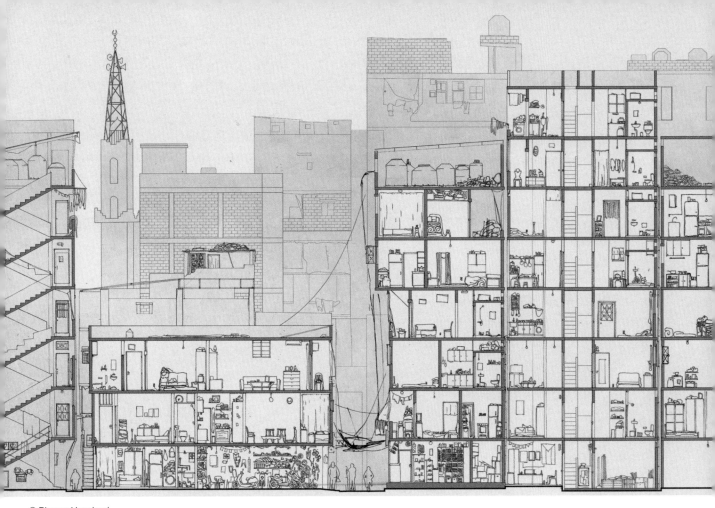

© Bjørnar Haveland

Bjørnar Haveland (BA U. Michigan), MA (BAS, Bergen) is a Bergen-based architect with a special interest in how the built environment affects human rights. As Raul Wallenberg '15 fellow at the University of Michigan he spent a year (2015-16) in the Shatila refugee camp in Beirut, Lebanon, conducting a study combining urban and architectural mapping with anthropological research methodologies to understand connections between the built environment and identity in protracted camps. Haveland now works at Kaleidoscope Nordic and is the leader of Byrop.

Initially comprising some 500 tents erected by the International Committee of the Red Cross as a temporary refuge, the camp has grown tremendously over the past decades. The camp has seen a predominantly vertical growth with units added on top of each other without either foundation or structures to support the building heights. The recurrent targeting and destruction of the camp has resulted in the extensive dilapidation of the housing and infrastructure the area is characterized by today. While there are just over 10,000 Palestinian refugees registered to the camp today estimates of the number of residents range from 20,000 to 30,000 people.

In his master thesis The Island of (in)stability, or a hotel for visiting foreigners in the middle of town (2019), Haveland created an imaginary aid project; a hotel for journalists and researchers funding the camp infrastructure, used as a narrative tool to provoke as well as highlight aspects of Shatila's politics and criticize the roles of western aid, NGOs and researchers.

Illustration: Section drawing through Shatila's built environment based on a composite of map data, typology studies and a wide sample of apartment interiors.

Acknowledgements
This article has been adapted from: Knudsen, Are John. 2019. "Emergency Urbanism in Sabra, Beirut." Public Anthropologist 1 (2): 171–93. https://doi.org/10.1163/25891715-00102003.

A taxi preparing to set off for Syria at the Charles Helou station in Beirut, 2015. © Lucas Oesch

Forced migration and living between cities: Young Syrian adults in Beirut

Lucas Oesch is a researcher at the University of Luxembourg. He spent several years doing fieldwork and lived in Jordan, Syria and Lebanon. He holds a PhD from the Graduate Institute of International and Development Studies (IHEID) in Geneva, and was a research fellow at the Universities of Neuchâtel, Lyon and Manchester. This research was supported by a Swiss National Science Foundation (SNSF) fellowship (161164).

by
Lucas Oesch

Upon arrival in Beirut, most of the young Syrian adults I encountered decided to settle and live in areas of the Lebanese capital which represent important poles of urban centrality

IN the context of the recent so-called refugee 'crisis', attention has been given to how train stations in large cities become important transit hubs for forced migrants, on makeshift camps of tents which appeared around such transit hubs, and on several urban infrastructures, such as old sport stadiums and airports which were used to 'host' or 'exclude' forced migrants. However, less attention has been directed to other dynamics around forced migration in urban areas. Through his research, Oesch looks closer at how the last decade's unrest in the Middle East and the resulting displacement have impacted the urban space in less visible ways. Or, put in other words, how cities play an important role in the lives of displaced for less visible reasons.

People gathering in front of a theatre showing a Syrian theatre play in Beirut, 2016. © Lucas Oesch

In my research, I examine some of the underexplored links between cities and displacement in the context of the Syrian crisis, focusing on the 2011-2016 time period. I do this by analysing how some young Syrian adults belonging mainly to the middle-class had progressively decided to relocate to cities in countries bordering Syria (Lebanon, Jordan and Turkey) since the start of the Syrian conflict. I begin by highlighting the importance of centrality for these migrants, i.e. of living in central areas of cities. I also underline the strategies used to secure accommodation. I then present how some young Syrian adults were living between urban centralities, commuting back and forth on a regular basis between multiple cities and countries, including sometimes their home town. Finally, I show how this search for new centralities was often perceived as a temporary move, before being able to either settle back home, or move further.

To illustrate these uses of urban space, and their impacts on cities, I will refer mainly to young Syrian adults who I encountered in Beirut between 2011 and 2016 while conducting field research . They were mostly moving alone, i.e. they were single and did not have any children. There was often a mix of motivations according to which they decided to move, and these reasons were often entangled. They were ranging from having lost their occupations in Syria, or part of it, because of the crisis, to avoiding compulsory military service or because of political views, and more generally due to the lack of security and (economic) perspectives in their country. Their move was thus situated somewhere between forced and voluntary displacement. Some young Syrians also noted that a large number of their acquaintances had come to Beirut, or travelled even further.

The Lebanese capital is only a few hours drive from the Syrian capital, Damascus. In 2016, Lebanon hosted about 1 million Syrian refugees . Among 30,000 of them were in the Beirut Governorate , which does not include surrounding municipalities connected to the municipality of Beirut. Many more resided in these peripheral areas of the capital. Moreover, these numbers only included people registered with the United Nations High Commissioner for Refugees (UNHCR). Many others took the decision not to register. This was the case for a majority of young adults I meet. They were generally stressing that the reason why they did not register was because they did not feel 'in need'. A report was mentioning an overall estimation of a number of 1.55 million Syrians in this situation in Lebanon. It is referring to them as mostly 'middle-class professionals and wealthy Syrians' . Some of them were already in Lebanon prior to the start of the crisis in their country, but from then on unable to return. This is certainly a simplified categorisation as, for example, numerous less well-off seasonal migrant workers should also be included in that group. And they also had been moving back and forth between Syria and Lebanon for a long time. Most of the young adults I met, however, fitted in the 'middle-class professionals' category.

Searching for centrality

Upon arrival in Beirut, most of the young Syrian adults I encountered decided to settle and live in areas of the Lebanese capital which represent important poles of urban centrality (mostly in the neighbourhoods referred to as Hamra and Achrafieh). These locations were important in terms of re-creating social networks, in part with other Syrians who had also moved to Beirut. It was also important in order to find work opportunities and to live in, or near, the vibrant areas of the city. For many, this search for urban centrality was however not completely new in their lives. Many of these young adults had in fact, already before 2011, been attracted by this centrality when in Syria, and above all in Damascus. For those who were not originally from Damascus, many had been living for some time in the Syrian capital. They had moved there from their hometown, mainly to complete their higher education, or in order to find work opportunities.

This search for centrality required finding an accommodation. When in Syria, especially if they were not originally from Damascus, and if they did not have any relatives living there, young Syrian adults were often renting rooms in old damascene houses and more recent flats in several central areas of the Syrian capital (e.g. the Old City, Sarouja, Shaalan). Some of them would even rent whole houses or flats, and sublet rooms to other young people. These accommodations would also often be shared with young foreigners who were coming for short periods to Damascus, e.g. to learn Arabic.

When they decided to move to Lebanon starting 2011, to be able to live in central areas of Beirut, where accommodation costs are high, many young Syrian adults belonging to the middle-class replicated the same system. They rented rooms in shared flats, or whole flats, either individually or collectively, and then sublet rooms, mainly to other young Syrians and foreigners. By comparison, only about 60% of Syrian refugees who registered with UNHCR in Beirut and its periphery were able at that time to find shelter in apartments, the remaining were living in informal settlements, substandard buildings and collective centers. The proportion of registered refugees living in apartments in, and near, the Lebanese capital was however higher in comparison to the rest of the country.

For the young Syrians who had never left their home town or even family house, moving to Beirut was a drastic change in their lifestyle. However, for others who had already moved in the past within Syria, mainly from their home town to Damascus, this was rather an extension of their 'mobility pattern' and a replication of their previous lifestyle. Majid, a young Syrian actor, would even see a form of intergenerational continuity in this mobility. He explained that, in the past, "to find work, our parents had to move from their villages to cities in Syria, and now, because of the war, we have to change cities again". Nevertheless, this time, it implied crossing an international border and going to another country. As a matter of fact, many of the young Syrians I encountered had never been to Beirut before, or only for very short visits. Rima, who had been in Beirut for about 9 months when I met her, would tell me in an amused way that "it is the first foreign country ever that I am visiting".

Beirut had since long ago been an important place to come for work or stay for Syrians. This was however mostly the case for seasonal workers (e.g. construction workers) whose number in Lebanon was estimated around 350,000 before the start of the crisis in 2011. It also concerned the elites, but not as much less well-off young adults of the middle-class.

In-between cities

When they arrived in Beirut and settled in some of its central areas, many young Syrian adults tried to pursue their previous activities. Some had even secured their new occupation before deciding to move. Arabic teachers found new language centres to teach in, a lawyer a new study to work in, an architect a new firm, a café manager started a new establishment, actors found new theatre plays and TV series to act in, and so on. For others, on the contrary, their move to Beirut signified a greater change in their life trajectories. They seized new opportunities, such as working for international NGOs dealing with the Syrian crisis. However, in addition to having family and friends still in Syria, some also kept part of their livelihoods there. They started commuting on a regular basis between Beirut and their home city in Syria, or adopted city. Actors would go back to Damascus as they were still involved in artistic projects, others were still pursuing their higher education and going back during exam periods, while some had to go back as they were still registered in professional associations (e.g. the bar association, and so on) and keeping part of their professional activities there.

These back and forth movements were possible as, until the beginning of 2015, Syria and Lebanon had an open border and free movement policy, until Lebanon started to restrict the conditions of entry and stay for Syrians on Lebanese soil. These movements from and to Damascus and other cities in Syria were also feasible by the fact that the Beirut-Damascus road was not cut-off by the fighting going on. Even if, as time passed by, more and more checkpoints of the Syrian army were set up along the road, extending travel times. Amina, a young Arabic teacher, estimated that before these delays started, to go from Beirut to Damascus "was taking barely two hours, similar to going from one Syrian governorate to another". The Charles Helou station in central Beirut remained most of the time a vibrant transport hub with taxis and buses regularly setting off to Damascus and other Syrian cities. Since 2015, and the change of entry requirements in Lebanon, it has however become more difficult for Syrians to continue moving back and forth.

Space of transit

Many young Syrian adults I met perceived their life in the central areas of Beirut as a form of transit. That is part of the reason why some kept strong links with their previous life back in Syria, such as with relatives and acquaintances, and even part of their activities, hoping to be able to fully and easily settle back there when possible. Others were thinking of a second move, mainly to Turkey or Europe. The perceived temporariness of their stay in the Lebanese capital was expressed in several, and sometimes colourful, ways. Rana, a young Syrian actor, would explain to me that she does not feel that "Beirut is a city which embraces you and makes you want to stay in like Damascus does". Majid, the young actor, would tell me that in the apartment he lived in Beirut, there was a storage with all the suitcases left by other Syrians who had lived there for a while, before deciding to pursue their journey further on. They would leave behind some of their belongings, which they did not have space enough to take along, imagining maybe being able to come back later to recover them. According to him, "Beirut is like a metro station", a place where you only transit.

The 'transitness' of Beirut for some Syrians was also manifested in other ways. With numerous international flights not going to Syria anymore, Beirut airport became a hub for international transport for Syrians. Buses and vans would even bring or pick up Syrian passengers from the airport to drive them directly to Damascus. Beirut also became an administrative centre for Syrians. With many Embassies closing in Syria, most Syrians had to come to embassies located in Beirut to file their visa applications to overseas countries.

While they were 'transiting', and either waiting for their flights to depart or their visa applications to be proceeded, or living 'between' cities, some places in Beirut became well known to some young Syrian adults; which hostels to sleep in, which restaurants to eat in, and in which cafés to spend time, and most importantly, to be able to meet acquaintances, commonly friends from back in Syria who had moved to Beirut.

Syrians, or the presence of Syrians in Beirut, also started to change the landscape of Beirut's streets. Syrian theatre plays were showed in Beirut's theatres, Syrian restaurants and cafés opened, some Syrian products and brands could be found easily (such as Kharta yerba mate packed in Syria), and so on. While this was not completely new in Beirut, the intensity of the phenomenon became greater after 2011, and it was carried out in new ways. For example, theatre plays performed by Syrian actors would not only be showed in Beirut, as this was already the case before 2011, but now also put on in Beirut, with actors rehearsing there. The visibility of Syrians, and of Syrian 'activities', increased in Beirut's streets. Amal, a young Lebanese woman, would explain that "before, for Lebanese, Syrian presence [in Lebanon] was limited to the army and migrant workers". She was referring to the presence of the Syrian military forces in Lebanon in the aftermath of the Lebanese civil war; presence which lasted until 2005. Amal explained that, since 2011, she now meets new categories of Syrians in Beirut, like young middle-class adults, and that this is becoming something 'normal'. Picard mentions that there had been other categories of Syrians in the past in Beirut as well, such as businessmen, but that they were mainly 'invisible'. However, the new interactions with

Beirut, 2019. © Urban-A / Ida Zeline Lien

Syrians and their visibility which started after 2011 have not always been perceived in a positive way by part of the Lebanese opinion, as reflected by a provocative article published by the newspaper An-Nahar in January 2015 entitled 'Al-Hamra is not getting Lebanese anymore… The Syrian growth has changed its identity' . It referred to Al-Hamra, one of the famous trendy and commercial areas of Beirut.

Besides, some of these 'Syrian places' also came to reflect the 'transitness' of the city of Beirut for some Syrians. Some establishments indeed closed after a short period of existence. This was the case for a Syrian snack restaurant which had started a branch in Beirut and shut down after less than a year, as well as a café opened and managed in part by Syrians, and which had become an important place where young Syrians would meet and spend some of their time. Oroub, a young Syrian lawyer, was explaining, about this café, that "it's a young Syrian who opened it. He used to run a café in Syria (…), and he tried to somehow recreate this place in Beirut". She considered that it was an important place as, "for Syrians in Beirut, there is a loss of identity, and they like to have places like [this café] where they can meet again"

Conclusion

By the beginning of 2016, most young Syrian adults who, at some point since 2011, I had the chance to meet in Beirut had moved further on. Some had relocated to Istanbul, while others moved to Europe 'with a visa' in order to study, work or re-unite with members of their family who had successfully settled there, as well as using so-called 'irregular' channels and roads. Overall, many Syrians are still in Beirut and living in some of its central areas, and Syrian establishments are still flourishing in the Lebanese capital.

This article has shown the importance of cities and urban centrality for some categories of migrants in a context of displacement. It has also exposed how some migrants in such a situation start living between multiple centralities and cities in different countries, sometimes including their home town, keeping links in and commuting between these different urban spaces. Finally, it has presented how this mobility between several urban centralities is often perceived as a temporary life 'in transit'.

● 1 — All names have been changed for anonymity purposes. Interviews were conducted in Arabic and/or English. ● 2 — UNHCR. (2016b). Syrian Refugees Registered, Lebanon, 31 March 2016. Syria Refugee Response. ● 3 — UNHCR. (2016a). Distribution of the Registered Syrian Refugees at the Cadastral Level (Lebanon: Beirut and Mount Lebanon Governorates), 31 March 2016. Syria Refugee Response. ● 4 — WB/UNHCR. (2016). The Welfare of Syrian Refugees: Evidence from Jordan and Lebanon. Washington: The World Bank. ● 5 — AUB/UN-Habitat. (2015). No Place to Stay? Reflections on the Syrian Refugee Shelter Policy in Lebanon, p.51. Beirut: UN-Habitat/American University of Beirut. ● 6 — Interview, 11.02.2013. ● 7 — Interview, 10.01.2014. ● 8 — Chalcraft, J. (2009). The Invisible Cage: Syrian Migrant Workers in Lebanon. Stanford: Stanford University Press; ICG. (2013). Too Close For Comfort: Syrians in Lebanon. Middle East Report, p.3. Brussels: International Crisis Group. ● 9 — Picard, E. (2006). Managing Identities: Expatriate Businessmen across the Syrian Lebanese Boundary. In I. Brandell (Ed.), State frontiers: Borders and boundaries in the Middle East. London and New York: I.B. Tauris. ● 10 — Interview, 08.01.2014. ● 11 — Interview, 03.01.2014. ● 12 — Interview, 11.02.2013. ● 13 — Interview 26.01.2014 ● 14 — Picard, E. (2006). Managing Identities: Expatriate Businessmen across the Syrian Lebanese Boundary, p.83. In I. Brandell (Ed.), State frontiers: Borders and boundaries in the Middle East. London and New York: I.B. Tauris. ● 15 — An-Nahar, newspaper, 06.01.2015. ● 16 — Interview 21.07.2014.

The Battle for Home: An Interview with Marwa Al-Sabouni

Interview by Alexis Kalagas

Marwa al-Sabouni is a Prince Clause laureate 2018, and has been named one of the Top 50 thinkers in the world by UK Prospect Magazine. She was listed as one of the top contenders for the Pritzker Prize 2018, was on BBCs 100 Women list in 2019, and her TED Talk has been viewed over one million times. Al-Sabouni is based in Homs, Syria, where she runs a private architectural studio.

Alexis Kalagas is an urban strategist and writer. The recipient of a 2018 Richard Rogers Fellowship from the Harvard GSD, he is exploring alternative development models for affordable housing, focusing on innovations in financing and the application of new digital technologies. Kalagas recently worked with Urban-Think Tank for four years, where he amongst other contributed to the development of this journal.

Illustrations taken from Al-Sabouni's book The Battle for Home: the vision of a young architect in Syria. © Marwa Al-Sabouni.

IN our interview with Marwa al-Sabouni we are privileged to get an up-to-date view on the Syrian crisis from Homs. Al-Sabouni has lived through the violence and destruction of the city's three-year siege, and has documented her experiences in her book The Battle for Home: Memoir of a Syrian Architect. Al-Sabouni offers an eyewitness account of the urbanization of the conflict, and explains how the built environment played a role in the eruption of sectarian violence. In this interview, al-Sabouni discusses the role of architecture and urban planning in the lead-up to and during the war in Syria, and how the conflict continues to impact peoples everyday life today.

Alexis Kalagas: One of the main ideas explored in your book, The Battle For Home, is that the modern transformation of Syrian cities contributed to the outbreak of the war. Could you explain what you mean?

Marwa al-Sabouni: I suggest that the urban configuration and settlement pattern, as well as the new kinds of architecture that were introduced over time, contributed to a process of social segregation. This affected the connections and daily encounters among people, and therefore their sense of belonging and tolerance - their sense of creating something together. The comparison between the old city and the new settlements in Homs is where architecture's role is most evident. Residents used to express their love towards their built environment, and consequently towards the neighbours who shared these places and structures. Compare this with the experience of people in high-rise blocks and informal areas. Once the conflict erupted, those informal areas were the first to be destroyed, and the first to become inflamed by violence and division. People were not only physically distant, but also mentally and socially distant from each other. The differences between the old city and the new settlements can be most clearly understood through four main elements: the connection to nature, the role of the marketplace, the openness of spiritual sites, and housing. There is a sheer and immediately visible contrast. For example, in addition to being a place of commercial exchange, the old marketplace is also a place of production. In the case of spiritual or sacred sites, I discuss in the book how mosques and churches used to be placed, the size of building they were housed in, and in what way they faced people in the street - how welcoming or inviting they were. I contrast this with the more isolated and oversized structures in other parts of the city. The size, configuration, and materiality of these urban spaces have in my view contributed to how people behaved and related to each other during their daily routines.

AK: It was interesting to hear echoes of Jane Jacobs' critique of modernist planning in a completely different cultural context. Were you already thinking through some of these ideas before the war began?

MS: I was actually only introduced to Jane Jacobs' work after the publication of my book. One of my friends recommended it, as he suspected I would find it very inspiring. The way that Jacobs looks at urbanism in terms of economic effects is enlightening. But what I think is missing in a comparison between American and Syrian cities is history. When you look at Syrian cities, history is the added element. It adds to the social aspect as well as the economic dimension. But going back to your question about how I was thinking before the war, in my graduate research I was addressing topics like globalization and the meaning of vernacular architecture. I was interested in comparing how we approach our traditional architecture, and the history of architecture that we have, to the way in which we were introduced to architecture as students - mainly to modern architecture. To me, there is a disconnect between what we've inherited in a historical sense, and what we're designing and implementing in our cities. And this extends to how the international architectural community defines the mainstream architecture that is being designed and built around the world, which was perceived in Syria as the ideal form for us to emulate locally. That was my area of interest, and that's where I had questions and tried to pursue research. But once the war began, the role of architecture in contributing to social divisions, as well as the broader role architecture can play in our lives, became very clear and very important to me.

> AK: There has been a very positive international reception to your book, but how has it been perceived within Syria?

MS: Zero interest. They all ignore it.

> AK: As I understand it, your family and friends have almost all left Homs. Why did you choose to remain despite the danger and destruction?

MS: Basically, I wasn't forced to leave. That being said, my family and I were, for over three years, caught in the middle of the battle line between the conflicting factions. We had to endure the straying bullets, mortar missiles, stationed tanks, kidnapping, snipers that we had above our heads, at our door steps, and even inside our home. It is like the case of today's global pandemic, some of us stay put hoping that things will be better, or as a result of not having real alternatives. We were a young family with little money and a belief that the only control we had over the situation was through the choice to stay and live the situation day by day, moment by moment. We chose to be patient, tried to be rational and avoid panic. We held to our faith and tried to keep positive, although we did not have much to do. Millions of Syrians were forced to leave during this war, but most of the people that I know who have left, were not forced. They chose to leave because they couldn't bear it anymore, or because they felt there was no future left, or that this was not a life. But I also recognize other cases where people were really forced in the true meaning of the word - having their children or young sons kidnapped, or forcibly conscripted into the military, or their home literally falling down on top of them. Those people had no place to go. But most of the people I know, they left by choice. And most of the people who reach Europe, many of them had choices, because the journey costs a lot of money. This kind of money would grant you other options, if you decided to remain here in Syria. Elsewhere in the Middle East, Syrians are often treated badly by the host communities. The people in some countries. For most Syrians, their stay in other countries in the Middle East is only a temporary phase. At the same time, it also depends on the country. For example, in the United Arab Emirates you have to have a lot of money to afford to live there. But then once you're there you're not treated badly, compared to living in Jordan or Lebanon. This is why it is temporary. Because it either costs so much, or you're not made to feel welcome.

> AK: Are there many people displaced from other villages or towns in Syria that have sought refuge in Homs?

MS: Yes, people from the countryside have moved to the cities, to safer neighbourhoods or safer villages. The demographics of Homs have changed drastically. Complete neighbourhoods have been transformed. But no construction or reconstruction is being done. You either rent a place, or you live in a partially destroyed building or a tent supplied by an NGO.

> AK: Thankfully, most people who read your book will never experience what it means to live through a conflict. How does daily life change in an urban environment?

MS: That's a hard question. It's very complicated to answer because we have so many different contexts depending on different phases of the conflict. People imagine that the worst part is the life-threatening part, and that is partially true. It's terrifying to worry about your life on a daily basis. But it's also nerve-wrecking to deal with the social impact of the war during moments of relative peace. I think that aside from the decline in services and amenities, and the sharp rise in prices as a result of the conflict, people have also changed. It's very hard to find someone you can trust, or someone you can talk to, or someone you can work with. It's like living in a desert of a place - there's just nothing there. There are no trees anymore. Heating is a problem in winter, and cooling is a problem in summer. Electricity is a problem all the time, although it's been good for months now, so I can't complain. But people need to run generators constantly, which hum and smoke. I don't have a car, so I don't have to worry about fuel, but I hear people waking up at 5am to line-up at the station to fill their tanks, and even then, sometimes, there's nothing. We call these crises. There's the crisis of fuel, the crisis of gas, the crisis of electricity. It fluctuates. Sometimes you have them, sometimes you don't. And never all at once. People are preoccupied with this most of the time. It's improved a lot though. I look back at the first years of the conflict, when we didn't have electricity for days or weeks, and now we have a system of power cuts. This affects street life, affects shops, and affects new businesses. The health sector represents another severe challenge. Hospitals, clinics, medications - it's all very corrupt. It's a sector of the economy that you don't want to deal with. It's become a business for so many people, and the most horrific crimes have been committed inside hospitals. To make it worse,

the sanctions mean you can't find certain medications, or they're very expensive. And then we don't have enough doctors because they've fled, or have been killed. The final thing I can think of is education, because I have two young children. My husband and I always worry about the quality of their education and the quality of their social experiences; where they can find friends that won't be a bad influence, or how they can be encouraged to seek out knowledge and have access to quality teachers. With the trauma suffered by so many people of all ages, it's a mess.

AK: Reading your book, I thought a lot about the idea of urban resilience. From what you described, it seemed like the old city was much more resilient during the conflict than the new.

MS: It all revolves around building materials, because they influence construction methods as well as the shape and form of the architecture. This boils down to a final aesthetic look, but also a sustainable building life and performance. I can't think of a more important element to differentiate between the old and the new city than the materials used. The new architecture - I cannot call it architecture - the new buildings introduced into our cities are like fast food. It's just commercial interests, nothing more. There are no considerations beyond profits for the developers and the city committees. People are excluded from the equation. Labels like 'sustainable' or 'green' are just a cover. But in the old city, it revolved around placing people, settling people. The means and aim were completely different, which is what we, as architects and planners, have to refocus on. That's the main lesson we can take from our old cities.

AK: You have written about the possibility for community to be expressed through architecture. When you look to the future, are you optimistic that this can still be the case given the fractures and divisions that have become so entrenched in Syria?

MS: Architecture can definitely contribute with a lot in this area. That is my conviction, and that is what I try to make a case for in the book. But I'm not really optimistic about the degree to which this message will be picked up and carried forward by others. I have to be realistic and look at how things are being prepared for the reconstruction of Syria. I also have to look at previous experiences in places like Sarajevo and Beirut - other cities that were affected by civil war - and what kind of reconstruction followed. At the same time, I still place hope in the work that I, and others, are doing, and this kind of growing global awareness about the role of urbanism and architecture in contributing to peace among people.

AK: Something that particularly struck me was when you described a new generation that has never known the sense of belonging through a shared identity. How difficult is it to recapture a sense of togetherness when an entire generation has lost the connection with its past and the sense of beloning?

MS: It is extremely difficult, because this neighbouring countries have acted with generosity and in a very welcoming way toward Syrian refugees. But generally, there is this perception that we are coming to steal jobs and be an extra burden on already challenging circumstances. So Syrians are not very welcome in surrounding to your question about how I was thinking before the war, in my graduate research I was addressing topics like globalization and the meaning of vernacular architecture. I was interested in comparing how we approach our traditional architecture, and the history of architecture that generation is suffering from so many problems, including the lack of a shared identity. Architecture alone cannot heal this, but if we look at the social codes that used to govern our cities, and how this aligned with the spaces people inhabited, there is a chance to relive and recapture this. There is always hope, especially if we look at the history of Syria and this land. How many times it was destroyed, how many times it has witnessed severe destruction, how many times it has been the setting for brutal battles and wars, and how many times it has risen again. But we are rising now at a time when technology is not helping. I will sound very old-fashioned, but technology and social media is not helping. My only hope is that there will be enough people to share these kinds of ideas and help in restoring what we had, rather than just continuing on the same path we were taking before. My focus is on delivering this message. As long as it's delivered, as long as the ideas we've been discussing are spread, and as long as there are people sincere and aware enough to act on them, then I don't care if I have a role or not. We are currently suffering from a mass disinterest in knowledge. I say this because I teach at a university. I encounter young people and future architects on a daily basis, and I see how disinterested most of them are in acquiring knowledge. For many young men, college is just a way to avoid military service, because if you're studying you don't have to go to the army. Very few students are interested in education, and for those who are, many do not have access because of the current stuation. Many have lost all hope. You have to imagine that the young people who are now 18 and 19 were 10 and 11 when the war started. They have developed a sense of apathy. They don't care.

AK: If that is the case, who do you think will lead the rebuilding of Syrian cities?

MS: I think it will be a combination of developers, and warlords, and international interests. We have to fight this. We can't leave it to that dark future. We have to fight it. And that is what I'm trying to do.

Part Two

FROM RESEARCH TO DESIGN
This section looks at work that reveals a renewed confidence in the responsibility of architects, non-architects and artists to recount and transform the world but also create places for meeting, confrontation and exchange of views.

From Rese to de

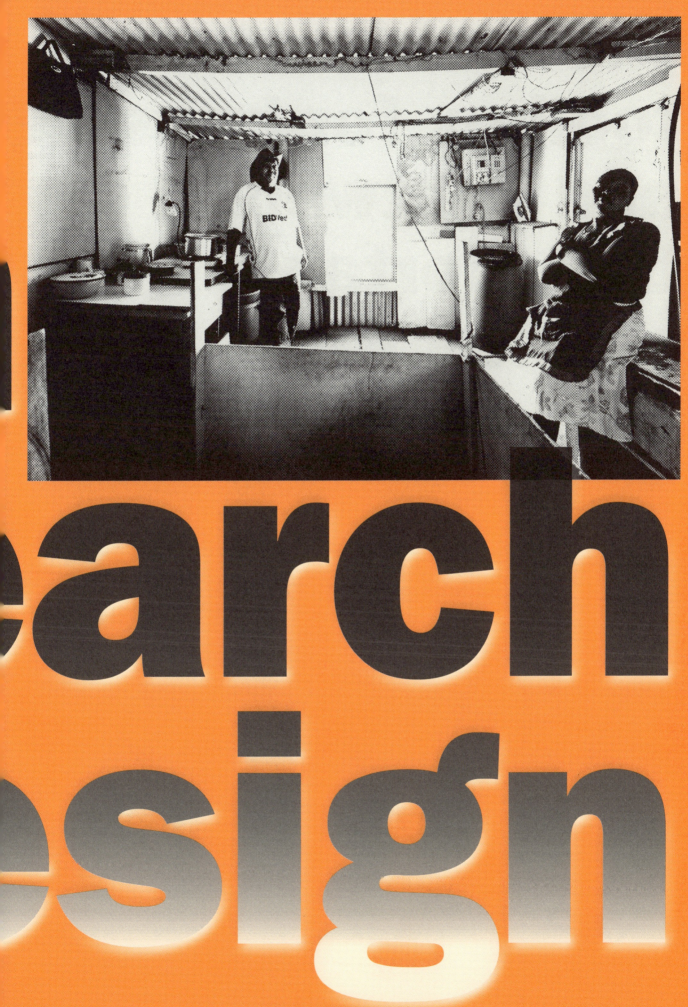

The architecture toolbox for housing and lightweight transportable architecture

FROM RESEARCH TO DESIGN

116

Village being constructed © Tamas Buynovszky

Sample of a bed © Tamas Buynovszky

(U-TT) design-build 'Project Village' for Hello Wood in Hungary was conceived as the 'Migrant House', a simple structure that provided the initial point of orientation for migrants arriving in Hungary. The vertical structure was designed to create a sense of identity for this disparate group of individuals, while its open frames were slowly filled in with the remnants of past lives. The resulting bricolage represented the collective embodied spirit of those that temporarily chose to inhabit its spaces, at the same time planting foundations within the broader Project Village.

A project by
Urban-Think Tank

Part 1:
Migrant Housing

Urban-Think Tank's proposal sought to transform the idea of the Migrant House into a dynamic concept of 'Transportable Housing'. Each team, consisting of students, professionals, and migrants, was given the task to design a house unit - a series of rotating frames that can configure into a multitude of spaces based on personal needs. These individual dwelling units have material limitations that prevents the construction of solitary housing. However, as the individuals inhabiting the units begin to form relationships - friendships, groups, romantic entanglements - the units can transform. The project led to a collective force of design, where the units fulfil their structural potential and permit a range of variations and combinations, allowing for community building.

Today, U-TT is developing a range of practical housing strategies for Townships in South Africa embedded within community-driven processes. The Migrant Housing project builds upon ideas of modular construction, community capacity building, rapid and incremental upgrading, and quick, prefabricated assembly and disassembly methods. Their ability to be transported and rapidly installed, transformed, and dismantled is key, and a major performative element. The project questions how displaced individuals begin to establish relationships with other traveling migrants. What are the spatial structures that allow assemblage, growth, reconfiguration, and transformation? Can architecture preserve individual identity while contributing to integration?

The 'Migrant House' design utilizes modular and prefabricated construction, and can be assembled within 12 hours by a small team without large equipment. The structure can be enclosed with a series of rotating frames and panels that allow for a variety of uses, while each panel has different surface materials (netting, nylon, plywood, cloth, recycled materials). In the housing scheme, each 'migrant' has the possibility to customize material interventions and transformation scenarios for an individual unit. As an individual 'migrant' forms relationships with others nearby, the structures change shape and grow in potential, creating the village.

The 'Migrant House' design utilizes modular and prefabricated construction, and can be assembled within 12 hours by a small team without large equipment.

Assembling a village
© U-TT

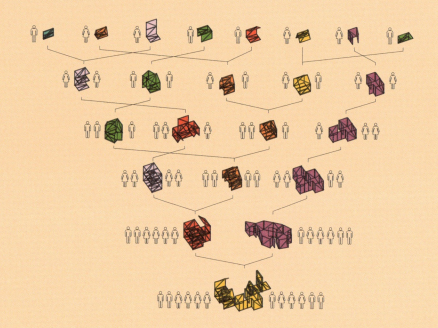

Kit of parts
© U-TT

Residential tower lookout point
© U-TT

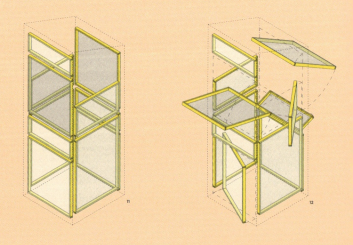

FROM RESEARCH TO DESIGN

The structure can be enclosed with a series of rotating frames and panels that allow for a variety of uses, while each panel has different surface materials (netting, nylon, plywood, cloth, recycled materials)

Flexible market project, Barcelona © U-TT

Part 2:
Lightweight transportable architecture

In addition to the 'Migrant Housing', the following three examples illustrate U-TT's method of creating something that is temporary in character but which could become permanent, working on three different themes in three different contexts: Barcelona flexible market building / playground; San Francisco homeless shelter; and South Africa Social housing.

Through their work, U-TT seeks to create an urban toolbox of "lightweight transportable architecture", proposing a working method for a new supportive architecture that functions as an infrastructure that empowers people at the margins of cities. The objective for devising and applying the toolbox is to shift the emphasis of contemporary architecture and architectural education from form-driven to purpose-oriented infrastructure and to eliminate the disconnect between design and its social impact. Rather than being driven by an artistic objective, U-TT is calling for an architecture that creates buildings from more efficient, locally produced, industrial materials, assembled as an infrastructure made by a kit of parts. The vision is to produce viable, quick-fix urban architecture that functions as a life-support infrastructure for the perpetually changing city that will, in turn, benefit other localities and cultures in urgent need of solutions.

FROM RESEARCH TO DESIGN

9 SIP Structure

12 Exterior Cladding

THE POWER OF THE COLLECTIVE
The first shack and the next houses were built as a pilot project to test the relationship between public and private space, social categories, and cultural identity. On a local scale, it changed living standards very quickly and gave the residents a two-floor house, safe above the waterline, with between 20 to 32 square meters of space on each floor. In terms of the millions of people around the world who are marginalized—geographically, politically, economically—what we learned and what we accomplished have much broader implications.

Inauguration of the homeless shelter / poets' corner by street musicians, San Francisco © U-TT

Homeless shelter / poets' corner, San Francisco © U-TT

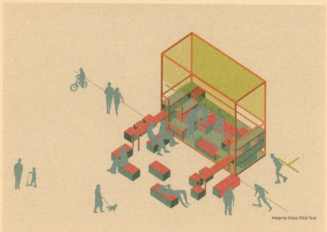

BOX HACK
© U-TT

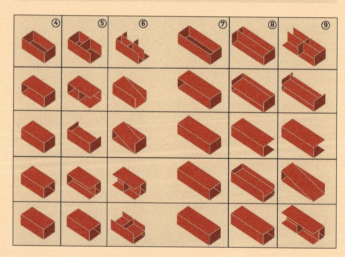

Event with designed boxes
© U-TT

FROM RESEARCH TO DESIGN

Empower Shack original settlement, South Africa © U-TT

Empower Shack first test shack, South Africa © Jan Ras

Empower Shack unit courtyard, South Africa © Klearjos Papanicolau

Empower Shack social housing project layout, South Africa © U-TT

FROM RESEARCH TO DESIGN

Social Furniture

© Paul Kranzler

A project by
EOOS

'SOCIAL Furniture' is a social design project by the Viennese studio EOOS, produced as part of the Places for People. Responding to the immediate pressures created by the increased flow of refugees into Europe, the collection consists of 18 pieces that can be constructed through a self-building process, and which were originally designed to furnish a former training facility for customs officers in Vienna that had been repurposed as a primary care facility and site of long-term accommodation for asylum seekers run by two Austrian NGOs.

Between March 2016 and June 2017, EOOS initiated a furniture workshop in the basement of a refugee housing. More than 150 people were joining the program and produced over 800 pieces of furniture in total for the residents' rooms, public spaces and for a community kitchen. The Social Furniture workshop helped to strengthen the community spirit and created a strong identity for the place. All the material (approximately 20 tons) and the workshop equipment were donated by Austrian companies within their Corporate Social Responsibility (CSR) programs. Because of legal issues the workshop had been moved to another project space in 2017. Today, the complete collection is available within a workshop program run by the NGO Caritas in Vienna, where the pieces are built by people who have difficulties integrating into normal working environments.

To mark the development of the Social Furniture collection for Haus Erdberg, EOOS published a catalogue (Koenig Books, 2016) modelled on Enzo Mari's Autoprogettazione, which contains simple instructions on how to assemble the individual pieces. Made out of yellow shuttering panels, the distinctive furniture forms places for collective activities: living, cooking, and working. Beyond its function in refugee aid projects, the collection positions social furniture as a concern of society at large, and can be applied flexibly at different scales and in response to various needs. Each of the designs are easy to assemble and can be mass produced depending on the context with a circular saw and power drill.

The entire edition of the Social Furniture catalogue has been sold out and more than 3500 downloads of the free online manual have been counted so far. The open design catalogue was used in a wide range of use scenarios, from other refugee projects to a recent European research project on new materials made from plastic waste, EOOS further invited users of the open design manual to submit their experiences and projects.

Part of the book project was the Social Furniture Manifesto. It should be read as a blueprint for designing furniture with a purpose – beyond furniture as fashion and status item.

© Paul Kranzler

© Paul Kranzler

FROM RESEARCH TO DESIGN

Manifesto

This manifesto was originally published in the catalogue Social Furniture by EOOS, on the occasion of the exhibition Places for People in the Austrian Pavilion at the 15 International Architecture Exhibition — La Biennale di Venezia 2016.

Link: PDF of the Social Furniture Open Design Manual: http://www.eoos.com/cms/index.php?id=353

I In its simple realization Social Furniture sets a basic standard for collectively used furniture.

II The use of Social Furniture is not dependent on financial need.

III Social Furniture is not second or third-class furniture – it is the expression of a worldview rooted in collectivity and common welfare.

IV Social Furniture is designed to stimulate communication.

V Social Furniture can be manufactured in a collective self-building process. The workshop is part of the project.

VI Materials must be carefully chosen, taking into account aspects of social and environmental sustainability and circular thinking.

VII Building the furniture only defines the material part of the project. The social construction (who uses the furniture) and the regulative level (the usage rules) must be determined in a collective (design) process.

VIII Representation, status, private property, and dependency are replaced by sharing, autonomous action, and collective use.

IX As a crown makes a king from the actor, Social Furniture makes the user an important protagonist of an alternative lifestyle.

X Social Furniture is like stage sets – simple and effective.

XI Social Furniture tells stories about the collective.

XII Social Furniture becomes an aesthetic common good through an abstract language.

XIII Social Furniture emerges in the interplay between social design, open design, the culture of self-building, and the concept of common goods.

XIV The functionality of Social Furniture is defined by the social functionality. Each piece of furniture represents its own functional unit.

XV Each functional unit must fulfill symbolic, ergonomic, and aesthetic requirements.

XVI The combination of the functional units creates scenarios for interpersonal encounters, for cooperation and exchange.

XVII Each scenario supports the role and the potential of the protagonists and their meaningful actions.

XVIII Ideally, the scenarios form the departure point for spatial planning. They define qualitatively charged spaces, even within difficult spatial contexts.

XIX Adaptation to local cultural or spatial realities is desired.

XX The sustained modification of the furniture results in countless personalizations or even in the creation of a new archetype. The latter is a virtuous objective in the spirit of the project.

© Paul Kranzler

© Paul Kranzler

FROM RESEARCH TO DESIGN

High Table
SF02

The construction method is identical to that of the SF 01 table. The table height of 850 mm was chosen to encourage interaction between seated and standing people. As it has the same height as the cooking tables, it can be docked beside them to temporarily expand the work surface for preparing food.

6–8 people
L x W x H: 2100 x 800 x 850 mm
Material quantity 2.70 m2

Scale = 1:20

Kitchen wall panel
SF09

All cooking utensils are stored on the kitchen wall panel. In this way, they are easy to find and can be hung back in their place in an orderly fashion. An organizational form used in workshops is transferred to the kitchen. Cookware can be attached with nails or screw hooks. Strong magnets can also be used to hold magnetic objects such as pots and knives. When there is a greater number of users, labels or outlines of the utensils can be added to the panel. Used as a plain back wall (e.g. in combination with SF 16), SF 09 can serve as an attractive information or graphic identity wall.

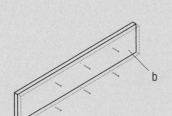

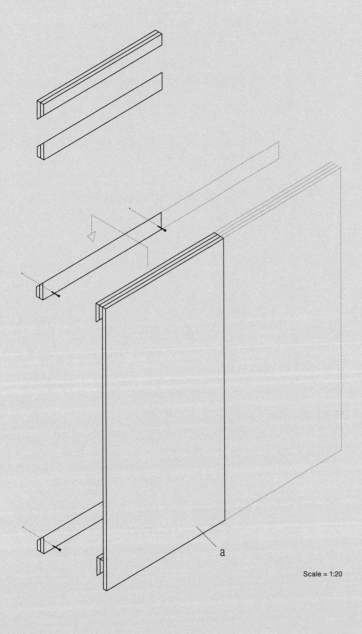

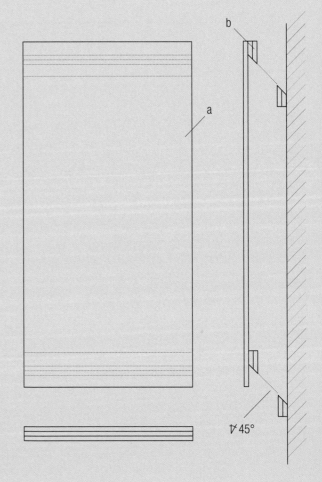

Scale = 1:20

3 panels: max. 20 people
L x W x H: 1000 x 81 x 2000 mm
Material quantity 8.4 m2

FROM RESEARCH TO DESIGN

Shelf
SF15

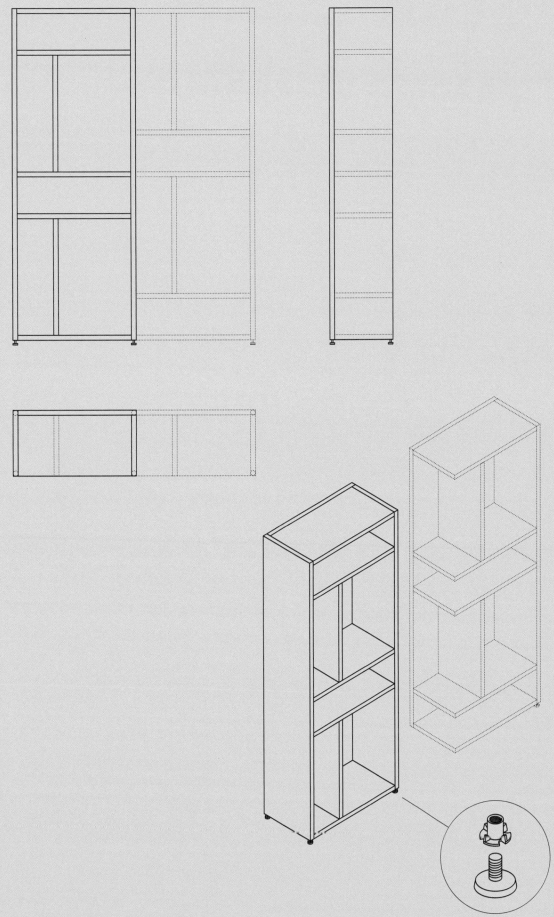

L x W x H: 687 x 357 x 1800 mm
Material quantity 3.65 m2 per element + side panel b

Border Materialities

A Research project led by
Nishat Awan and Aya Musmar
at Sheffield University

Nishat Awan is a Lecturer in Architecture at University of Sheffield. Her research interests include the production and representation of spaces of migration, including borders, and exploring how these can be addressed through spatial practice.

Aya Musmar is a PhD candidate at Sheffield School of Architecture (SSoA). Through her research, Musar investigates humanitarian response in Za'atri refugee camp, focusing on the spatial configurations of the camp environment.

INTRO The Border Materialities design studio for the MA in Architectural Design at University of Sheffield focused on the Za'atri refugee camp in Jordan, near the Syrian border. The camp hosts 81,000 Syrian refugees and is considered the second largest in the world. Michel Agier describes such camps as places for 'managing the undesirables'[1]. These pseudo cities spring up at the edges of established cities, near borders, or in the middle of a desert, and are designed to provide refuge for vulnerable refugees. Yet, unlike standard cities they are often closed spaces where entry and exit is controlled, and where political representation is not possible. These places are usually governed by the United Nations High Commissioner for Refugees (UNHCR) alongside the host country government, as is also the case in Za'atri.

Initially, the camp was organised through cluster planning but as the numbers increased rapidly UNHCR resorted to grid planning, an arrangement that in many ways severed social relations within the camp. Our studio explored the consequences of this change in planning the everyday lives of refugees and on issues of governance. And furthermore, we explored these social relations through their spatial materialisations. During their visit to the camp, students were taken on guided walks. It is interesting how these first impressions shaped their future responses. Some asked about the fence that surrounded schools in the camp; the image of the wired fence was not only an element of surprise for them but of shock! Why would a primary school for children be fenced off and why could they not use other materials that were not as harsh?

The studio applied two main design methods, scenario games and parametric modelling, in order to explore the spatial, social and economic relations within the camp. We explored topics such as agency, normality, the role of women and honour within the camp. Scenarios have been used extensively by large-scale organisations and the military to predict future outcomes. Herman Kahn of the RAND corporation was perhaps the first to develop scenarios as a narrative technique, where stories apparently by people from the future predicted a possible world to come[2]. In architecture and other design disciplines, scenarios have been used to imagine future possibilities, with the group Chora developing one particular methodology of making board games that simulate urban processes[3]. The technique uses role playing to respond to a changing and often unpredictable situation, with the important introduction of chance events into the game, for example through the roll of a dice, or cards that denote environmental events. In our design studio, students created games situated in the Za'atri camp taking on roles based on interviews they had conducted with people living and working in the camp. It allowed us to model the ways in which everyday lives, governance, spatial and environmental conditions came together to create opportunities for design intervention.

While parametric modelling is most often used to generate forms, where certain variables are added into the computer model so that a change in one variable can be predicted across others, our use of this technique did not model physical properties. Instead, the variables we

FROM RESEARCH TO DESIGN

used related to social life, political commitments and economic conditions. For example, in the RefuSHE project described below, students used parameters related to the familiarity of a space, how much it exposed or made visible, as well as shading in order to identify useful spaces for activities for a women's support network. We also used a technique of parametric modelling that did not require computers but instead used physical models to simulate the effects of the change of one parameter on to another, while at the same time critiquing the paradigm of flexibility within such approaches[4]. This is the case with the model shown in figure 5 that combines spatial interaction with an analysis of various services as they were introduced in the camp over its initial five years.

The following pages introduce two projects from the Border Materialities studio: I am a RefuSHE and [De]constructing Normality in the Camp.

I am a Refu[She]
By Tahira Al-Raisi, Ebru Sen, and Xinfei Zhao

This project was concerned with creating spaces that could empower women in the camp by extending their social networks based on shared interests, values and activities. It combined a thoughtful analysis of gendered social and cultural relations within the camp, with an understanding of the harsh environmental conditions of the desert landscape. The starting point was a careful mapping of spaces in one district of Za'atri according to the familiarity of that space for a group of women, based on where family, friends and

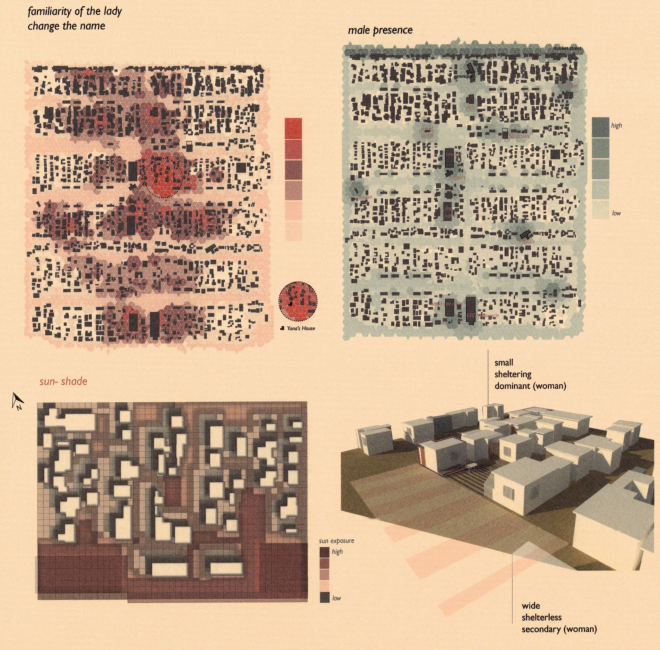

acquaintances lived. Male presence in the camp was also an important factor as it often determines the movement of women. For example, at specific times of the day mosques can become very busy as men gather for prayer, and so these areas are often avoided by women. The mapping visualised this fluctuating spatial and temporal territory that women negotiate daily. In the design, environmental factors such as shade and privacy were combined with social concerns to create a network of temporary spaces. These could be activated at various times of the day through the clever use of materials available in the camp.

The design intervention proposed corresponded to the teams' speculations on "women empowerment". It sought to help women claim some communal powers in the society. The scenario-based analysis women agencies as necessary catalysts for this intervention.

By mapping the spatial tactics that women had performed in the camp to transgress patriarchal norms the design intervention responded to women continuous movements between the centre (highlighted in blue - where men gather - and the margin (highlighted in pink - where women find each other (figure 1). Developed from one of the scenarios that students have dwelled on to understand women everyday life, the food cart design (figure 3) allows women to reclaim certain communal powers.

[De]Constructing Normality in the Camp
By Tan Ke, Ziwei Liu, Nidal Majeed, and Zhuoying Wang

This project revolved around the socio-cultural necessi-

Aya// Yana's neighbor Cooking

scenario 3

Aya, 32
Marriage status: married to an unemployed husband
Personality: shy
Skills: cooks well

Step 1
Aya with her shy personality wants earn money and help her family. She cooks in her kitchen; in front of their house, her son sells the food on fridays. After lunch prayer the men who get out from the mosque can buy the food.

Step 2
Through this activity many women can enter to this business. Buy making a foodcart by themselves with the materilas in the camp.

Proposal 3 / Sustainable Foodcart

Foodcart is a tool for them to widen their business and by making it with the tools that can be applied in the camp, they can build a sustainable cart.

Foodcart making progress

Materials that is being used in the camp can be used to build a sustainable foodcart.

The wheels that used to carry caravans can be used again to build foodcart. Spare wheels can be taken and assembled.

Spare panels can be taken from recycling center

Drawer can be made with woods and panels from recycle centre

Spare wood sticks can be taken from recycling center to build the structure of the cart.

The fabric which is being used for covering caravans can be taken.

FROM RESEARCH TO DESIGN

ties of living that are beyond the bare essentials required to sustain life. Starting with a critique of UNHCR's outdated Handbook for Emergencies that is the blueprint for setting up refugee camps anywhere in the world, the team identified what constituted 'normality' within such spaces. From the perspective of UNHCR, normality is conceptualised through the provision of basic infrastructure and services that can enable people to survive in what are extremely challenging circumstances. Yet, for a camp like Za'atri, which was established in 2012, normality also means much more than the provision of basic services.

By playing scenario games and taking on different roles, the project evolved by identifying the types of everyday practices that often are taken for granted, but which are extremely difficult, if not impossible, to conduct within the setting of a refugee camp. The drawings and mapping sought to understand the various layers of infrastructure, social and physical, that make up the camp space. The design proposals were based on this careful analysis and through an understanding that since most refugees cannot leave the camp, the only way to build a 'normal' life is through mutual help and social interaction within the camp itself.

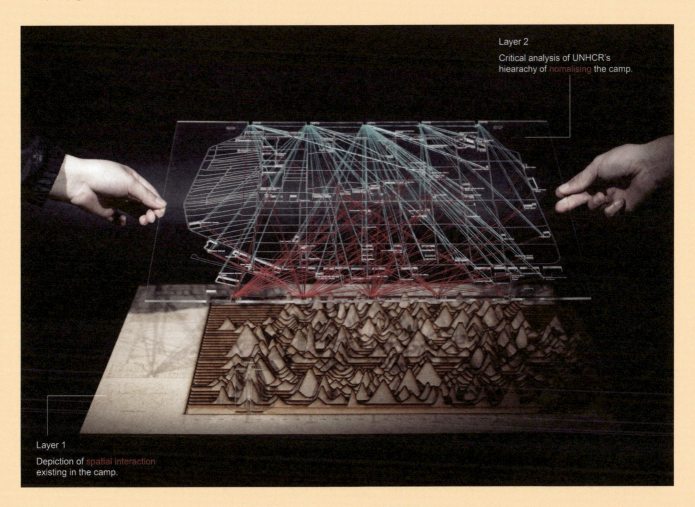

Layer 2
Critical analysis of UNHCR's hiearachy of nomalising the camp.

Layer 1
Depiction of spatial interaction existing in the camp.

● 1 — Agier, Michel. 2010. Managing the Undesirables. 1 edition. Cambridge: Polity Press. ● 2 — Chermack, Thomas J., Susan A. Lynham, and Wendy E. A. Ruona. 2001. "A Review of Scenario Planning Literature." Futures Research Quarterly 17 (2): 7–31. ● 3 — Bunschoten, Raoul, Hélène Binet, Chora, and Takuro Hoshino. 2001. Urban Flotsam: Stirring Agier, Michel. 2010. Managing the Undesirables. 1 edition. Cambridge: Polity Press. ● 4 — Langley, Phil, and Femke Snelting. 2015. "Parametric Truth(s) | Possible Bodies." May. http://possiblebodies.constantvzw.org/inventory/?075. ● 5 — UNHCR Handbook for Emergencies. 2007. Third edition. UNHCR.the City. Rotterdam: 010 Publishers

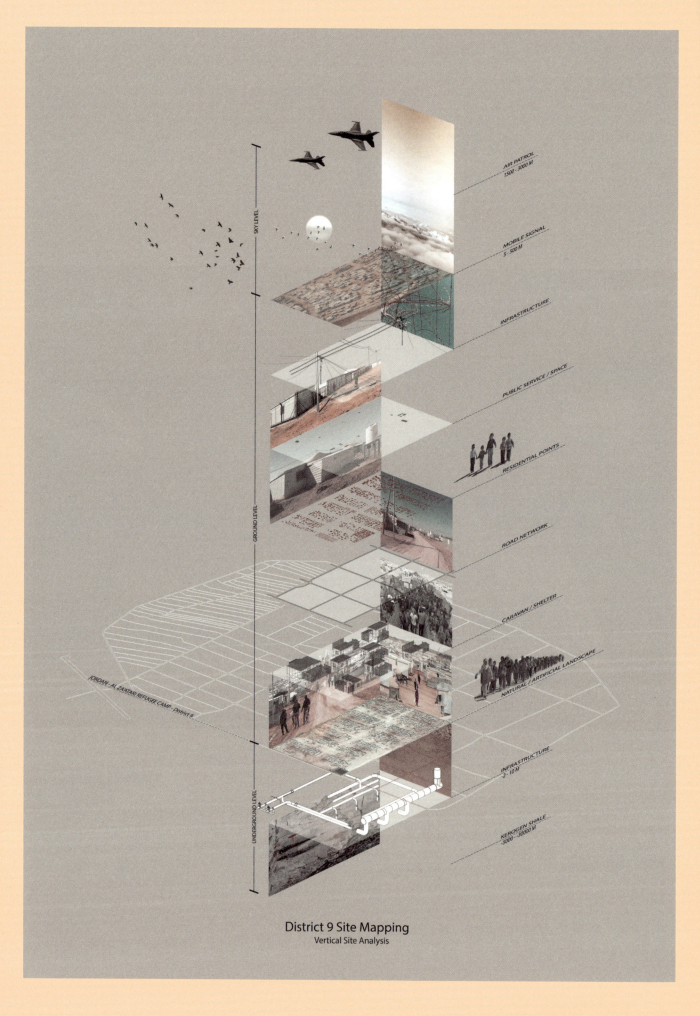

District 9 Site Mapping
Vertical Site Analysis

FROM RESEARCH TO DESIGN

Phase 4

Classroom

Textile workshop

5 Years and 6 Months
The development of the centre through various phases has rendered it an integral part of refugee life that works for the improvement of refugee life.

Collage of Phase 4

Phase 5

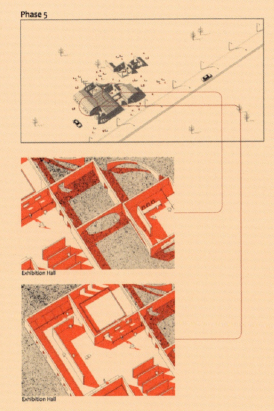

Exhibition Hall

Exhibition Hall

12 Years
Life in the camp is over with the refugees going back to their home country. The permanet structures evolve to develop as a museum that depict the unique stories of refugee life.

1   2   3

137

FROM RESEARCH TO DESIGN

RUSAIFAH - an edge city 10 km northeast of Amman, located in the Zarqa Governorate, Jordan's industrial center. Formerly it was an agricultural and recreation zone along the Zarqa River. Now it is home to a large and growing population of displaced people and refugees. Around two-thirds Rusaifah's population is under age 25.

© Alfredo Brillembourg

The Restless Earth

Fondazione Nicola Trussardi

Edited by
Massimiliano Gioni and Micola Brambilla.

Published by
Electa 2017/La Triennale/Fondazione Niccola Trussardi
ISBN 9788891814081

ABSTRACT The Restless Earth—borrowing its title from a collection of poems by Édouard Glissant, a Caribbean—tries to describe this unstable and agitated present as a polyphony of voices and narratives. Through the works of more than sixty artists from thirty-nine countries the exhibition charts both experiences and perceptions of migration and the current refugee crisis as an epoch-making transformation that is reframing contemporary history, geography, and culture.

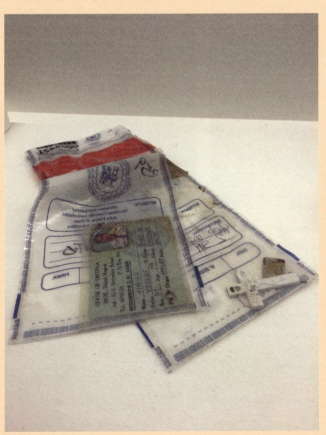

Through installations, videos, documentary images, historical sources, and material artifacts, The Restless Earth explores real and imaginary geographies, reconstructing the odyssey of migrants through personal and collective tales of exodus inspired by varying degrees of urgency and longing.

Following the unequal and often exploitative exchanges of labor, commodities, and capital in our globalized economy, The Restless Earth attempts to trace a choral history of the multitudes of migrants who too often remain nameless.

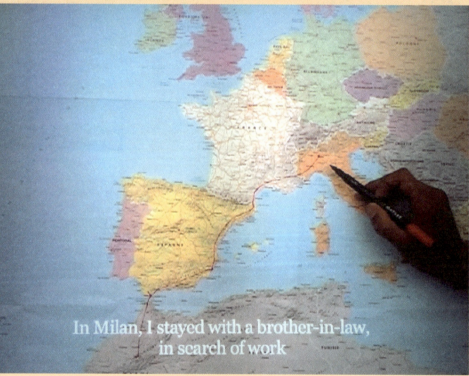

The Mapping Journey Project by Bouchra Khalili

Eight-channel video (color, sound)

The Museum of Modern Art New York 2016
This project aims to draw attention to draw an alternate practice of map-making elaborated and shaped from the perspective of individuals forced to cross borders illegally. Each still is based on videos made with one long static shot. A hand holding a permanent marker draws literally on the map, tortuous and complex roads across borders that forced illegal journeys generate, while off-screen the narrators recounts factually the journey.

FROM RESEARCH TO DESIGN

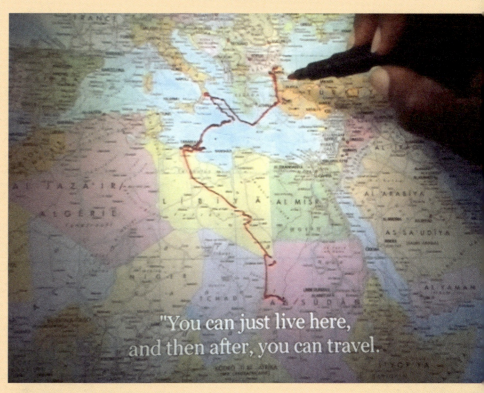

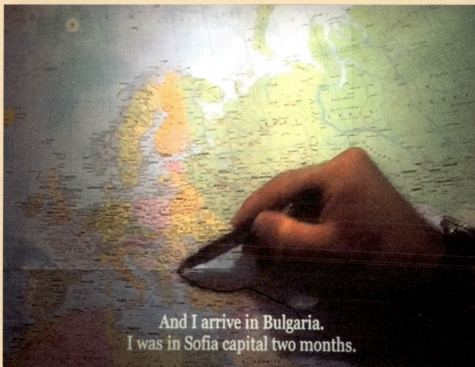

Part Three

STATE CONTROL, illustrates some of the ways in which state control is used to regulate, suppress, divert, redirect, steer, or in other ways managed movement flows through physical and spatial measures, as well as separate, exclude and control temporary or permanent presence of people. Across the globe, state control of migration and displacement flows is implemented through the application of different physical instruments and actions. This can include the construction of physical structures for separation, such as wall; designating specific and separated land areas for settling; or tearing down structures and moving people from their place of living. The physical manifestations are often violent and intrusive structures that – as the following articles illustrate - might produce surprising, unexpected or counterproductive spatial results.

In a time where more and more people move across borders, what are the acceptable spatial control measures for the protection of nation states versus the protection of human rights and the environment?

PARANGOLÉ #1, MOTHERLAND

The ephemeral thresholds of Europe

The Jungle "high street". © Irit Katz

Irit Katz is an affiliated lecturer in the Center for Conflicts Research, and Director of Studies in Architecture at Girton College, University of Cambridge. She has co-edited the book, Camps Revisited: Multifaceted Spatialities of a Modern Political Technology (2019).

by
Irit Katz

AS the numbers of asylum seekers and undocumented migrants entering and traversing Europe spiked in 2015, both makeshift and institutionalized camp spaces proliferated across the continent. The most visible expression of broader mechanisms of exclusion, Irit Katz suggests that these camps appear when the shifting forces of migratory movement encounter systems and architectures of control.

During its existence, 'the Jungle' in Calais changed overwhelmingly. The makeshift camp, which became one of the symbolic spaces of Europe's migration 'crisis', grew rapidly between September 2015 and January 2016, when arrivals spiked to 150 people per day. Camp dwellers and NGOs reshaped the site through the frantic construction of new shelters to replace existing tents before temperatures dropped. In February and March of 2016, when its population exceeded 6,000 people, construction and expansion were superseded by attempts to deal with, and struggle against, waves of demolitions, which bulldozed almost half the camp. Meanwhile, a new semi-closed enclave of converted shipping containers opened at its heart, though many were reluctant to relocate despite the temptation of heated shelters[1]. Within a few months, the entire makeshift camp would be demolished, and most of its residents dispersed to other regions in France.

The shifting actions and attitudes of the diverse protagonists influencing the fortunes of the Jungle and other camps in the area was one of the few predictable characteristics of these spaces of refuge. At the beginning of April 2016, after the southern and western parts of the Jungle were erased, and its northern zone became dense with relocated shelters, no one was invested in further construction. The shock of the demolitions, together with threats to continue clearing the rest of the camp, suspended all building. At the same time, less than 35 kilometers to the east, informal construction works were at their peak in the La Linière camp in Grande-Synthe, near Dunkirk, which had been opened a month earlier by Médecins Sans Frontières (MSF). The new site's prefabricated timber shelters had been built to host 1,500 refugees, who had spent the winter in squalid conditions in a muddy tent camp nearby.

The constant change in these two camps was evident not only in their layouts and typologies, but also their very existence. Similar to other camps along Europe's migration routes, they were created, altered, demolished, reappeared, and erased again due to multiple factors, including persistent and intense migration flows, border closures, and the subsequent actions of NGOs, local authorities, national governments, and migrants themselves. While the future of such camps, and the ways in which they will develop, is

A Sudanese house in progress in the northern part of the camp

A mosque in the northeastern part of the camp

A Libyan tent in the central part of the camp

STATE CONTROL

148

A frame for a shelter in the northern part of the camp

A duplex in the Eritrean area

An orthodox church under construction in the south-central part of the camp

Grande-Synthe -Graffiti - good luck my brothers and sisters

© Marco Tiberio

The Jungle and the "container camp" © Irit Katz

usually unknown at the time of their existence—the Jungle was cleared by French authorities in October 2016 and the La Linière camp burnt to the ground in April 2017—it is also difficult to predict when and where new camps will appear. Unlike the planned detention and reception centers that form part of the more permanent border apparatus managed by states, these camps feed into an everchanging spatial and geopolitical reality.

Migration Routes, Borders, and Camps

The 'Jungle Books' complex remained an isolated island in the erased southern part of the Jungle before it was demolished together with the rest of the camp. In the spring of 2016, residents gathered there for language lessons, free Wi-Fi, and to enjoy the well-stocked library and each other's company. On the wall was a map of Europe with yellow post-it notes attached. They described fragments of the long and difficult journeys made by migrants who managed to enter Europe and cross the entire Schengen Zone only to find themselves stuck one step from their desired destination[2]. Every night, many tried to make it to the United Kingdom (UK) in what they called 'the jump'. Groups and families walked a few kilometers to the parking lots next to the harbor and attempted, usually not for the first time, to hide in one of the cargo trucks ferrying goods through the Eurotunnel.

The liberal world has always been characterized by an unequal system, wherein the free movement of goods goes hand-in-hand with firm control over the movement of people. In the period since, more barbed wire fences, cameras, guards, dogs, and 'advanced security methods' (such as infrared cameras, carbon dioxide probes, and heartbeat detectors) have been employed to detect those attempting to smuggle themselves through to England. Crossing has become almost impossible. The Foucauldian systems employed at the port are the result of a 'comprehensive action plan' agreed by the UK and France in 2014, which included a British pledge of €12 million a year to keep migrants away from Europe's most fortified territory.

The location of the Jungle near the Channel Tunnel was not arbitrary. Together with the La Linière camp a few kilometers from Dunkirk's port, and the makeshift camps that developed in Paris—one above the Eurostar railway tracks—each site formed in proximity to fiercely controlled routes to the UK. This is similar to many other European camps that have appeared along heavily controlled or temporarily blocked migration routes, leading to 'bottleneck' spaces of suspension[3]. Some emerged adjacent to border crossings, such as near the Slovenian-Croatian border in September 2015, on a motorway at the Serbian-Hungarian border, or near Idomeni close to the Greek-Macedonian border, where approximately 10,000 migrants spent the winter of 2016 in appalling conditions.

Comparable camps have also been created at the heart of major cities, such as the several makeshift camps which existed, were demolished, and reappeared under bridges in Paris, the camp created in Budapest near and within the Keleti train station, or those that sprung up in public parks in Belgrade, Brussels, and Athens. Others, like the camps near Calais and Dunkirk, or the site that materialized near Mytilene's harbor in Lesvos, form on the outskirts of port cities. While the physical characteristics of these spaces may sometimes be reminiscent of urban slums or favelas, and other sprawling refugee camps around the world have been labeled as the 'cities of tomorrow', makeshift camps that appear along migration routes should not be confused with alternative forms of urban informality[4].

As opposed to a different kind of 'arrival city', they could be better described as 'departure camps'[5]. These spaces do not form due to the wish of their dwellers to become part of the urban fabric to which they were pushed or pulled, but rather as a result of their persistent will to reach their desired destination, and their refusal to surrender to any enforced restriction on movement. The residents of these spaces do not seek to remain in their current location, but to move on. The camps are created to potentially facilitate long stays, but not permanent relocations. In part, this distinguishes these makeshift camps from other informal 'slum' and 'squatter' situations—they are mechanisms of exclusion that call into question the normative relations between space and citizenship on a biopolitical basis[6].

Although makeshift camps are not surrounded by barbed wire like institutionalized refugee or detention camps, they are nonetheless related to the altered geographies shaped by such enclosure[7]. They are often erected near new fences fortifying international borders in all their forms and settings, from rural landscapes to urban train stations. Once sealed, these borders are transformed from abstract territorial markers on a map into physical barriers. When they block the movement of migrants, they in many cases produce visible spaces inhabited by those forbidden from crossing. For instance, following Austria's introduction of border controls at the Brenner Pass on the Italian-Austrian border in April 2016, warnings were flagged of a probable appearance of a 'second Idomeni' on the Italian side[8].

Paradoxically, these camps effectively 'belong' to the state on the other side of the border. By blocking migration flows, a government creates suspended frontiers in neighboring countries. These camps are in-between spaces par-excellence—not only in relation to time, but also vectors of movement, which become fragmented. Ever-changing policies and practices have led to the appearance and disappearance of camps, as well as to shifting social and humanitarian networks between them. Migrants who slept under the Pont Charles-de-Gaulle in Paris in June 2015, for example, also spent periods in the Jungle. As recorded stories testify, many migrants passed through several camps on their way to and within Europe[9]. Similarly, local and international NGOs work in different camps, transferring donations and other forms of aid across the continent.

Beyond these ephemeral realities, it is equally important to highlight the deeper, and possibly more permanent, political meaning of such temporary spaces. The appearance and existence of the camps sometimes creates a reality of solidarity, both among migrants themselves, and between the migrants and activists who support them. By producing spaces that visibly highlight the political problem that created them, migrants may sometimes influence the attitudes and awareness of the general public and policymakers, while also altering their own subjectivities[10]. The makeshift camps that flourished in Europe can also be analyzed, therefore, as part of an emerging network of spaces of exclusion that symbolize a degree of marginalization and helplessness, but at the same time produce new forms of politics and political subjects[11].

Permeating Powers, Hybrid Typologies

The constant change and unstable reality of the camps extends to their formation, function, and resulting spatial typologies. The institutionalized purpose-built camp and the makeshift self-built camp are usually seen as two discrete typologies, which are created and function separately[12]. A closer examination of the recent camps in Europe, however, shows that this formal/informal dichotomy is much less rigid and stable than imagined. While in some cases the typologies are indeed spatially and functionally separate, in other cases formal and informal typologies are closely connected, intersect, and sometimes transform one another.

The opening of a semi-closed container camp at the heart of the Jungle in January 2016 is an example of this intersection. After bulldozers cleared an inhabited area of around 500 people, 125 white shipping containers, equipped with heating, bunk beds for 12 people each, and cutout windows, were placed in a rigid grid and surrounded by a fence. The identical containers were labeled with large colored number plates, and a plan of the camp was fixed on a sign to prevent confusion and disorientation. With no cooking facilities in the camp, its 1,500 inhabitants were supposed to receive a daily hot meal at the Jules Ferry Center two hundred meters away.

The constant change in these two camps was evident not only in their layouts and typologies, but also their very existence. Similar to other camps along Europe's migration routes, they were created, altered, demolished, reappeared, and erased again due to multiple factors, including persistent and intense migration flows, border closures, and the subsequent actions of NGOs, local authorities, national, governments, and migrants themselves.

Movement through the camp's vertical turnstile gates was controlled by fingerprint scanners, with entrance restricted to those inhabitants that registered with the prefecture and consented to a biometric scan of their hands before moving in. This biometric system, which transforms the body of a migrant into a key, has far reaching legal implications as a result of the Dublin Regulation mandating that responsibility for an asylum seeker lies with the European Union state in which they first made an identifiable claim. Rumors circulated about migrants who managed to reach the UK, but had their asylum applications rejected because their fingerprints had been registered previously in France. This is also why migrants often use fake names, attempting to remain anonymous until they reach their destination.

Conceived and funded by the French state, the camp's design, fabrication, and implementation were delegated to the private company Logistics Solutions, which also builds military facilities. The camp's maintenance, administration, and control was outsourced to La Vie Active, an association that specializes in working with elderly people and the disabled. This combination of a military-like space controlled by experts in the management of specific vulnerable populations goes together with the creation of the 'container camp' as a biopolitical facility at its core. It strips away the particular life, culture, and social needs of migrants, reducing them to mere biological bodies. They are identified only according to their fingerprint pattern, and stored in minimal, dense spaces 'like animals' (as described by one inhabitant).

Because the container camp was created at the heart of the Jungle, its residents spent long hours in the surrounding informal area, using its public institutions, communal kitchens, and 'high street' for social gatherings and other everyday needs. With its basic, yet complex, materiality and articulated spaces, the Jungle offered a much richer environment than that of the institutionalized camp. A consistent stream of people walked or cycled on the main muddy street that curved between the Jungle's 'neighborhoods'. Grocery stores displayed soft drinks, cigarettes, and batteries, adjacent to several barbershops, pita bread bakeries, and shisha restaurants, which were usually packed with residents, activists, and visitors. Afghans ran most of the businesses, maintaining supplies through contacts with fellow migrants in the city.

This busy street developed from what was initially a collection of tents. Many of the shops were built first as robust informal shelters, which were then developed by their owners, who often continued to use them as sleeping quarters. The businesses also formed part of an informal real estate market, in which shelters were sold, let, sublet, or passed on to friends after their owners moved elsewhere. Some makeshift institutional structures featured traditional architectural characteristics, a form of intangible heritage that crossed borders. The mosque was large and wide, while the Ethiopian Orthodox church had vertical articulated sections that distinguished it from the other

Grande-Synthe camp "cigarette factory". © Irit Katz

shacks. Similarly, certain neighborhoods were organized by place of origin—for instance, Eritrean, Syrian, or Afghan—and retained specific traditional spatial qualities, such as the homely circular compounds of the Darfurian communities[13].

Most of the densely placed timber frame shacks, covered with colored tarpaulins that flapped in the wind or more sturdy plywood boards, included an additional layer expressing the personal signature of their occupants. Flags of original and desired nationalities, as well as graffiti, constituted an iconography of pride, protest, and hope. These creative gestures became a sophisticated form of anonymous participation in the politics from which migrants are excluded—the same (bio)politics that compels them to use fake names and identities. The material improvisation evident in doors, windows, and chimneys, as well as details like the plastic milk lids that separated nylon and nails to prevent tearing, also revealed an inherent inventiveness and resourcefulness. The various spaces created were a product of the Jungle's heterogeneity, where residents' personal experiences were translated into a shared public reality[14].

Migrants did not create the Jungle alone. NGOs and independent groups of volunteers were responsible for many of the shelters and institutions in the camp. Sometimes they only supplied materials. In other cases, huts were built by volunteers, especially for populations in need like unaccompanied minors. L'Auberge de Migrant was the main NGO on site that was responsible for the building and distribution of shelters. The organization had an informal factory for prefabricated shelters in a warehouse in the Calais industrial zone not far from the camp. Volunteers in Calais established similar centers in their back gardens. Other infrastructure that existed in the camp, such as street lighting, portable toilets, and communal water stations, was provided by the French authorities. French courts had ordered the city of Calais to improve conditions in the camp following appeals led by several NGOs[15].

The intersecting relations between different typologies have been replicated in other camps in Europe and beyond, which do not obey a distinct 'formal' or 'informal' mode of creation and function. For example, the semi-carceral mobilities of the Gradisca asylum seekers camp in northern Italy led migrants to establish makeshift camps just outside its walls, providing spaces for social activities. Similar settlements were also created near Moria Reception Center in Lesvos, where migrants camped outside as they waited for registration. The Jungle was also initially created near a 'formal' state facility. When the Jules Ferry Center was opened by the French government in January 2015 to host migrant women and children, other migrants were forced to relocate their makeshift camps in and around Calais next to the remote site, which provided toilets, showers, and hot meals, but was also intended as an instrument of control.

The La Linière camp is another example of intersecting, shifting, and hybrid typologies. Although also designed to host 1,500 people—in organized rows of four-person timber shelters dubbed 'chicken houses' by their inhabitants—it was very different from the container camp. Initiated by the local municipality, MSF was invited to plan and build the facility on a land parcel purchased in advance, and the organization Utopia 56, known for organizing rock concerts, was entrusted with management responsibilities. While subject to building and services regulations, the camp was designed and managed as a place that offered a degree of autonomy to its residents, such as communal kitchens and the ability to reshape the shelters. Less than a month after the camp opened, many of the prefabricated huts had already been reappropriated, altered, and expanded by their occupants according to personal needs and preferences.

The camp was created on a long, thin strip of land, physically enclosed by a highway and railway. Police and volunteers supervised its narrow openings, but it was not a confined space. Visitors and migrants were free to enter and leave without identifying themselves. Although in essence a 'top-down' camp, it was founded and developed in line with principles of solidarity and flexibility, which respected residents and acknowledged their agency. In effect, the site was reminiscent of planned refugee camps that have undergone an incremental process of informalization. While its inhabitants, who still aimed to make 'the jump', perceived the La Linière camp only as a 'station' on a longer route, this in-between space still allowed everyday life to develop. A small, informal 'cigarette factory',

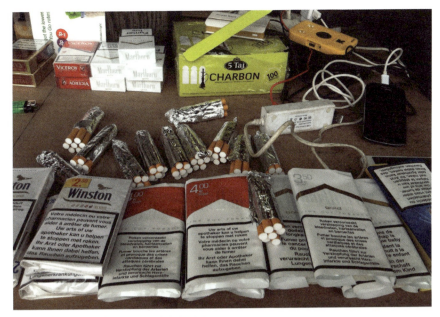

Grande-Synthe camp "pop-up shop" © Irit Katz

and other small shops, were opened near and on the small stalls in the communal area.

The experiences in Calais and Grande-Synthe demonstrate that while different political attitudes materialize into distinct architectures and camp typologies, these also intersect, transform, and are reshaped in various and multiple ways, according to shifting realities and everyday needs. Container camp occupants used the makeshift facilities in the Jungle, and the institutionally created camp in Grande-Synthe was undergoing a rapid process of informalization. The simplistic formal/informal binary opposition disguises a complex situation in which migrants retained partial autonomy. It is important to remember, however, that while the Jungle, and later La Linière, offered less controlled environments, they were still camps. That is, violent spaces of exclusion defined by their separation from human surroundings and suspension from the normal lives their dwellers aspired to.

When Two Forces Collide

Any attempt to map and fully categorize the intersecting and changing typologies of the camps in Europe, with their innumerable networks and dynamic complexities, seems pointless. These camps were, and still are, created and altered rapidly. They disappear, change, and reappear through humanitarian support, violent state measures, and the day-to-day actions of their inhabitants—people on the move who strive to survive in uncertain conditions. It is clear, however, that these camps are formed at the ephemeral meeting points of several strong forces, two in particular. The first is 'biopower', which attempts to control human beings as mere biological life, manage their movements, and strip them of their specific form and power. The second is the power of human life, and its ongoing search for better places and forms of existence.

Situated where migratory movement encounters systems and architectures of control, and practices of destruction, these camps appear when the two forces collide. They are not only spaces, but also ongoing political processes—actions and counteractions that attain a materiality. They do not result from a force majeure, but a humanitarian crises produced by political decisions and acts. Vulnerable people are abandoned to the elements, to the violent and arbitrary intervention of authorities, to traffickers, to vigilantes, and to other criminals. After the demolition of the southern part of the Jungle, which had sheltered over 3,400 people, 129 unaccompanied minors could not be found (and remain missing). Days after the camp was 'cleared', refugee children were still sleeping rough in the demolished site. The very existence of these camps shows that human power can sometimes be stronger and more persistent than attempts at biopolitical control. But they also create new forms of risk, when one population is abandoned in favor of another.

● 1 — See 'Calais "Jungle" Migrants Resist Container Move', BBC News (15 January 2016) accessed at http://www.bbc.co.uk/news/world-europe-35322374 ● 2 — By 'migrants' I refer to all people 'on the move' who flee their home for a variety of legitimate reasons. On the problematic and changing categorization of 'refugees', 'asylum seekers', and 'economic migrants', see Heaven Crawley et al, Unpacking a Rapidly Changing Scenario: Migration Flows, Routes, and Trajectories Across the Mediterranean (MEDMIG Research Brief 1, March 2016). ● 3 — Irit Katz, 'A Network of Camps on the Way to Europe' (2016) 51 Forced Migration Review 17. ● 4 — See 'Refugee Camps are the "Cities of Tomorrow" Says Humanitarian-Aid Expert', Dezeen (23 November 2015) accessed at http://www.dezeen.com/2015/11/23/refugee-camps-cities-of-tomorrow-killian-kleinschmidt-interview-humanitarian-aid-expert/ ● 5 — Doug Saunders, Arrival City: How the Largest Migration in History is Reshaping Our World (2011). ● 6 — Nezar Alsayyad & Ananya Roy, 'Medieval Modernity: On Citizenship and Urbanism in a Global Era' (2006) 10 Space and Polity 1. ● 7 — Claudio Minca, 'Geographies of the Camp' (2015) 49 Political Geography 75. ● 8 — See 'Warnings of "a Second Idomeni" at Brenner Pass', The Local (19 April 2016) accessed at http://www.thelocal.at/20160419/warnings-of-a-second-idomeni-at-brenner-pass-austria-italy. ● 9 — See Irit Katz, 'The Global Infrastructure of Camps', Insecurities: Tracing Displacement and Shelter (2017) accessed at https://medium.com/insecurities/the-global-infrastructure-of-camps-8153fb61ea30 ● 10 — Irit Katz, 'From Spaces of Thanatopolitics to Spaces of Natality – A Commentary on "Geographies of the Camp" (2015) 49 Political Geography 84. ● 11 — See also Kim Rygiel, 'Bordering Solidarities: Migrant Activism and the Politics of Movement and Camps at Calais' (2011) 15 Citizenship Studies 1. ● 12 — See eg, UNHCR, Policy on Alternatives to Camps (2014) ● 13 — See Irit Katz, 'Between Bare Life and Everyday Life: Spatializing Europe's Migrant Camps' (2017) Architecture_MPS [forthcoming]. ● 14 — Dalibor Vesely, Architecture in the Age of Divided Representation: The Question of Creativity in the Shadow of Production (2004) 8. ● 15 — See 'French Court Orders Water, Latrines and Garbage Pickup at Calais Refugee Camp', The Guardian (2 November 2015) accessed at http://www.theguardian.com/world/2015/nov/02/france-calais-refugee-camp-improvements

The Jungle panorama, November 2015. © Irit Katz

The Jungle panorama, April 2016. © Irit Katz

STATE CONTROL

Valencia school, camp El-Aaiun. © Iwan Baan

STATE CONTROL

156

Interwoven Sovereignty

Manuel Herz is a Professor of Architectural, Urban, and Territorial Design at the University of Basel, and principal of Manuel Herz Architects. His research focuses on the relationship between the discipline of planning and (state) power.

by
Manuel Herz

IN this article, Manuel Herz calls for a re-examination of how we come to understand and define sovereignty and a new model for statehood. Building on his experiences working with the Sahrawis to bring the Sahrawi Arab Democratic Republic to the Venice Biennale of Architecture, Herz provides an in-dept account of what a novel type of statehood can look like.

What we can draw from these examples is that statehood should not be seen as an absolute category, of black and white. Instead, a range of different types and "shades" of sovereignty and statehood exist.

Everyday life. © Iwan Baan

What makes a state a state? How do we define sovereign statehood? The most widely accepted response is the Montevideo Convention of 1933, which lists four conditions of statehood: (a) a permanent population; (b) a defined territory; (c) a government; and (d) a capacity to enter into relations with the other states. The convention also declares that the "political existence of the State is independent of recognition by the other States." The Montevideo Convention is thus a clear de jure definition, in contrast to a de facto definition of statehood.

When we look at contemporary case studies, we come to understand the limits of the Montevideo Convention. Syria's population has tragically become impermanent, with more than half of its inhabitants having either fled the country or having become internally displaced. Ukraine lost control over a substantial part of its territory with Russia's occupation of the Crimean Peninsula. Belgium did not have an elected government for a period of almost two years during 2010-2011. In none of these cases, though, could one argue that the concept of statehood doesn't apply to Belgium, Syria, or the Ukraine. And conversely, several territories or countries that have declared independence, and that fulfill the conditions of statehood of the Montevideo Convention—such as Somaliland—but are not recognized by any other state, also show the limitations of the de facto practice of statehood. What we can draw from these examples is that statehood should not be seen as an absolute category, of black and white. Instead, a range of different types and "shades" of sovereignty and statehood exist.

What type of statehood does the Western Sahara represent? The Sahrawis declared the independence of the Western Sahara (officially: the Sahrawi Arab Democratic Republic, SADR) on February 27, 1976. The SADR has a constitution and a functioning government, with a president, a prime minister, several ministers with distinct portfolios, and a parliament consisting of fifty-three seats. The Western Sahara is a full member of the African Union, exchanges ambassadors with most of the nations that have

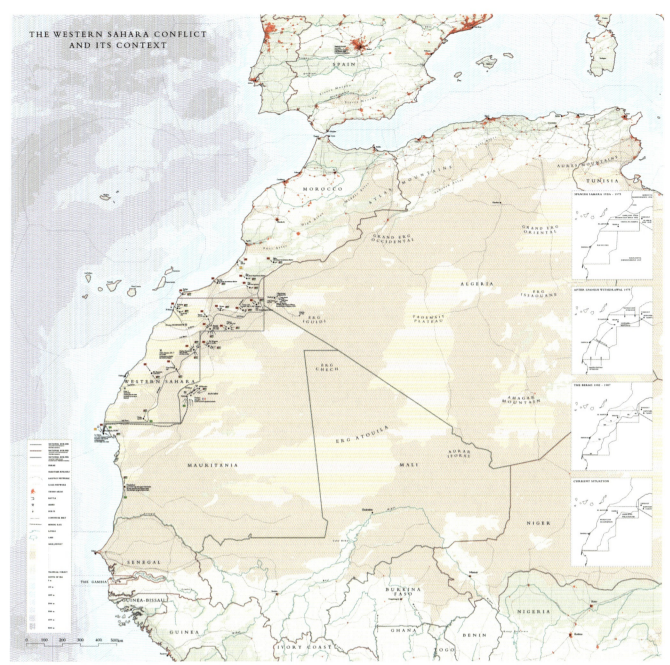

Conflict in Western Sahara. © Manuel Herz Architects

recognized its sovereignty, and has representatives in several other nations that do not officially recognize the SADR, such as most European-Union countries, the United States, and Russia. Territorially though, the situation is more complex. The Sahrawis' control of their own country's territory is limited to a thin sliver along the Algerian and Mauritanian borders, representing approximately 20-25% of the Western Sahara. This so-called 'liberated territory' is only scarcely and temporarily inhabited by the Sahrawis, as settling there would be interpreted as the acceptance of the status quo. The Sahrawi government though, has almost full control over the Algerian territory where the refugee camps are located. While the territory's limits are not demarcated and precisely defined, almost all aspects of political, social, cultural, and economic life are administered by the Sahrawi government. The refugees have Sahrawi identification cards, Sahrawi driver's licenses, learn according to Sahrawi curriculums, are judged by Sahrawi judges, and are protected by the Sahrawi army. But, at the same time, Algerian sovereignty still applies to this region as well. Algerians living in the same region pay taxes to Algeria, have Algerian driver's licenses and Algerian IDs, and are judged by Algerian judges. Hence, two sets of sovereignties coexist at the same time and are woven together across the same territory. The Sahrawi government does not see itself as a government-in-exile, as it does control territory, and also regularly meets in Tifariti, located in the "liberated territories" of the Western Sahara. What we are witnessing, therefore, is the emergence of a novel type of statehood and sovereignty, that overlaps and is interwoven with other sovereignties, a sovereignty that is incomplete but also prefigured, and a statehood that is performed rather than static. This model of an interwoven and performed notion of statehood, championed by the Sahrawi refugees, represents maybe a much more relevant model of statehood in the coming years.

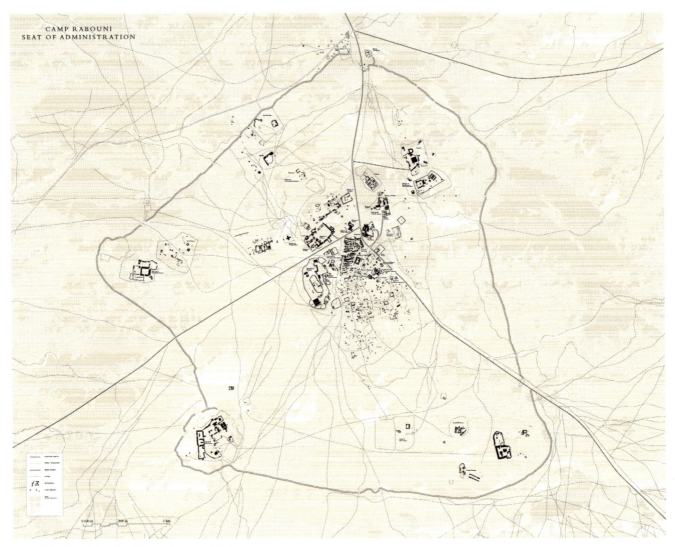

Camp Rabuni administration. © Manuel Herz Architects

Weaving a Nation

Having flown for two hours over mostly uninhabited terrain, the lights of Tindouf emerged suddenly out of the darkness. We landed in the middle of the night in this former garrison town at the edge of the vast Algerian territory, close to the Moroccan border. Despite the late hour, the dry heat of the day still lingered as we descended to the tarmac. Our airplane was parked next to an assortment of ageing military aircraft, as well as a large cargo plane whose presence seemed mysterious amid the sparse desert landscape. Making our way into the ageing terminal building, a remnant from the French colonial era, we were greeted by a representative of the Sahrawi refugees. Eventually our convoy, which consisted of Algerian military vehicles at the front and back, and three ancient Sahrawi Land Rovers sandwiched in between, set off into the desert.

Approximately half an hour later, we came to a checkpoint where the Algerian soldiers handed us over to their Sahrawi counterparts. After another half an hour, we arrived at Boujdour, one of five Sahrawi refugee camps (alongside Laâyoune, Ausserd, Smara, and Dakhla, as well as the administrative camp Rabouni) situated in the southwestern region of Algeria.

The Western Sahara is located at the western edge of the African continent. Formerly a Spanish territory, and since 1975 occupied by Morocco, it has been called the world's last remaining colony. At the onset of a guerrilla war against Morocco, that was fought from 1975 to 1991, most of the Sahrawi population fled into Algeria, settling in refugee camps that today house approximately 160,000 people. While the Sahrawis do not control their own country, they asserted independence of the Sahrawi Arab Democratic Republic on 27 February 1976. Forty seven countries recognize that claim of sovereignty, though it remains disputed.

By now, this was the fifth time I had visited the Sahrawi camps. My first trip, ten years earlier, was motivated by a hunch. More precisely, a hunch that the camps, located in one of the most inhospitable locations on the planet, could potentially offer a counter-model to the predominant notion that such sites represent prison-like spaces of misery and waiting. The self-organizing quality that I had read about would ultimately reveal itself in astonishing ways, through the collective territorial, urban and architectural strategies of the refugees. This time though, I had not travelled to continue the research and documentation project. Instead, I had arrived to pick up a set of large tapestries that would be exhibited at the Venice Biennale, placing the Sahrawis at the center of an international architectural discourse for the very first time.

Entry to Boujdour is via a checkpoint—a familiar ritual in the global landscape of refugee camps. Yet the situation in Boujdour differs in an important aspect from nearly all other comparable examples worldwide. It is neither

Sahrawi National Parliament. © Iwan Baan

staffed by military personnel from the host nation (in this case Algeria), nor by representatives of the United Nations High Commissioner for Refugees (UNHCR). Instead, Sahrawi refugees themselves man the gate. The refugees decide who can and cannot enter. The Sahrawi camps represent some of the rare instances in the world where refugees control access to their own settlements. Far more than an administrative detail, this fact points to a more significant, and also unique, phenomenon: the semi-sovereignty that the Sahrawi refugees have assumed and practice within the territory of their camps.

When Morocco invaded the Western Sahara with a civilian 'Green March', a military occupation soon followed, igniting a conflict between the well-resourced Moroccan army and poorly equipped Sahrawi soldiers. Seeing their country being taken over, the non-combatant members of the Sahrawi population–mostly women and children–escaped across the border into western Algeria. As Morocco and Algeria had been adversaries for years, indeed clashing over other parts of their territories, the Sahrawis were natural allies. The Algerian government supported the refugees in their attempts to establish camp infrastructure, providing them with resources and aid. Unlike most other camps internationally, the UNHCR was not involved in setting up these sites, and it continues to have little role in their administration today.

Boujdour now occupies an area of around five square kilometers, and is inhabited by roughly 10,000 Sahrawis. From one of the few hills in the mostly flat landscape, one can see the camp stretching out to the horizon. A relatively dense fabric of single-story buildings, huts, and tents is interspersed with larger institutional facilities such as schools, and denser clusters of shops and small markets. Sahrawi families have constructed residential compounds that often consist of a number of huts arranged around a small central open space. The huts, built of adobe bricks, are typically mono-functional: one for cooking, one for sleeping, one for drinking tea and receiving guests, and so on. Depending on the size and financial situation of each family, these compounds can consist of one or two huts, or grow to include up to seven or eight.

Given the long history of the camps, the fact that improvisational architecture such as tents remains in place requires explanation. There are a number of functional considerations: In the heat of the summer, when temperatures rise above 50°C, the tents provide a comfortable nighttime climate, as they cool more quickly than the adobe huts and allow a breeze to enter. They also reference the nomadic tradition of the Sahrawis, alluding to the time before their country was lost to Morocco. Beyond questions of culture and comfort, another reason for using tents is symbolic. The tents serve as an architectural signifier of the fact that the Sahrawi refugees have not surrendered to living in exile, but instead are still struggling for a return to the Western Sahara.

The tent—signifying temporality—employs this architectural typology to signal that the situation is not settled. It expresses through architecture the ongoing political demand of the Sahrawis to return to their home country. Similarly, the question, for example whether to use clay or cement bricks is not only a technical question of construction method, but also one that hints at issues of permanence. The same calculus between durability and ephemerality is evident in different choices of roofing material, or whether interior decorations are made with textiles such as tapestries, and are therefore movable, or instead with stucco. This tension shows how every architectural element, every detail, has additional messages and meanings. Architecture is never neutral, never innocent.

The autonomy evoked by the Boujdour checkpoint has a far more significant substantiation in Rabouni. In fact, nowhere does the notion of using camp spaces to materialize (self) governance become more evident than in this administrative settlement, even if first impressions are less obvious. The center of Rabouni is marked by a large parking lot-cum-bus depot, surrounded by improvised petrol stations, repair yards, and shops selling everything from groceries to building materials (usually simultaneously). The scattered vehicles, mostly ageing Land Rovers from the 1950s and 60s, have seen so many repairs that they appear like moving—or depending on their state of decay, immobile—bricolage. Combined with the hot, dusty desert wind that covers everything in a fine layer of sand, the sensation is akin to visiting an alien civilization on a desert planet in a scene from Star Wars.

North of this area lies a large compound enclosed with a giraffe-patterned wall, the Ministry of Defense. The surrounding urban fabric is dotted with all the other ministries that comprise the conventional bureaucratic apparatus of public administration in a regular nation state. As with the other physical constructions in the camps, each of these institutions are single-story compounds, built with cement bricks and covered in cement plaster to withstand the very rare—but then very heavy—rains and frequent sandstorms. The institutions occupy large swaths of ground within the urban fabric of Rabouni, but their low-rise profile does not allow for grand symbolic gestures. Nevertheless, their appearance is marked by a certain unconventionality.

Further to the west stands the Ministry of Foreign Affairs, with a cross-shaped floor plan that looks like it was lifted directly from the Swiss flag. To the east lies the large compound of the National Hospital, located next to the Ministry of Public Health. Just a few hundred meters further is the Ministry of Construction and Development, a building whose symmetrical layout is marked by four main corner rooms that are each roofed by prominent domes, giving the structure the look of a wedding cake. Inside, the Minister of Construction showed us a proposed scheme for housing units combined with an education center. A few minutes further out from Rabouni's center one reaches the key to this unique setting, the Sahrawi National Parliament.

The Sahrawis are the only refugees worldwide who have achieved semi sovereignty in the territory of their camps. They have built up their own system of administration and political representation. Rabouni is the capital for a nation in exile. It is the place where public health decisions are made, cultural policies are devised, new school curricula are developed, and codes of law are written. Rather than another example of 'humanitarian space' shaped by a dominant NGO culture, Rabouni is testimony to the self-reliance of the Sahrawis. With Rabouni, the camps are being used consciously by the Sahrawis as a political project. Not only in charge of their own lives, the refugees are also developing expertise and experience in running a country. Though still in exile, they are preparing themselves for the nation yet to come.

Rabouni also introduces something not typically considered when thinking about refugee camps: everyday life. Each morning, hundreds of ministry employees commute the ten kilometers or so from residential camps such as Smara by public bus or private taxi. They work in their offices, go for lunch, and in the evening return home. This ordinary routine, shared by billions worldwide, is significant precisely because it is so quotidian and unremarkable. We imagine a refugee camp to be a place of extremes—a place constructed to save lives, a place dedicated to pro-

In stark contrast to perceptions that camps are spaces where politics is not permitted, political activity is both facilitated and promoted. The Sahrawi population is encouraged to engage in political matters, while the camps themselves are seen and used as political projects in their anticipation of the Sahrawi nation state.

STATE CONTROL

Ceuta

STATE CONTROL

STATE CONTROL

STATE CONTROL

STATE CONTROL

The nation against nature: a report from San Diego-Tijuana

Trump's border wall prototypes, Otay Mesa, California. Estudio Teddy Cruz + Fonna Forman. © Jona Maier

Teddy Cruz is a professor of Public Culture and Urbanism in the Department of Visual Arts at the University of California, San Diego. He has conducted extensive urban research of the Tijuana/San Diego border, advancing border neighborhoods as sites of cultural production from which to rethink urban policy, affordable housing, and public space.

Fonna Forman is a professor of Political Theory and Founding Director of the Center on Global Justice at the University of California, San Diego. A theorist of ethics and public culture, her work focuses on human rights at the urban scale, climate justice in cities, border ethics, and equitable urbanization in the global south.

Cruz & Forman are principals in Estudio Teddy Cruz + Fonna Forman, a research-based political and architectural practice in San Diego, investigating issues of informal urbanization, civic infrastructure and public culture, with a special emphasis on Latin American cities

STATE CONTROL

THE construction of the Mexico-US borderwall holds social, economic, and political consequences for people living on both sides of the border. In this article, Teddy Cruz and Fonna Forman gives us an addition lens in which the borderwall manifests, describing the environmental implications of the border as a wall traversing the bioregional systems, representing a collision between natural and jurisdictional systems, and ecological and political priorities.

Written and Photographed by
Teddy Cruz + Fonna Forman

From its foundation, our research-based architecture practice has forwarded the Tijuana-San Diego border region as a global laboratory for engaging the central challenges of urbanization today: deepening social and economic inequality, dramatic migratory shifts, urban informality, climate change, the thickening of border walls and the decline of public thinking.

The current global climate of protectionism and border-hysteria that has reconfigured continents into walled geographies of closure, resonates powerfully for us here, transforming our local border conditions into a global hot-spot. Last year, for example, San Diego became a testing-ground for Trump's $4 million border-wall prototypes. Eight vertical monstrosities hovered ominously for months over the informal communities on the Tijuana side before they were disassembled. They were an overt slap on the face of our neighbour, and exemplified an architecture of violence and division, a protagonistic icon of exclusion, fear and border-building everywhere.

This is nothing new. The incremental hardening of division and surveillance has long been part of everyday life for border communities in our region: A chain-link fence in the seventies, a steel wall constructed with temporary landing mats discarded by the US military after Operation Desert Storm in Iraq in the nineties, and a see-through concrete pylon wall in the early 2000's, crowned by electrified coils and panoptic night-vision cameras. But the specter of Trump's new 30-foot high continental wall has re-ignited worries about the delicate cross-border ecosystems it will violate, compromising the health of human communities on both sides of the border and their shared environmental assets.

Only the most myopic of politics can conclude that building a wall across the continent will solve 'our' problems, ignoring the damage this political artifact will continue to exert on the cross-border bio-region. But this wall has collateral damage too rarely considered: As the United States builds its new wall against the 'other,' it also violates its own natural resources, as well as Mexico's. While the wall has been sold to the American public as an object of security, Trump's borderwall is an artifact of environmental, social and economic insecurity. This was demonstrated in the lawsuit brought by Arizona-based Center of Biological Diversity against the Trump administration for ignoring the environmental impact of the new border wall.

One example is the current condition of the Tijuana River watershed system, a bi-national environmental asset (25% of it is in the US, 75% in Mexico) truncated by the border wall. Here a new set of walls have wreaked havoc at the precise moment where the hydrological cone of this watershed drains into the Pacific Ocean. Before culminating in the ocean, water moves through Mexican canyons, tributaries and informal settlements, and crashes against the wall, where it seeps precariously into the U.S, infiltrating an environmentally protected Estuary in San Diego, a zone that is now heavily layered with militarization.

Here we witness the collision between: 1.) the Laureles Canyon, an informal settlement of 85,000 people in Tijuana, and the site of arrival of thousands of Central American Refugees in recent months; 2.) the Estuary in San Diego, a delicate bi-national environmental asset; and 3.) Trump's new multi-layered border walls, equipped with robust surveillance infrastructure. The collision between natural and jurisdictional systems, and between ecological and political priorities is profound. This is where most of our cross-border research is sited: a juncture where geo-political borders, global environmental crisis and human displacement is localized, and physicalized.

Rapid construction of these new borderwalls, and the addition of new dirt and concrete dams with small drains beneath, has accelerated northbound waste-water flows from the informal canyon settlements, which sit at a higher elevation, syphoning tons of trash and sediment into the Estuary with each rainy season, contaminating the "lungs" of the bio-region. These impacts have intensified in recent years because of poor water and waste management infrastructure in the Mexican settlement, and lack of collaboration between San Diego and Tijuana.

With our local partners on both sides of the borderwall, we resist an American perception that regional pollution is Mexico's problem: that they caused it and thus have to fix it. Instead we claim that this site of environmental insecurity is a challenge shared by Tijuana and San Diego, and must be tackled collaboratively. Much work in the next years will be dedicated to increasing awareness that this border region, like others across the world, is a laboratory for interdependence and new strategies of co-existence. Reimagining exclusionary borders through the logics of bioregional systems and social-ecologies will shape the future of this binational region and others.

Photo-tile demonstrating the conflict between the US Estuary and the Mexican informal settlement (above), and that new dams and drains will accelerate the wastewater flows from the Mexican settlement into the Estuary in San Diego (below). © Estudio Teddy Cruz + Fonna Forman.

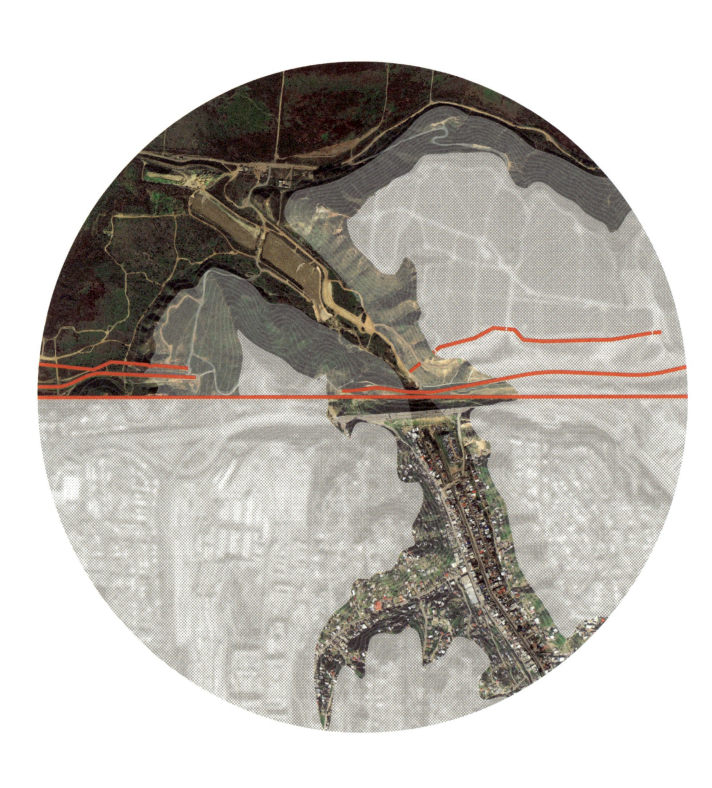

The collision between the Estuary in the US, the new borderwalls built by the US in recent months, and an informal settlement located in the Mexico's Laureles Canyon. © Estudio Teddy Cruz + Fonna Forman.

Ceuta

STATE CONTROL

STATE CONTROL

182

STATE CONTROL

STATE CONTROL

STATE CONTROL

The nation against nature: a report from San Diego-Tijuana

Trump's border wall prototypes, Otay Mesa, California. Estudio Teddy Cruz + Fonna Forman. © Jona Maier

Teddy Cruz is a professor of Public Culture and Urbanism in the Department of Visual Arts at the University of California, San Diego. He has conducted extensive urban research of the Tijuana/San Diego border, advancing border neighborhoods as sites of cultural production from which to rethink urban policy, affordable housing, and public space.

Fonna Forman is a professor of Political Theory and Founding Director of the Center on Global Justice at the University of California, San Diego. A theorist of ethics and public culture, her work focuses on human rights at the urban scale, climate justice in cities, border ethics, and equitable urbanization in the global south.

Cruz & Forman are principals in Estudio Teddy Cruz + Fonna Forman, a research-based political and architectural practice in San Diego, investigating issues of informal urbanization, civic infrastructure and public culture, with a special emphasis on Latin American cities

STATE CONTROL

THE construction of the Mexico-US borderwall holds social, economic, and political consequences for people living on both sides of the border. In this article, Teddy Cruz and Fonna Forman gives us an addition lens in which the borderwall manifests, describing the environmental implications of the border as a wall traversing the bioregional systems, representing a collision between natural and jurisdictional systems, and ecological and political priorities.

Written and Photographed by
Teddy Cruz + Fonna Forman

From its foundation, our research-based architecture practice has forwarded the Tijuana-San Diego border region as a global laboratory for engaging the central challenges of urbanization today: deepening social and economic inequality, dramatic migratory shifts, urban informality, climate change, the thickening of border walls and the decline of public thinking.

The current global climate of protectionism and border-hysteria that has reconfigured continents into walled geographies of closure, resonates powerfully for us here, transforming our local border conditions into a global hot-spot. Last year, for example, San Diego became a testing-ground for Trump's $4 million border-wall prototypes. Eight vertical monstrosities hovered ominously for months over the informal communities on the Tijuana side before they were disassembled. They were an overt slap on the face of our neighbour, and exemplified an architecture of violence and division, a protagonistic icon of exclusion, fear and border-building everywhere.

This is nothing new. The incremental hardening of division and surveillance has long been part of everyday life for border communities in our region: A chain-link fence in the seventies, a steel wall constructed with temporary landing mats discarded by the US military after Operation Desert Storm in Iraq in the nineties, and a see-through concrete pylon wall in the early 2000's, crowned by electrified coils and panoptic night-vision cameras. But the specter of Trump's new 30-foot high continental wall has re-ignited worries about the delicate cross-border ecosystems it will violate, compromising the health of human communities on both sides of the border and their shared environmental assets.

Only the most myopic of politics can conclude that building a wall across the continent will solve 'our' problems, ignoring the damage this political artifact will continue to exert on the cross-border bio-region. But this wall has collateral damage too rarely considered: As the United States builds its new wall against the 'other,' it also violates its own natural resources, as well as Mexico's. While the wall has been sold to the American public as an object of security, Trump's borderwall is an artifact of environmental, social and economic insecurity. This was demonstrated in the lawsuit brought by Arizona-based Center of Biological Diversity against the Trump administration for ignoring the environmental impact of the new border wall.

One example is the current condition of the Tijuana River watershed system, a bi-national environmental asset (25% of it is in the US, 75% in Mexico) truncated by the border wall. Here a new set of walls have wreaked havoc at the precise moment where the hydrological cone of this watershed drains into the Pacific Ocean. Before culminating in the ocean, water moves through Mexican canyons, tributaries and informal settlements, and crashes against the wall, where it seeps precariously into the U.S, infiltrating an environmentally protected Estuary in San Diego, a zone that is now heavily layered with militarization.

Here we witness the collision between: 1.) the Laureles Canyon, an informal settlement of 85,000 people in Tijuana, and the site of arrival of thousands of Central American Refugees in recent months; 2.) the Estuary in San Diego, a delicate bi-national environmental asset; and 3.) Trump's new multi-layered border walls, equipped with robust surveillance infrastructure. The collision between natural and jurisdictional systems, and between ecological and political priorities is profound. This is where most of our cross-border research is sited: a juncture where geo-political borders, global environmental crisis and human displacement is localized, and physicalized.

Rapid construction of these new borderwalls, and the addition of new dirt and concrete dams with small drains beneath, has accelerated northbound waste-water flows from the informal canyon settlements, which sit at a higher elevation, syphoning tons of trash and sediment into the Estuary with each rainy season, contaminating the "lungs" of the bio-region. These impacts have intensified in recent years because of poor water and waste management infrastructure in the Mexican settlement, and lack of collaboration between San Diego and Tijuana.

With our local partners on both sides of the borderwall, we resist an American perception that regional pollution is Mexico's problem: that they caused it and thus have to fix it. Instead we claim that this site of environmental insecurity is a challenge shared by Tijuana and San Diego, and must be tackled collaboratively. Much work in the next years will be dedicated to increasing awareness that this border region, like others across the world, is a laboratory for interdependence and new strategies of co-existence. Reimagining exclusionary borders through the logics of bioregional systems and social-ecologies will shape the future of this binational region and others.

Photo-tile demonstrating the conflict between the US Estuary and the Mexican informal settlement (above), and that new dams and drains will accelerate the wastewater flows from the Mexican settlement into the Estuary in San Diego (below). © Estudio Teddy Cruz + Fonna Forman.

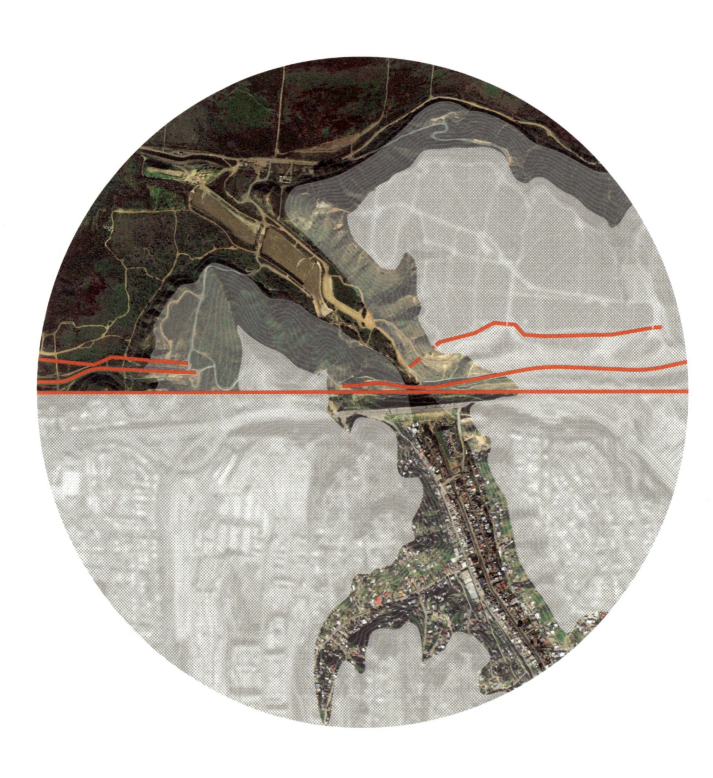

The collision between the Estuary in the US, the new borderwalls built by the US in recent months, and an informal settlement located in the Mexico's Laureles Canyon. © Estudio Teddy Cruz + Fonna Forman.

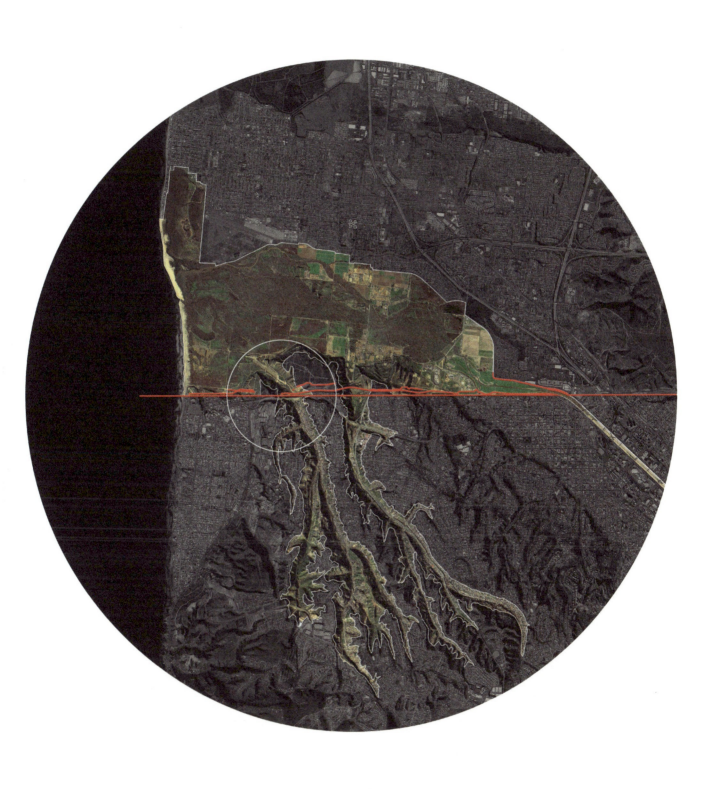

Laureles Canyon in Tijuana, B.C. Mexico, an important finger of the bi-national watershed, crosses the new multi-layered border wall, and drains into a militarized Estuary in San Diego. © Estudio Teddy Cruz + Fonna Forman.

View from Tijuana towards San Diego, with the informal settlement to the left, the new borderwalls and the estuary to the right, and the pacific ocean beyond. Estudio Teddy Cruz + Fonna Forman. © Lorena Branks

TEETER-TOTTER WALL

"The wall became a literal fulcrum for U.S -Mexico relations and children and adults were connected in meaningful ways on both sides with the recognition that the actions that take place on one side have a direct consequence on the other side,"

Ronald Rael

Ronald Rael, Professor of architecture at the University of California, Berkeley, and Virginia San Fratello, an associate professor of design at San Jose State University

Stories of displacement from Israel and Palestina

IN the years between 2011- 2018, Urban-Think Tank (U-TT) has documented and tried to understand the Israeli-Palestinian conflict, traveling extensively in the region. What we have witnessed over the seven years is by no means exhaustive, but it serves to document histories and lived experiences of people. During our travels, we trekked through a terrain of violence and toured architecture predicated upon violence. This is a marked contrast to U-TT's normal analytic gaze, which has focused on spatial problems rooted in economic inequality and social marginalization. In those contexts, we have sought to develop a new mode of architectural practice that can foster spaces of mediation, often with an overarching goal of stitching fragmented cities together. In Palestine and Israel, the political violence inscribed in the environment clearly called for different communication strategy, rooted first and foremost in the voices of locals who live creative political resistance every day. In our meetings with people and activists on the ground, we were always aware that we were part of an endless stream of researchers, journalists, and activists asking similar questions. And yet, those we spoke to engaged us with candour.

With the publication of this Motherland journal, the information and impressions from our trip resulted in a condensed travelogue, excerpts which are presented here. While the trip took place over an extended time period, much of the experiences unfortunately remains relevant today. To a large extent, the grim realities reported here have changed little.

Marielly Casanova is a Venezuelan architect. Before starting her doctorate at the University of Duisburg-Essen in Germany, Casanova worked at Urban-Think Tank as a senior designer and researcher.

Charlot Boonekamp is a Dutch architect focusing on socially and environmentally orientated spatial design. Boonekamp was a guest researcher at Urban-Think Tank.

Daniel Schwartz is an American filmmaker, photographer, and artist based in Zürich and Atlanta. His work focuses on stories about urban transformation from social, spatial, and political perspectives. Schwartz worked as a filmmaker, photographer, and researcher for Urban-Think Tank.

by
Urban-Think Tank

U-TT Research Team
Marielly Casanova
Charlot Boonekamp
Daniel Schwartz

Edited by
Alfredo Brillembourg
and Synne Bergby

Photography by
Daniel Schwartz

Els Verbakel (the architect)

Verbakel is a Belgian architect who migrated to Israel a decade ago. She has since established a thriving Tel Aviv practice with her husband, and is now the Head of the Department of Architecture at Bezalel Academy of Arts and Design Jerusalem. Having researched urban transformations in the city, she agreed to take us on a short tour of several local neighbourhoods. As we began our walk among the skyscrapers downtown, Verbakel explained how Tel Aviv existed before the creation of the state of Israel, as an expansion project of the port town Jaffa (also known as Yafo in Hebrew or Yafa in Arabic).

In 1910, the giant sand dune next to ancient Jaffa grew into a new settlement based on the British 'garden city' model, which shaped what was then called Ahuzat Bayit. As the population of Jaffa expanded rapidly at the beginning of the 20th century, its Jewish habitants moved to Azuyat Bayit and renamed the town Tel Aviv. The massive wave of Jewish immigration between 1918 and 1939 caused Tel Aviv to develop even faster, as nearby Jaffa was the main port of arrival. These mostly educated immigrants arrived with money, which contributed to the economic, industrial, social, and cultural development of the city.

In an effort to fill a planning vacuum in the early 1920s, the Mayor of Tel Aviv, Meir Dizengoff, invited Patrick Geddes to design an urban scheme. The 1925 'Geddes Plan' proposed a garden city laid out over a gridded street plan. Although ratified, the plan, which was predicated upon low densities, failed to anticipate the city's accelerated growth over the next 25 years. Tel Aviv attracted people from around the region due to its economic and leisure opportunities, placing pressure on municipal infrastructure and services. The declaration of the state of Israel, and ensuing conflicts between Jewish and Arab residents, further undermined the planning process. Verbakel paused our walking history lesson in front of a decaying four-story house, which sat incongruently in the expansive parking lot of a waterfront high-rise tower. It was a rare holdover from an earlier era, when the built identity of the city, and nation, was being defined. "Despite years of inconsistent planning, the Zionist government that took shape in Tel Aviv possessed some specific spatial visions for the region", she explained. From the head of government down to the municipal level, authorities felt an urgent need to unify and consolidate the new nation state. The city's boom came at the expense of existing inhabitation and surrounding areas, including the forcefully annexed Arab villages Salama and al-Shaykh Muwannis. Today, Tel Aviv is a cosmopolitan, vibrant city, which anchors the Israeli economy. Verbakel insisted the Tel Aviv region was a good place to begin to understand how much of the modern territorial conflict and displacement we would soon witness could be traced to ideological planning policies. By this time, we had reached the end of the waterfront, arriving at a lush park dividing the beach from a busy coastal road. "This is Charles Clore Park", said Verbakel. "It was made in theearly 1970s, and is one of the few places that hasn't been paved over for parking or high-rise development". The park is a wide stretch of grass and palm trees, covering a landfill formed by the ruins of Manshiya, the mixed Arab-Jewish suburb of Jaffa that was demolished during and after the creation of the state of Israel, mostly by urban planners designating the area as an uninhabitable slum. A kilometer away, a much older town perched behind a tree-lined hill overlooking the Mediterranean. "And that's Jaffa. It looks Arab from here, right?" she asked with a knowing smile, "Well it is, and it isn't, just like this park". Arab families were sitting throughout the grassy expanse, under young trees, or in the sun around picnic blankets and hookah pipes. Jewish families were also visible. There were, of course, more secular park visitors, as well as a presumably high number of tourists like us. Verbakel let our eyes wander before directing them toward an odd, rectangular building not far from where we stood. A double- story glass box was planted in what appeared to be the ruins of an ancient sandstone house. It was the Beit Gidi Etzel Museum, she explained. The museum commemorated the battles of the Irgun, a Zionist paramilitary organization that operated in Mandate Palestine until the creation of Israel. During the 1948 war, the Irgun continuously shelled Jaffa to force Arabs to leave. At the time, Jaffa was the largest Arab town in the region. Its location in the middle of the planned Jewish state, combined with its violent resistance against Jewish control, made it an important target of Jewish nationalists. After several years of fighting, the Irgun captured Jaffa. In what appears to be a particularly ironic architectural gesture, the museum honoring the group's victory was inserted on top of the only remaining home of Jaffa's northern- most neighbourhood. It took some imagination to recognize that we were standing on the ground of a former battle zone, and before that, a mixed Arab-Jewish neighbourhood. The memories of the houses and people that had lived, worked, and died there seemed buried particularly deep beneath the manicured landscaping and beach bars nearby. The thousands of families that fled during and after the battle for Jaffa still felt like the footnote in a classroom history lesson. In the coming days, however, we would meet some of those people and their descendants, living surprisingly close, and yet insurmountably far, from where we stood. The sun had begun to set, and Verbakel had to return home.

Saleh Abu Hasan (the driver)

Our strategy of beating the lines had worked too well. When the taxi dropped us off at Sheikh Hussein Border Crossing, a 20-minute drive from Tiberias, there was no

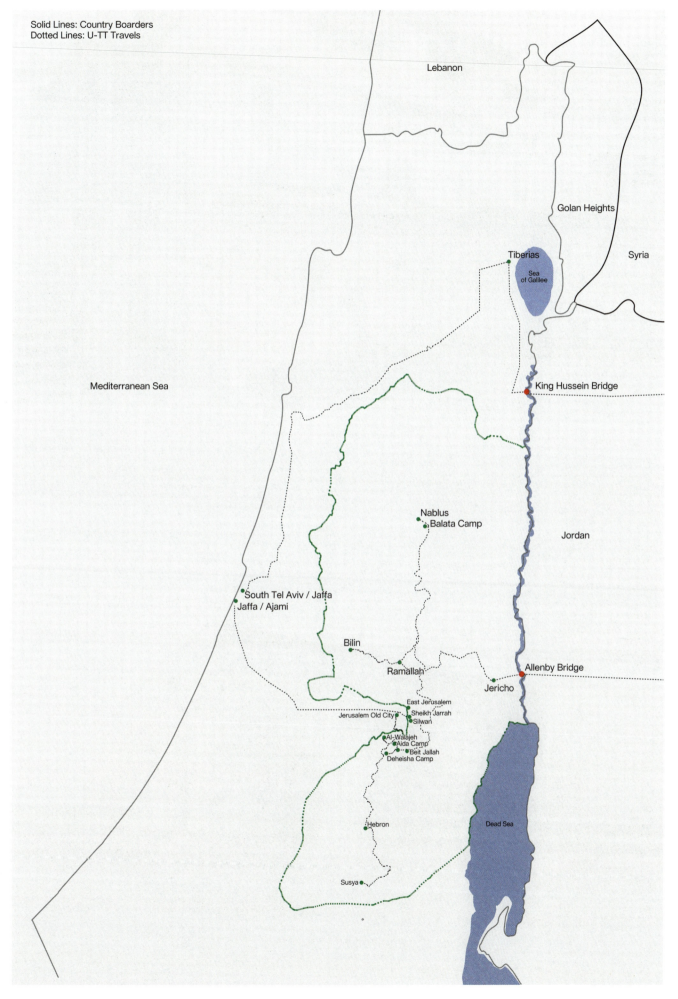

Map of Israel and Palestine

Tel Aviv Jaffa. © Daniel Schwartz

one outside. We had the driver cruise the full length of the fenced building to ensure we were indeed at the border. When we made it inside, our paperwork was processed smoothly, and we boarded a special bus to cross the no-man's land, dusty and pocked by several watchtowers and rusted jeeps. The Jordanian police on the other side were far more sceptical about our tourist claims, but we were eventually allowed to enter.

We had arranged to be picked up by a driver named Saleh Abu Hasan, who had guided Alfredo Brillembourg on a previous research trip to Jordan in 2010. Abu Hasan had been born and raised in Jordan. His parents came from Palestine, however, and had settled at a refugee camp near Amman around 1948. Abu Hasan turned out to be very well-informed, and supportive of the project, so we had arranged to not only work with him during our brief stop, but also to stay in his family's house.

Soon we were driving up rocky slopes, emerging out of the Jordan Rift Valley toward the vast plateau where the metropolitan Amman sprawled. We had scheduled to spend most of the day in one of the larger refugee camps near the capital, known as Marka. The camp, which was established in 1968 some10 kilometres from Amman, was one of ten official refugee camps in Jordan that together host 346,000 registered Palestinian refugees This equated to 17 percent of the approximately two million Palestinian refugees residing in Jordan in total.

To understand how so many people could be displaced for so long, it is worth reviewing some history. In 1948, the area of British Mandate Palestine—covering Israel and the Occupied Palestinian Territories (OPT)—became a conflict zone after Zionists unilaterally declared the Independent State of Israel. While both Jews and Arabs had fought with the British army against the Ottoman Empire in exchange for independence, the British only contractually guaranteed support for an eventual Jewish state. When Britain transferred Mandate Palestine to the newly established United Nations (UN) in 1947, it was expected that the territory would be divided into a Jewish state consisting of 56 percent of the land, and an Arab or Palestinian state on the remaining area .

Because this plan unequally distributed both people and private property, the Arab coalition rejected the proposal. Capitalizing on the climate of diplomatic instability, Zionists began a campaign to forcefully seize land. While they used a variety of tactics to empty villages and expel Palestinians from their land, the British army and UN failed to intervene. The Zionist leadership made their unilateral declaration on the same day the British army left, causing fury among neighbouring Arab states. The next day, these countries declared war, eventually culminating in a cease-fire in 1949.

By then, Israel had expanded to approximately 78 percent of the area of former Mandate Palestine. Zionist fighters had targeted Palestinian civilian communities during the war, and many fled the violence with the intention of returning in calmer times. In total, half of the pre-war Arab population had been expelled, while one-fifth of the Arabs that remained in Israel were forcibly displaced. This massive dispersal of 700,000 to 900,000 Palestinians is commonly denoted by Arabs as the 'Nakba', which translates to nightmare or catastrophe.

Following the Nakba, most of those who were expelled or escaped the violence settled in refugee camps in surrounding states, namely Jordan, Syria, Lebanon, and the remaining parts of former Mandate Palestine (primarily the Gaza Strip and West Bank, then ruled by Egypt and Jordan, respectively). Because Israel prevented these Palestinians from returning, they remained refugees, and in many host countries their descendants have been born into that status. This was the UN's first large scale confrontation with a refugee crisis. In 1949, it established the UN Relief and Works Agency (UNRWA) as a temporary organization to provide humanitarian relief to the displaced Palestinians.

In 1967, a second war between Israel and the Arab powers culminated in the occupation of East Jerusalem, the West Bank, and the Gaza Strip, placing both Palestinian citizens and refugees under Israeli control . The violence drove away a further 400,000 Palestinians from the occupied territories to surrounding countries . Almost 70 years since the beginning of the Nakba, Palestinian refugees are still denied the right of return as stipulated by the UN General Assembly. And because the Palestinian refugee issue continue to exist, the UN has repeatedly prolonged UNRWA's mandate. Although the agency does not administer camps, it is responsible for many camp services and infrastructure.

We cruised past Amman on Highway 25. Abu Hasan turned the van onto a dusty, uneven road, which led to a dense and haphazard settlement. We left for Abu Hasan's house, in Amman's largest refugee camp, Rusaifah. His father had built a spacious, suburban home outside the camp's dense centre. Abu Hasan's wife and two children lived on the second floor, while his brother's family occupied the ground floor. Together, we enjoyed a dinner cooked by Abu Hasan's wife. When asked about the recipes, she began to describe joyfully how she had been entrusted with this knowledge as a way to remember her grandmother's West Bank village and Abu Hasan agreed they would move to their ancestral village if given the chance. "Our memory is like this food", he said, pointing to a plate filled with bread and olives. "It is what has sustained us and will sustain our children". In the morning, we said goodbye to Abu Hasan's family and drove west.

Sae Osawa (Marka Camp commissioner)

Austere concrete buildings huddled tightly together left little space for movement and transport. Hand-painted signs added small hints of colour to the otherwise grey and yellow shop fronts. A growing stream of people crowded the poorly paved streets and sidewalks. We had arrived in Marka Camp. The camp's Japanese commissioner, Sae Osawa, was waiting for us outside its administrative headquarters, and ushered us in for coffee and a lecture on Marka's institutional structure.

Marka was established in 1968 by the independent Jordanian Department for Palestinian Affairs (DPA), which represented the Palestinian refugee population in Jordan, and acted as an intermediary between UNRWA and the Ministry of Foreign Affairs. In Jordan, decisions concerning the expansion, upgrading, and renovation of Palestinian refugee camps had to be approved by the ministry. Camp committees had been appointed to take charge of the social and physical infrastructure of the camps, collaborating closely with UNRWA to provide residents with services and facilities. Refugees residing in the camp's immediate surroundings also used these facilities.

As Osawa explained, the definition of a refugee, at least in the eyes of UNRWA, was complicated. For UNRWA, a Palestinian refugee was an individual who had resided in Palestine between 1946 and 1948, and lost their home and livelihood as a result of the first Arab-Israeli conflict. In addition, the offspring of registered refugees were automatically registered too, regardless of where they lived. These so-called '1948' refugees represented the largest portion of the total Palestinian refugee population (4.8 million). At the time of registration in 1950, however, not all refugees were able, or wanted, to do so. Even today, UNRWA consistently updates registration cards, and continue to register 'new' refugees if refugee status could be determined.

There were an additional 2.2 million unregistered refugees, most of whom were displaced during the 1967 war and other crises in the OPT since 1950. As UNRWA had softened its requirements in various ways over the years, many unregistered refugees had moved into the camps. "But", Osawa noted with some resignation, "only registered refugees can access UNRWA's services and facilities, such as healthcare and education". This made for a politically contentious bureaucracy in many camps, though he assured us that "most of the refugees in Marka are registered from 1948 and happened to be displaced a second time in 1967". Osawa took us on a tour of several UNRWA facilities, most concentrated along a large, central street. We visited a health clinic filled with mothers and babies, state-of-the art laboratory equipment, and a chain-smoking doctor. After, we passed through a neighbourhood of dilapidated houses, some constructed on and around the original brick structures built in the early 1970s. Health problems plagued many residents, as deteriorating homes, pollution, and a harsh climate contributed to chronic ailments like asthma and autoimmune diseases. We spoke to a mother of three, whose husband had begun suffering from both physical and mental health issues and could no longer work. The family survived due to a modest UNRWA allowance. But her husband, who was an unregistered refugee from Gaza, struggled to receive necessary treatment.

We concluded our tour at a youth centre, where 20 teenagers had been waiting for us. A group conversation began, focusing on life in the camp and access to education. It soon turned toward more abstract expectations for the future. Most participants possessed a sense of innate nostalgia that caught us by surprise. "The label of refugee has caused me a lot of suffering. I only know Palestine through the stories of my grandparents. But I am prepared to do anything in order for Palestine to return to the beautiful country it once was. Wherever I am, I will work for my country. I am here now, but my heart is in Palestine", one of the boys told us.

A girl seated across the room interjected. "Your home village is here, not where your grandparents are from. Here you can vote, there you would have nothing", she said, referring to Jordan's extension of suffrage to its long-term refugee population. Yet most of the group seemed to share the boy's perspective. While they understood the need to build a community in Jordan that would have an impact on their immediate futures, they had also been taught that their true home was on the other side of an impenetrable border. Civic life in the camp and better integration into municipal services were important, but the teenagers did not exude a sense of long-term investment.

Osama Hamdeh Ramalla (city architect) and Farhat Muhawi (RIWAQ Planner)

The sun woke us at daybreak, heating up our stuffy hotel room and encouraging us to get out and see the city we had entered amid the darkness of the previous night. We were staying close to the centre, near al-Manara Square. Ten kilometres north of Jerusalem, Ramallah was settled in the 16th century and grew as a stop on an important trade route to Nablus. Al-Manara was the city's central intersection, and both Ottoman and British rulers built important administrative offices and military outposts in the surrounding area. As Ramallah grew, especially with an influx of displaced people during the Nakba, al-Manara became a symbolically important core for Palestinian culture.

We strolled around the traffic circle that now occupied the square and bought some cheese-filled bread from a bakery. The adjacent buildings were four or five stories tall, most constructed with the white Jerusalem stone quarried locally. There were very few pedestrians at such an early hour, and traffic had yet to swell to the same level we had witnessed the previous evening. It felt like Ramallah was a sleepy town rather than the administrative and economic hub of the West Bank. Any misconceptions would be dispelled, however, at our first stop for the day, a meeting at City Hall. The Deputy Mayor, Mahmoud Abdullah, greeted us, before welcoming us into a small conference room.

Once inside, we were introduced to city architect, Osama Hamdeh, and Farhat Muhawi, a planner at the architectural heritage group RIWAQ. "Ramallah is the capital of Palestine, even though we do not want it to be", Abdullah began, as we sat down. "We should be in Jerusalem, but we are here, and for this Ramallah grows. People continue to come here to live and work". Checkpoints and other limitations in movement that arose from the occupation continued to encourage people to settle close by. As a result, Abdullah explained, Ramallah had the highest growth rate of any city in the West Bank and was suffering from its own popularity.

"We have over 40,000 residents, but that number doubles during the day... in 2008, the municipality prepared a strategic plan for the development of the city, which included many projects. In the past, there was no strategic plan, and because of the occupation infrastructure developed very slowly. For example, we can compare Ramallah today to the 1980s. Back then, 60 to 70 percent of the city was connected to the sewage network. By any normal logic, the rate of connection in the years after should increase. But in 2010 we discovered that the rate had actually gone down to 50 percent. The demand on housing—on new buildings in general—is too much for us to handle".

"Do you know about the designations of land in the Occupied Palestinian Territories?" asked Hamdeh. He was referring to the subdivision of the West Bank following the 1995 Oslo II Accord, which split the territory into Area A (17.7 percent), controlled exclusively by the Palestinian Authorities (PA), Area B (18.3 percent), administered jointly by the PA and Israeli Defense Forces (IDF), and Area C (61 percent), over which Israel would retain full civil and security control. "Well, we need to build new sanitation and waste treatment facilities, but the only suitable land is in Area C. We've been waiting for 15 years for permission to begin building. It was only a few years ago that we were allowed to begin conducting engineering studies with the help of German partners. In the meantime, our city won't have the infrastructure it needs". The strategic plan for Ramallah, the officials explained, was to encourage decentralization through the construction of additional apartment towers, to reroute and expand public infrastructure, and to create new commercial centres. Abdullah was emphatic. "The traditional way of living in houses with gardens must be abolished. It has to make space for the new way of living, which relates to Palestinian maturity and modernization". The UN, as we would later learn, estimated that the housing shortage in the OPT was approximately 450,000 units and growing. In order to meet this need, over 40,000 units would have to be built annually. "Is the government or the private market to build these houses? That is the question". Before he or anyone else in the room could provide an answer, Abdullah excused himself for another meeting.

Jordan. © Daniel Schwartz

STATE CONTROL Jordan / Palestine. © Daniel Schwartz

Almost immediately, the tone in the room shifted. Muhawi lit a cigarette and spoke up for the first time. "If we're honest, we have to admit that the PA has done a bad job at institution building. In one sense, this is understandable. We don't want to invest in this capital that we don't want to live in. But such a big housing shortage is evidence that the government vision is not good enough, and that the private market is not striving to meet a demand, but rather looking for easy profits". According to Muhawi, the blame fell on a mentality of greed. Both the government and private real estate developers were trying to maximize profits rather than address real needs.

"Due to the limited land available for construction, prices for a plot are easily the equivalent of $1,000 per square meter in Ramallah. Land in Area B is much cheaper as it is located further from the Palestinian urban centres in Area A. But because land in Area B is cut off from Area A by Area C, daily commuting is uncertain and time consuming. If anything, it should be used for agriculture or industrial development. But instead, real estate developers get it, promise the government a lot of tax revenues, and then construct housing priced at European levels. The majority of Palestinians don't have access to these lands". Hamdeh confirmed that annual income per capita was about $2,000, meaning many of the new housing projects remained out of reach for most people.

Dr. Samih al-Abid
(Palestine Investment Fund)

We had set up an appointment with Dr. Samih al-Abid in order to get a private sector perspective on housing in the OPT. Al-Abid, a former architect and peace negotiator for the PA, had taken a position as planning and real estate consultant at the Palestine Investment Fund (PIF). The PIF was a sovereign wealth fund dedicated to 'national economic empowerment'. With assets of close to $800 million, PIF had played a significant role in much of the real estate development in Ramallah and other West Bank cities in the last decade.

The fund's office, which was located in a quiet residential neighbourhood, was small but refined. Glass and chrome fixtures dominated most surfaces, and the few employees we glimpsed as we waited in the reception area were dressed in fine suits and seemed far removed from the more casual disposition of those at City Hall. Al-Abid, a tall man of about 65, greeted us and directed us to his office on the building's ground floor. Our conversation turned quickly to housing—in particular, whether there was a lack of vision among Palestinian planners.

"The housing sector is mainly private" explained al-Abid. "We don't have a public housing sector here, and the reason for that is because 80 percent of the people of the West Bank own property within the towns and villages. So, government land is scarce and not meant for housing for the poor. We don't like social housing, because if we build social housing for the poor, people will remain poor, like in refugee camps. You see this in the social housing projects of Europe and the United States. I think they created their own problems for the future".

Al-Abid expressed his faith in enlightened market-driven projects. "What we will do is find the ways to give the people the right to own property by using credits and lowering the interest. And we make people live within a community—poor, middle-class, and rich together". Unfortunately, many of the private development schemes had failed or stalled when confronted with territorial restrictions imposed by Israel. A post-occupation national 'Protection Plan', which al-Abid helped conceive in 1998, mapped out regions in the West Bank for various types of development, environmental protection, and cultural heritage. Because the occupation never ended, however, the plan was eventually abandoned. Echoing the views of the Deputy Mayor during our morning meeting, al-Abid agreed that "the most viable and abundant land for development is in Area C, which Israel makes practically inaccessible". A major development proposal in the Jordan Valley that would include tens of thousands of units of housing, agriculture, and industrial projects, had been stalled indefinitely due to Israel's refusal to grant permits. "The just solution to all of this is a two-state solution. Palestine and Israel both deserve sovereignty over separate lands".

We asked about what urban development plans existed for after any political agreement. "If hypothetically there is a two-state solution, of course that will bring a bigger population. Are there plans? Yes, and I helped finish them with the previous peace negotiations. So now we have to see if the pragmatic need for infrastructure and resources that come with this current political reality is something to discuss endlessly in the present, or something one just deals with in the hypothetical future".

Al-Abid ended the meeting by showing us various maps and development plans that he had helped create over the previous fifteen years. By the time we left his office, we had begun to feel numb. Drawn on his maps were not just politically complex and spatially nuanced proposals for how to improve a region, but what seemed to be the dashed hopes of a generation. Bold lines, shaded regions, and dotted cities all seemed to circumscribe an impression of geographic disorientation and frustration.

Khaldun Bshara
(Ramalla RIWAQ director)

Having studied both conservation architecture and anthropology, Bshara was uniquely positioned to understand the importance of Palestinian heritage within the built environment. At RIWAQ, he had helped manage and design numerous preservation projects around the West Bank that sought to use architecture as a force for civic engagement. When we arrived at the organization's beautiful 1930s villa, Bshara was parking his bright red Volkswagen Beetle. The office was empty, Bshara unlocked the door and flipped on several antique light fixtures. As we explained the nature of our research, he made us coffee and replaced his sunglasses with a pair of rectangular spectacles with frames that matched the colour of the car. After listening intently, he began; "We at RIWAQ believe architectural heritage has to do with identity, so we're trying to blur the boundaries between modernism and post-modernism, memory and heritage, architecture and art, space and social space. We think about space as an essential element for social change. And we try to reverse the colonial condition, seeing heritage as non-static. Heritage is more than a product of a moment in history".

He paused to sip his coffee. "The colonial condition disturbed the flow of culture in a structural way, imposing its own norms. We want to reverse that condition. We add a new layer that was cut from its normal flow—that is what restoration can offer, a reflection on how we can carry on". We asked Bshara to clarify the identity Palestinians could claim through space. "There is no single identity that is called Palestinian. I'm not just Palestinian. I'm also Roman, Syrian, Ottoman, Arab, Muslim, Christian, Jewish. And the stories we tell ourselves about who we are, they are told for certain reasons, for example to fight against alienation after being colonized or exiled. Refugees were made a class. A refugee is somebody who moved involuntarily, by nature or by war, and in doing so, they are made into a class who has nothing to do or offer but themselves and their bodies".

Warming to the theme, Bshara led the discussion back to the defining issue of contested territory. "This is why there will be no solution to the Palestinian-Israeli problem without a just solution for the refugees. Palestinian identity increasingly constitutes refugeehood and nothing else. Sometimes, I admit to myself that this land we glorify is so stupid. It might even be the most boring area in the world, Israel and Palestine. But we Palestinians also created this metaphor of Palestine beauty, and there is a moral commitment for Palestinians to remember that metaphor and those who lost the beauty". We were slightly taken aback by Bshara's forthright challenge to the terms through which we had heard other Palestinians frame these topics.

He went on to describe why the pursuit of statehood was a destructive and ultimately futile effort, more likely to result in alienating national identities and corrupt institutions than an authentic liberation process. For Bshara, it was clear that a positive future for Palestinians was tied to a more flexible cultural and social sphere rooted in place-making. The land allegiances that had frozen Palestinian identity were destructive, and modern ideas such as a nationalism based on loss or religion would further cement such identity politics. When the coffee cups were empty, Bshara proposed that we visit al-Kamandjati Music Association, a project RIWAQ had realized several years earlier, near the centre of Ramallah.

We parked the car near the entrance to the Old City and walked through a labyrinth of alleys and small streets. Bshara explained that the project was built with a French-Palestinian NGO, which wanted to extend musical education to a wider and more diverse portion of the youth in Ramallah. Traditionally seen as a hobby or vocation reserved for the elite, music lessons and training were now being offered to everyone. The new facilities were a great success, Bshara proclaimed proudly, with similar centres already built or planned in numerous Palestinian refugee camps and villages, as well as in East Jerusalem.

RIWAQ's unique sense of post-modern preservation was obvious as we approached the building from a side street. What appeared to be an Ottoman-era cluster of houses had been carefully renovated and furnished with contemporary and tasteful design elements. Two massive steel plates, connected to form a skewed box, jutted out from the white stones. A large door in one of the plates was open, revealing a beautiful courtyard inside. The sound of music emanated from a second-story classroom in one of the interior buildings, and Khaldun led us up to observe a group of about ten teenagers rehearsing. The domed roof inside was original and created an acoustic balance for the gathered musicians.

"This was a partial ruin before", Bshara beamed, ushering us back outside into the courtyard. "You see we replaced many of the broken stones, added a wooden porch, re-plastered the existing walls, and even developed some low-cost but fancy design elements. Through preservation, the evidence of the existence of cultures inhabiting a specific area during a certain time will be maintained and can be used to defend the right to be present. But to be sure that we are not just creating an identity based on conflict and the right to a territory, creative cultural heritage takes a decisive role". He excused himself, as he had many appointments elsewhere in the city, leaving us to listen to the end of the rehearsal.

Zvi Efrat (architect and historian)

The public bus from downtown Ramallah delivered us to Bil'in after about half an hour driving down an arid road with small, vernacular villages breaking up the sunbaked fields. When we arrived, there was little to distinguish Bil'in from the other villages we had passed. But as we walked into the centre of the quiet cluster of cinderblock houses, we began to see Arabic slogans spray-painted across countless walls. Electrical poles were decorated with yellowing vinyl banners that depicted militants and martyers plus numerous political signs in both Arabic and English declared anti-Israeli messages. Settlement construction was at the heart of the protests.

We spoke to the Israeli architect and historian, Zvi Efrat, who referred to Zionism's 'territorial syndrome', and identified its essence as the quest to conquer the 'Land of Promise'. According to Efrat, it was a unique form of colonialism 'immersed in an autochthonous imaginary, programmed by anti-urban precepts, articulated through reformist social doctrines, and propagated by a paramilitary frontier culture'. His writing resonated as we climbed a hill away from Bil'in's centre. At its crest, a large valley swept down the other side, before rising again and revealing a large Jewish settlement sprawling across the opposite hill. The late afternoon sun was imbued with a golden hue, and the white bricks of the Modi'in Illit bloc glowed.

With its 45,000 inhabitants and 60 births per week, Modi'in Illit was the largest and fastest-growing Jewish settlement in the West Bank But it was by no means the only one. The settlement movement had its roots in the Zionist movement's commune building that began well over a century prior. Efrat had recounted this history, writing, 'in the century between the 1880s and 1980s, about 700 new villages, rural towns, and garden cities were built in Palestine by and for Jewish immigrants (about 250 settlements before Israeli statehood, 450 after)' . This settlement building was connected to both an ideological and pragmatic need for the Jewish state to control its territory.

In pre-Israel times, the Zionist movement was explicitly anti-urban, perceiving cities as corrupting spaces for the emerging National project. But with the actual realization of the Jewish state, planners embraced the model of a semi-urban towns as a means to develop the nation, preventing uncontrolled sprawl, and as a way to control socialization patterns of a largely immigrant-based population. Throughout the 1950s and early 1960s, Jewish settlement building continued along a government-initiated master plan referred to as the 'Israeli Project'. Arieh Sharon, a Bauhaus graduate and one of the prominent architects of the new state, was assigned with the national task to provide temporary housing to the flow of Jewish immigrants.

Ibrahim (Mod'in Illit farmer)

Housing also served to consolidate the 1948 armistice lines and prohibit the return of Palestinian refugees, especially to peripheral areas. The 'Sharon Plan' envisaged the development of the physical environment of the Israeli state through centric planning and construction, embodied in the concept of the 'Israeli New Town'. Notwithstanding its larger size, the structural organization of these new towns mimicked the morphological structure of an agricultural community (Kibbutz). Over time, the architecture changed, adapting to a rightward shift in Israeli politics that favoured private development and American-influenced suburbia. With control of the OPT new land became available, but it lacked Jewish identity

Ramallah. © Daniel Schwartz

STATE CONTROL Israel. © Daniel Schwartz

and needed to be domesticated. Similarly, the threat of a counter-attack demanded fortification measures.

The 'Allon Plan' proposed defensible borders in heavily Palestinian populated areas - namely, a strategic strip of land in the Jordan Rift Valley, and mountain ridges to the west from Nablus to Hebron. The plan envisaged the construction of a defensive line of settlements in the annexed territory. Their interconnection would fortify the Israeli presence and secure desired areas. The border crossings at Allenby Bridge and Sheikh Hussein could easily be occupied in times of unrest, allowing Israel to execute full control. Although the plan was officially rejected by political leaders at the time, it still shaped much of Israel's settlement policy in the West Bank from 1967 to 19778. By 1973, there were 9,800 settlers living in the OPT (including East Jerusalem) . Although Israel agreed in 1995 to stop settlement construction, building intensified during the Second Intifada, culminating in the presence of 330,000 settlers in the West Bank by 2011 (not including East Jerusalem) . The growth of Modi'in Illit fit this pattern. Although construction began in 1993, Jewish colonies had been present since the 1980s. According to Bil'in's 'official' website, Israel subsequently annexed 60 percent of the village's territory for settlement construction, cutting villagers off from their agricultural lands. While the challenge to the security wall's route had succeeded, the settlement had continued to expand. Clashes between settlers and villagers were common. As a result, the IDF had an outsized presence, intervening routinely in conflicts or occasionally meeting the weekly protests of pro-Palestinian activists with lethal force.

With this in mind, we were surprised by how tranquil the area seemed. In the centre of the valley, we glimpsed the new route of the security wall, with a smoothly paved road running along its edge and an Humvee driving on the side of the settlement. It was eerily quiet, and we struggled to see any movement from within or around the tower blocks. The terraced structures, ranging from one to ten stories tall, were clustered along the hilltop in a circular formation, spreading across the ridgeline. The architecture evoked an aggressive posture, as boxy balconies jutted out toward Bil'in. It did not require much imagination to envision the buildings as a massive defensive line. Caught in the moment, we were startled by shouts from behind us.

"Hey! Hey!" We turned and saw a man, perhaps 50 meters away, in the olive orchard that ran along the hillside. He waved enthusiastically, gesturing for us to come toward where he was standing beneath a tree. With stories of local violence weighing on our minds, we felt tense. But as we approached, we saw that he appeared to be a young, stylish Palestinian farmer. He wore faded jeans, a purple t-shirt, and sunglasses. If not for the pick-axe in his hands and a sweaty brow, it would not have been clear that he had just finished digging a small trench nearby. When we reached him, he grinned widely, shook our hands, and introduced himself in broken English as Ibrahim. He put down his axe and motioned for us to follow him to the other side of the orchard.

In the shade of the trees, Ibrahim explained haltingly that we were on his family's land. Pointing back to Mod'in Illit, he said that they wanted it. To reinforce the point, he paused and plucked one of the green fruits dangling above. He put it in his mouth, pointed to the rocky ground on which we stood, and then placed his hand flat across his chest. The symbolism was clear. On the other side of the orchard, we found Ibrahim's small party, consisting of his wife and baby, as well as his brother and sister-in-law. They were sitting on a blanket, with a large hookah pipe, a mobile playing Middle-Eastern electronic music, and a small fire on which a pot of tea was simmering. It was a bucolic scene, contrasting sharply with the conflict that seemed to define life in the area.

Mustafa Farrah
(Nablus Cultural Center)

We soon reached the outskirts of Nablus. With more than 170,000 inhabitants, it is one of the largest Palestinian cities, and home to three refugee camps, including the West Bank's largest, Balata. When we arrived at the camp, the taxi maneuvered slowly through the dense concrete fabric, which was commonly referred to as 'the Brick' and stopped in front of the mural-clad Yafa Cultural Centre. Its name a variation on the port of Jaffa, the centre had recently expanded its facilities with a guesthouse. That night we would be some of its early guests. After checking in, we agreed to walk to the historical centre of Nablus with an employee named Mustafa Farrah. Jocular, energetic, and sporting a baseball cap that seemed to perpetually swivel on his head, Farrah proved to be a good guide.

As we entered the Old City, he stopped us in front of the crumbling stone façade of a three-story house with grand arched windows and elegant pillars. "The Old City of Nablus traces back to 2,000 years ago, but these days we're distracted by more recent history", he said, pointing first to the deteriorating building, and then to a poster plastered on one of its doors that depicted a deceased martyr. "The Battle of Nablus during the Second Intifada was one of the bloodiest and longest in the West Bank. The hiding spots, cellars, and maze organization of the Old City were very useful for the resistance fighters building rockets. But when the Israelis came, they hit hard and destroyed much of what you see around us".

Farrah led us down the alleyways of the souk, with crevices between buildings that appeared to be growing together. "With violence increasing, a special Israeli military division was sent in 2002 to dismantle resistance. A raid in Balata, which was successful but deadly for the Israelis, made them worried that the hundreds of armed Palestinians in the Old City could cause a lot of casualties. So they fired rockets, armoured bulldozers cleared the barricades, and then an infantry brigade entered. By the time the Palestinians surrendered, hundreds were killed, and many buildings were severely damaged or destroyed". According to UNESCO, more than a dozen had important heritage value. Farrah showed us where some buildings had been partially restored. But many more were still collapsed, and the signs of violent conflict were evident on bullet-punctured facades.

The smell of the famous local cheese pastry, knafeh, wafted around us. We walked into several shops and businesses, from a centuries-old soap factory, to one of the city's famous candy and spice shops. "Even after the battle ended, Israeli restrictions on the transportation of materials and products have caused a lot of suffering. We used to be one of the most important industrial centres in the West Bank, and now, these factories are some of the only businesses that were able to re-open". The military sealed all entry points to the city and surrounding villages through checkpoints, before erecting huge earth mounds, even within the city itself. Home to the largest West Bank university, students and teachers were frequently blocked for days or weeks from attending classes. These conditions lasted for nine years. "People and investors turned to other cities like Ramallah, and we had a very high unemployment rate", Farrah said as we approached the edge of the Old City. "However, we're working hard on our tourist industry, trying to get foreigners to visit, and apparently the economy is growing". We walked back into the souk, which began to light up as the evening sky darkened to a deep blue, and the streets swelled with people enjoying fresh air without the oppressive heat. We could not help but notice the graffiti scrawled everywhere. As we walked back toward Balata, Farrah laughed awkwardly with us as we passed a café that had fixed both Osama bin Laden and Rambo posters to its door.

Farrah had agreed to show us several Balata neighbourhoods. At 24-years-old, he was too young during the Second Intifada to have fought, but old enough to remember what Balata went through. "Arrests, shootings, nightly military raids, and killings became normal", he said grimly as we walked toward the centre of the camp. Hundreds were killed or injured. More than 12,000 were imprisoned at various points, with 400 still languishing in Israeli jails . "The families of these men also lost their main source of income, and Balata today is much poorer than before. Like in the Old City, Israel restricted the movement of residents for years following the conflict, which worsened unemployment and kept our market depressed. Things have improved, but many people still suffer from those years of trauma".

The Yafa Youth Centre was located near the top of the hill on which most of Balata perches. We walked from its entrance along one of the main roads, and noted how many of the businesses lining the street had similar English-spelled names. "Yafa Chicken, Jaffa Bakery, Yaffa everything", Farrah joked. UNRWA first erected Balata in 1950 to provisionally host about 5,000 Palestinian refugees arriving in the area, many fleeing from Jaffa and the surrounding Arab villages. The camp was deliberately established at a distance from the centre of Nablus to under-line its temporariness, and authorities only allotted 250 square meters of land, rented from local landowners for a symbolic period of 99 years.

Farrah pointed to the street that began Balata's urban grid. "Each family was given a tent and could use the land around the tent for private purposes. Space between the rows functioned as pathways to access the tents and sanitary facilities, which were placed every couple of rows. Larger tents on the edges of the camp had facilities like a school, food distribution, and a medical centre. A fence around the perimeter kept the camp from growing bigger". Many of the families arriving to the site came from the same neighbourhoods, he explained. "People tried to keep the same social organization they knew from before the war. So even though Arab families are very big, they stuck together".

Just as we had heard in Marka Camp, Farrah emphasized how the intended temporariness of Balata ultimately settled into an improvised permanence. "The climate is hard here, cold in the winter and very hot in the summer. So after a couple years, the UN replaced the tents with single-room concrete shelters. These were better than tents, but too small for big families, and they had no sanitation facilities. The communal toilets and water taps began to break as we became bigger, and there were many disease outbreaks during that time". In the 1960s, UNRWA upgraded many of the shelters with basic sanitation infrastructure, but population growth placed increasing pressure on the camp to expand.

With camp officials at the time occupied with provision of healthcare, education, and social services, refugees began enlarging their homes. Public space was claimed, and the camp's urban fabric changed gradually as it began to densify. With the arrival of more refugees displaced during the 1967 war, plots of land were subdivided further. As the camp's horizontal boundaries were fixed, houses grew vertically, rising to two, three, and sometimes even four-stories high. The camp started to transform into what we could see all around us, a congested and hyper-dense urban cluster of more than 25,000 people. We left the main road and began to walk down a shoulder-width set of concrete stairs between two homes. The morning light barely penetrated between the buildings, and the air smelled stale with a faint hint of garbage. The bricks on the bottom of the buildings were different from those above, and Farrah confirmed that those were the original UNWRA structures built 50 years earlier. They were clearly not designed for the added loads, and we could see how the houses rose crookedly—perhaps a result of bad foundations as much as haphazard construction techniques. We were reminded of countless other informal settlements around the world that U-TT had studied and worked within.

"In the 1970s, Balata became more militant. The difficult living conditions and the new refugees arriving who were not part of these original families created disturbances. People lost hope that they would return to the homeland. People got angry", Farrah said. We knew he was referencing the growth of the political party Fatah, which under the guidance of refugee and leader Yasser Arafat, called for the liberation of Palestine through armed resistance. With the First Intifada, and then its more violent sequel, Balata was primed to become a hotbed of resistance. Farrah gestured for us to follow him up a metal staircase. At the top, a door opened into a small living room with a family seated on a couch watching television. A man stood and introduced himself as Ahmad. Farrah translated as Ahmad described growing up in the house during the Intifada. His older brother, Saher, was an active fighter killed by Israeli spies in the neighbourhood. He showed us a large poster commemorating his memory. It featured a young man dressed in black fatigues, leaning on his knee with a gun in hand and a stoic expression. The image was overlaid with pink Arabic script and other graphic flourishes. Ahmad brought over a young girl and explained that this was one of his nieces, who he was raising as his own. "The house is too crowded, but that's normal".

After we left, Farrah explained that though residents did not have land titles, they did own the investments they had made in the construction and expansion of their houses. This had resulted in an unofficial real estate market, both in Balata and other camps. Families that had been designated plots of land were able to subdivide, rent, or sell the rooms they built on top. Families like Ahmad's could live on the second floor, while renting out the ground floor to another family. "This has encouraged further densification. And you know, it's gotten extreme", Farrah said. "In some neighbourhoods, the homes are so packed that the only way to move furniture and coffins from a house is over the rooftops. This type of density changes our psychology. The organization of our homes starts to organize our heads".

Nidal al-Azza
<u>(professor and community leader Aida)</u>

The light was fading, so we retraced our steps and hailed a taxi to Aida Camp. With only 6,000 residents, Aida was relatively small. But it occupied an outsized role in conversations about territorial control within the OPT.

Israel / Palestine. © Daniel Schwartz

Nablus. © Daniel Schwartz

Nablus. © Daniel Schwartz

STATE CONTROL Bethlehem. © Daniel Schwartz

Located on the northern out-skirts of Bethlehem, two-thirds of its perimeter was enclosed by the Israeli separation wall. A 20-meter high arch supporting a giant sculpture of a key flanked the official entrance to the camp, which had been left inaccessible by car. More than double the height of the nearby wall, it was a powerful symbol referencing the keys that many Palestinians kept to the homes they left behind. As we passed through on foot, several men sat and smoked beneath the key.

Walking through the camp, we searched for the house of our contact, Professor Nidal al-Azza, a legal scholar at Birzeit University, co-founder of the non-profit human rights organization BADIL, and a community leader in Aida. When we knocked on the wooden door of his family's three-story home, he greeted us warmly and invited us inside for tea. A tall and slender man of about 50, al-Azza carried himself with dignity but could not hide his exhaustion. He apologized for speaking slowly, explaining that he had just come back from a lecture in Europe and many work obligations awaited. Yet despite this, al-Azza insisted that we share some tea and stay to discuss the camp's current situation. "For the people here in Aida, the wall has brought constant surveillance by the Israeli army, which follows our whereabouts 24/7. This state of permanent observation severely affects the mental state of the camp inhabitants, bringing about a range of psychological conditions. During the night, for instance, giant spotlights brightly light the camp, penetrating peoples' homes and disturbing them from having a proper sleep. Raids by soldiers are less common now, although they still happen".

"To be a refugee is to be seen as lower. Not just by the Israelis, but also by Palestinians. We still feel that we are a lower class of citizen. When the PA organizes municipal elections in Bethlehem, all three refugee camps in the area are excluded. We are forbidden from participation. So this oppression creates unity amongst us, and actually amongst refugees in general. Refugees have typically been the ones who raised and maintained the fight for national unity. Sometimes we unite against outsiders, but that does not mean we are inherently aggressive". We asked al-Azza about a broader rights-based vision for the Palestinian territory. "I reject a two-state solution", he said quickly. "History has taught that before the creation of the Jewish state, people in Palestine coexisted in peace, no matter their religion and cultural-ethnic background. A democratic secular state, with equal rights for everyone, is the only workable solution for ending the conflict. Seventy percent of the Palestinian people are refugees, and 80 per-cent of them have been refugees since 1948. A state based on 1967 territory does not have any value to them; it would only be a temporary solution until they start wanting to return to their homes".

"At the same time, the repatriation of refugees shouldn't result in the displacement of Jewish people". Al-Azza took a breath and sipped his tea. "Only rights-based solutions for everyone, including Zionist settlers, will facilitate coexistence and prevent new conflicts. It will take time to adapt to a new state and legal system, to accept the new national situation. And I mean this. I come from a family that used to be rich—the largest landowners in our village. I don't want to reclaim the land my grandfather once owned. I'm willing to share. There is a kibbutz in the village now, and they should be allowed to stay. To move forward, we need to create a new culture of human rights and equality".

Mohamed,
(street vendor at Gilo Checkpoint)

We got up at early dawn to be on time to see one of the 15 gateways that allowed Palestinians to cross the separation wall. Gilo Checkpoint, also known as Checkpoint 300, was located between Bethlehem and the Gilo settlement on the outskirts of Jerusalem, and served as a vital access point for 7,000 Palestinians who commuted to work in East Jerusalem and Israel. This was only a fraction of the 58,000 Palestinians holding Israeli work permits, or the 30,000 employed in Jewish settlements in the West Bank. But the checkpoint was one of the busiest and most popular conduits for those visiting the al-Aqsa mosque and other holy sites in Jerusalem.

The checkpoint's presence, like the entire wall, was illegal in the eyes of the international community. Israeli authorities were quick to cite statistics suggesting the wall's effectiveness at lowering the rate of suicide bombings and other terror attacks. But the PA, international observers, and even the Israeli Supreme Court—in numerous rulings—saw ulterior motives. According to many, it was not the wall, but instead better Israeli intelligence gathering and political stability between Palestinian factions, which could explain the decrease in terror attacks in Israel . The wall itself had become a tool for territorial control. According to UNRWA's Barrier Monitoring Unit, almost 90 percent of the planned 708-kilometer route would run inside the West Bank, 'effectively appropriating 9.4 percent of its territory and cutting Palestinian communities off from their lands'.

As our taxi pulled up to the Gilo Checkpoint, the concrete barrier looked particularly intimidating. Bright lights lining the top cut through the morning darkness, revealing an area busy with activity. Men milled around the entrance to a series of gates, where a dozen vendors had set up tables or wheeled small carts laden with cigarettes, crackers, and hot drinks. We bought mint tea from a man named Mohamed, who explained that the checkpoint had become more institutionalized in 2004, outfitted with high-tech security systems. The actual checkpoint was not visible from the outside. You first had to enter the gated waiting line and then pass through a series of turnstiles and control points. Palestinians wishing to cross had to obtain special travel permits, but this was not easy.

We approached the wall, which was adorned with political graffiti, and walked next to the roofed gate that ran parallel to the barrier for 50 meters before terminating at a locked entrance. Commuters—almost all men—shuffled down the corridor and began to form a line three-to-four bodies wide. We walked alongside them on the exterior, starting to feel uneasy. As we reached the end of the line, men of all ages were sitting smoking in silence. Some looked at us indifferently, or not at all, but others made eye contact.We became very self-conscious of our position on the outside of what looked like a physical and symbolic cage.

We were about to walk back when a man called us over. He appeared around 30 years old and spoke in slow and accented English. After asking about our research project, he seemed eager to talk, as long as we did not use his name. "I've been waiting here since three in the morning", he said, leaning against the bars. "I work at a garage in Jerusalem, and have to be there at six, so I can't take any risks arriving here late. My boss would fire me if I'm not on time". He explained that the checkpoint consisted of four inspection areas: personal identification checks, metal detectors, a baggage check, and an area with sniffer dogs.

"The whole thing can take several hours. Sometimes the soldiers are in a bad mood and close the checkpoint for no reason. So better safe than sorry".

Listening to the conversation, a greying man behind him leant over and said something in Arabic. The young man translated, saying that his neighbour in line did not bother to go home most days of the week. He came back across the wall so late, and had to return so early, that he slept in fallow land nearby. He was not the only one, we surmised, observing the blankets and garbage scattered behind us in the tall yellow grass. Turning back toward the end of the line, we saw that it had begun to overflow, and the hum of voices grew louder. While still mostly men, several women with children also pressed against each other, trying to secure a comfortable place to stand.

We had heard from others that Palestinians often try to seek better-quality healthcare in Jerusalem, sending children across the border when special surgery was required. At that moment, the call to prayer began to reverberate from a mosque nearby, and most people in line stopped jockeying for position and turned to the east. Those already trapped behind the bars found it difficult to kneel, but the ones who could crouch down began to pray with their heads against the cool dirt. We remained until the first turnstile was unlocked and people started to filter through, taking small, halting steps and repeatedly clipping the heels of the person in front as they approached the wall's opening.

Al-Atrash al-Walajeh (village elder) and Omar (guide in al Walajeh)

Al-Walajeh had a long history of Israeli harassment, which began with the seizure of three-quarters of its land in 1948, and then formal occupation post-1967. Much of its territory had eventually been designated as part of Area B or C, allowing Israel to exert a high degree of control. While not all residents had been forcefully displaced, the villagers had received refugee status due to the amount of agricultural land annexed. Since 1980, the nearby settlements of Har Gilo and Gilo—the latter so established that many of its 40,000 inhabitants did not realize it illegally occupied West Bank land—had expanded steadily toward al-Walajeh. The village had been reduced to approximately 13 percent of its original size. Villagers who found themselves pressured to move on account of military surveillance, home demolitions, unemployment, and settler violence, would follow in the footsteps of many before who ended up in camps like Dheisheh. By now it had turned into a particularly hot day, and we asked our driver to drop us off in the shade of a tree abutting the property of Adnan al-Atrash, a village elder who had agreed to a meeting. Al-Atrash and his English-speaking nephew, Omar, welcomed us inside their single-story home, seating us on a plastic-covered couch in the living room. The sheet-rock walls were bright yellow, and a large poster of Yasser Arafat smiled down from behind the chair al-Atrash relaxed into. "I'm from here, but I actually grew up in a refugee camp in Bethlehem. We don't have papers that allow us to build, but we do have papers that prove we own the land. We heard what was happening to al-Walajeh, so we came back and started to build in 1980, until in 1987 when Israeli forces demolished our two-story house. I came back again in June 1990, and I began to rebuild the house where the old one was. But the Israelis have continued to demolish houses here", he said, speaking slowly and occasionally rubbing the crest of his tanned, bald head.

The 1,700 inhabitants of al-Walajeh were doing everything they could to remain, resulting in diverse tactics encompassing marches, demonstrations, and petitioning. But beginning in 2007, the construction of the wall had added a new dimension to their struggle. "We were surprised when the wall was built. It extended to almost two-thirds of the remaining land of al-Walajeh—about six square kilometres—and surrounded all the houses so no farms or agricultural land were accessible. It restricted the movement of people even more. We couldn't breathe or expand naturally", al-Atrash said. "They want to make only one entry and exit point. The Israelis will have full liberty to close it whenever they want, and then we will really be trapped". An informal coalition of villagers, international civic groups, and Israeli activists had been successful with a legal challenge to postpone the construction of the wall around al-Wa-lajeh. But work had recently begun again, and al-Atrash suggested that Omar accompany us to go and see the building activity in person. We set off down the gravel road that sloped away from the houses of al-Walajeh, cutting alongside the hilly terrain. Pine trees provided some semblance of shade, but by the time we had moved little more than 100 meters we were all already dripping with sweat.

Omar explained to us that many people referred to al-Wa-lajeh as an "imprisoned village". We had seen the wall from afar as we arrived, but we did not fully understand what he meant until we rounded the next bend. There, we witnessed a deep gash being cut into the hillside, before being slowly stitched together by towering concrete plinths. Construction workers were pouring concrete around some recently placed panels, and several bulldozers were scattered across the site. The path of the wall curved down the slope, responding gracefully to the topographical complexity. On either side of the barrier, the ground had been cleared of vegetation, creating a 30-meter orange scar.

Omar pointed to the workers. "Look at them closely. They're Palestinian. Not from this village, from other villages nearby. We don't blame them personally, because we know how much they need the money, but we're being locked up by our brothers". Besides the 8-meter tall concrete panels, each one apparently 30 to 40 centimetres thick, the wall would be flanked by a patrol road. While exact figures for the cost had not been disclosed, the wall had consumed an estimated four percent of the Israeli government's annual budget since 2005, making it the nation's largest real estate project in terms of total investment . Yet the Department of Defense, which was tasked with managing the wall, and the Department of Regional and Strategic Planning, which oversaw its design and construction, continued to refer to the project as a 'barrier' or 'fence' in order to counter claims of building illegal 'structures' on occupied land. As we saw one of the newest sections materialize before our eyes though, its architecture seemed anything but temporary.

Noam Chayut (Breaking the Silence leader)

We drove to Jerusalem in the morning, aboard a special Palestinian minibus licensed to use Israeli roads. We had arranged a tour with Breaking the Silence, an Israeli NGO that collect testimonies from former soldiers who had served in the West Bank, East Jerusalem, and the Gaza Strip. The organization's mission was to give voice to Israelis who 'discover the gap between the reality which they encountered in the [occupied] territories, and the silence which they encounter at home'. We had heard that their tour of Hebron provided a particularly insightful view into

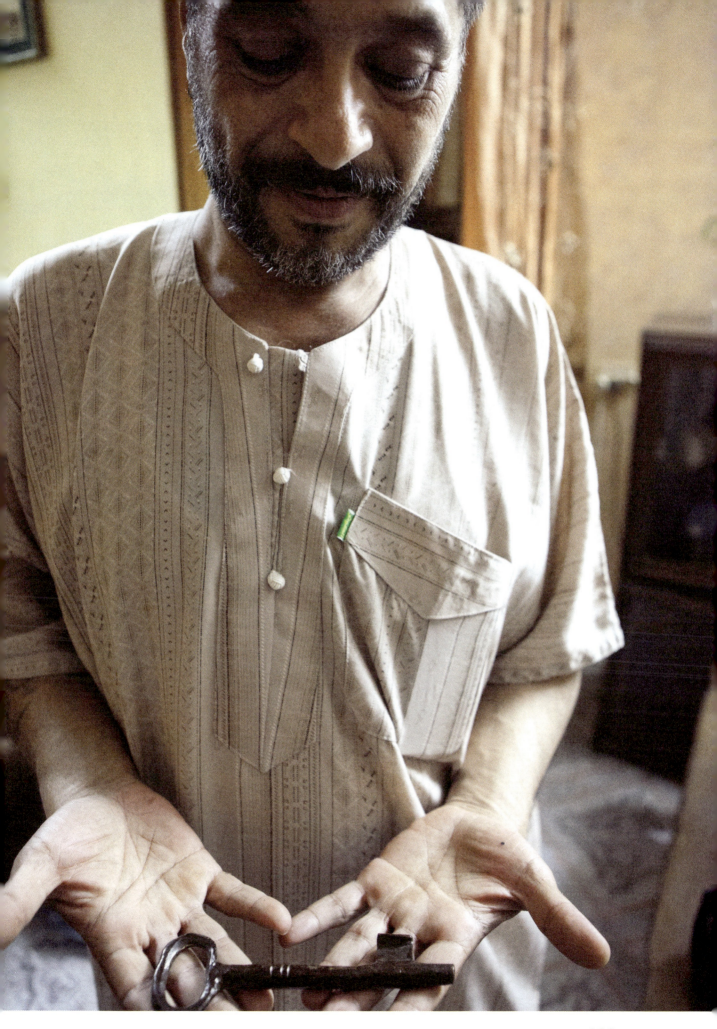

Nablus. © Daniel Schwartz

Nablus/Bethlehem. © Daniel Schwartz

Bethlehem. © Daniel Schwartz

Hebron. © Daniel Schwartz

Hebron. © Daniel Schwartz

STATE CONTROL Bethlehem. © Daniel Schwartz

the ways in which spatial conflict and control had resulted in a destructive urban transformation.

We met Noam Chayut, one of the leaders of Breaking the Silence, outside a bagel shop in Jerusalem. A former Israeli soldier in his mid-thirties, Chayut had served in Hebron and helped form the organization after his deployment ended in 2004. Chayut had served in the IDF for five years in total, participating in numerous operations throughout the West Bank, though focused particularly on Hebron and its surrounding Arab areas. He looked like an ordinary Israeli his age, sporting a short beard, sunglasses, and a black polo shirt. If anything, Chayut struck us as more hiking guide than human rights activist. We took our seats in the minibus that Chayut had hired, and as we drove, he began to tell us about the history of Hebron, or al-Khalil as it was known in Arabic. Hebron's fertile surroundings and natural resources had attracted diverse groups for thousands of years, evident in the concentration of elegant buildings dating back to Ayyubid, Mamluk, and Ottoman times. The city was also renowned as the burial place of the biblical Patriarchs and Matriarchs, with the Tomb of the Patriarchs considered the second holiest site in Judaism after Jerusalem's Western Wall. Christians also ascribed the site sacred importance due to scriptural references, while Muslims traditionally viewed Hebron as one of the four holy cities of Islam.

During the Ottoman era, Jews were not allowed to enter the holy tombs, as the Ibrahimi mosque had been built over and around the burial cave, forcing them to pray from outside. Although there had been shifting hostilities between religious communities for hundreds of years, the city's population had always been mixed, and was home to an economically and culturally vibrant Jewish community. This changed relatively quickly after the brutal 1929 Hebron massacre, in which Muslim rioters killed 67 Jews. Arab neighbours hid the remaining 435 Jews, before they were evacuated. Some families moved back several years later, but the British eventually evacuated the entire Jewish population during the Arab unrest in 1936. After 1967, Hebron fell under Israeli control, and it became a primary target for Jewish settlers looking to repopulate the Old City and claim it as a Zionist hub for scholarship, worship, and living. By the early-1970s, several groups of settlers had established illegal communities in the area. In 1979, Jewish extremists founded the first settlement of Beit Hadassah in the Old City, and soon the settlements Avraham Avinu, Beit Romano, and Tel Rumeida were also established, together housing more than 100 families. Notwithstanding that these settlers were contravening both Israeli and international law, Chayut said, the movement had continued to expand the Jewish presence in the centre of Hebron. Chayut emphasized that for the tour it was crucial to understand the recent spatial politics. In 1997, the Hebron Protocol was a central part of the Oslo Accords. The agreement divided the city into two sectors, H1 and H2. The first, home to about 140,000 Palestinians, was placed under PA rule, while the second, which included the holy sites of the Tomb of the Patriarchs and Ibrahimi mosque, and was home to about 35,000 Palestinians and 500 Israeli settlers, would remain under Israeli control. Ever since, ongoing terrorist attacks and outbreaks of unrest in the Old City had led the Israelis to restrict Palestinian access to much of H2. This segregation was enforced by a large military presence—one that Chayut had been part of for several years.

As we neared the city centre, Chayut described how the city had come to be divided. "The violence of the Second Intifada, and the lethal clashes between Israeli settlers and the Palestinian population, caused the Israeli authorities to impose a security regime based on the 'separation principle'—a legal and physical separation between the populations living in the Old City. As a consequence, in H2 Palestinian shops in H2 were closed, houses abandoned, and the Palestinian community was cut into two parts disconnected from each other. Israel frequently imposed a curfew on the Palestinian population, requiring Palestinians to stay in their homes day and night for weeks or months. They were only allowed to leave for a few hours each day, or every several days, to replenish provisions". It sounded like a confusing and bizarre arrangement, but Chayut reassured us that we would understand better after we saw it for ourselves.

Once we parked the car and began walking into the Old City, Chayut pointed out how a network of checkpoints, walls, and defensive installations allowed the military to enforce the barrier and monitor the movement of Palestinians in H2. He calmed us, however, that as we were obviously not Palestinian and arriving in a bus designated for tourism, we should have no problems entering or moving around. There were almost no pedestrians or shops open, and the old souk buildings were largely dark and shuttered. Several soldiers stood in the shade nearby, and a Humvee parked across the street appeared to be filled with more.

Chayut led us several blocks away to an open space, surrounded by crumbling buildings dating from the Ottoman era. "This clearing in the city was part of Hebron's market space", he said. "It was divided across different locations corresponding to products, but all together served as the biggest market for the southern population in the West Bank. The spice and vegetable market, where we're standing, has been closed by the Israeli military since 2000, as it is very close to the settlement of Avraham Avinu, and was viewed as too dangerous for the Jewish population".

Chayut explained how since the 1980s, when the illegal settlement was built with the tacit support of Israeli authorities, Arab residents had striven to resist the incursion through non-violent means. The settlement happened to be built in the old Jewish quarter dating from the 15th century, whose original Jewish habitants escaped the violence of the 1929 riots. The settlers had been outspoken in their right to the property, which had come to house offices, apartments, a synagogue, a nursery school, and a health clinic. Although the Supreme Court had ordered the residents of Avraham Avinu to surrender the land and buildings they had seized in the area, the ruling had not been enforced.

Chayut showed us pictures of the area before the closures, when the marketplace bustled with activity. It was hard to reconcile the image with what we saw in front of us. Decay, silence, and dust had replaced what was evidently a lively and chaotic neighbourhood. The absence of an effective rule of law was disheartning. Palestinian police could not enter the area, and Israeli soldiers were only present to protect Israelis and tourists. Organized crime was common, causing many Palestinians to leave for H1 where they felt safer from soldiers, settlers, and fellow Arabs.

We walked toward what was once a gateway to the Kasbah. Large iron doors blocked any access, except by the IDF in case of security threats. Previously, Palestinians who snuck into H2 were arrested. Chayut recalled being stationed in the centre of Hebron, terrified that a sudden Palestinian intrusion might occur. He was now more attuned to the fear of settlers entering H1. Once inside, settlers would harass Palestinian residents and damage property, sometimes resulting in bloodshed. "The recent history of terrorist attacks is long. Dozens of civilians have been killed... each side has their excuse for deadly revenge", Chayud explained. As recently as March 2016, two Palestinians had stabbed an Israeli soldier stationed near the market. They were both shot and killed by nearby soldiers, one after being disarmed.

But the small-scale violence of the settlers, consistently and quietly perpetrated, had in some sense influenced the transformation of the city in more profound ways. According to the Israeli watchdog organization Bet'selem, settler harassment was often committed for both ideological and strategic ends. Bullying helped to expand the Old City settlements, making the lives of Palestinians intolerable to the extent that they would vacate more properties. Describing the spatial tactics of local settlers, Chayut emphasized that "they understand the dynamic of the area, and they create the dynamic of the area. It is a matter of gaining centimetres and meters, with the idea that even if they can't succeed in one place, they will be able to get somewhere else by using this particular place as a diversion".

The IDF presence was predicated upon the need to protect Israeli citizens in the settlements. Attempts at evicting settlers had resulted in violent clashes between soldiers and settlers, and thus an odd stalemate had been reached, which contradicted court orders and international law. The IDF sought to avoid confrontations, and in return, the settlers treated soldiers with kindness, preparing Shabbat dinner and offering refreshments on hot days. But the military presence not only helped to protect the nascent Jewish population, it also contributed to the transformation of the built environment in the name of precautionary defence. The large majority of Palestinians that owned buildings in the Old City as of 1997 were prohibited to enter the restricted area and take care of their property. Many of these structures, considered historically monumental, were deteriorating rapidly. "Without renovation, they will likely perish", said Chayut. "The physical disappearance of a Palestinian presence—both people and buildings—could be used as an argument by settlers to contest the Palestinian claim to the territory. This city's memories, going back thousands of years, are being threatened by the argument of providing security to illegal settlers". In every shape and form, we were walking through a territory undergoing urbicide. We were nearing the end of the tour. Suddenly two Jewish boys rode by on bicycles. It was the first time we had seen any of the settlers up close, and their apparition in the form of children on oversized mountain bikes caught us by surprise. The boys circled back behind us and then rode in loops nearby, eyeing us suspiciously. Chayut stopped and pointed to some blue graffiti scrawled on a stone façade behind the boys. "That says something like, 'For evacuating the property, we will kill Arabs'. It refers to this practice of 'price tagging', which settlers do when the Israeli military kicks them out of occupied territory. Sometimes, instead of taking their anger out on fellow Israelis, they'll go and destroy or hurt Palestinians. It's their way of incentivizing the government not to get in their way". The implications of the graffiti were sickening, and we had to turn away. Chayut was contrite about his time in the service but spoke about it matter-of-factly. Years of reflection had resulted in activity rather than paralysis, including a need to testify to what he had seen and knew. "I understand the psychology of the soldiers, because I was one. We at Breaking the Silence agreed with the argument of security in its initial stage here. It was called for by an Israeli official. But if you look at the city ten years later, it is a twisted concept of security", he said, pausing. "There are a lot of problems whenever officials control a society without the ability to complain, because the army here commits the law, writes the law, and judges according to the law. The army is everything".

Khaled Husseini (Mayor of Hebron) and Alaa Shahin (architect)

After crossing over into the Palestinian-controlled side of Hebron, we had spent the night with Leila, a friendly middle-aged woman who ran a textile shop in the H1-designated portion of the Old City. She also rented out rooms in her family's large house, located in the heart of the Kasbah. The traditional house had been slowly constructed over many generations, with various rooms organized around a central patio, and stacked up to three stories high. Stone staircases wrapped around the patio, leading to each room. It was a tranquil space, only offset by Leila's stories of how difficult it had been to feed her family given the depressed economy. Our morning in Hebron would be spent trying to understand how the local city government was striving to deal with the past decade of challenges. Hebron was the most concentrated example of how territorial conflict in the West Bank created an endless array of urban planning problems, and we wanted to understand how Palestinians were attempting to address these from a top-down perspective. Through some fortunate coordination, the Mayor of Hebron, Khaled Husseini, had agreed to meet us. We walked through a bustling part of the Old City, confused by the strange contrast to what stood no more than 200 meters behind the separation wall. Exiting the Kasbah, we arrived at the large modern building housing the City Hall.

Flanked by his public relations assistant, Husseini greeted us with a warm smile in his air-conditioned office. His assistant stacked a small tower of municipal publications in front of us, asking us to later look at many of the city's accomplishments and goals. Husseini described his background as a businessman before being elected to public office, and he wanted to project a private-market mentality in order to find efficient and economical ways to govern Hebron. The conversation quickly turned, however, to the political reasons that explained why his goals were being impeded.

"Commerce in the souk has been severely affected, forcing many salesmen to leave. Over 500 shops in the Old City were closed by Israeli military orders, while another 1,140 went out of business as a result", he said, quoting figures from the Ministry of National Economy. "This represents threequarters of all the business establishments in the Old City. Additionally, just over 1,000 housing units have been vacated by their occupants—almost half the total housing stock". Husseini explained that movement restrictions between H1 and H2 had prevented many development and preservation plans, despite confirmed funding from the PA and European countries. And because much of Hebron was surrounded by Area C territory, the municipality had to seek Israeli approval to build on prime land.

"The Turkish government committed to investing $500 million for the development of an industrial zone near Hebron, in the town of Tarqumiyah. This was supposed to create 10,000 jobs, but it failed because the IDF rejected our request for building permits. Hebron has 40 percent of the West Bank's economy. By preventing Hebron from developing, they're preventing all of the West

Hebron. © Daniel Schwartz

STATE CONTROL

Hebron. © Daniel Schwartz

Hebron. © Daniel Schwartz

Bank from growing". Speaking about housing problems, Husseini noted that 51 percent of Hebron's population was under 18 years old. "Unless we have sport and cultural infrastructure, they will go to sleep, or do other things you might be able to imagine", he said, subtly referencing growing extremist activity. "These young people should not be preoccupied by an occupation of their city".

We shifted the conversation to more pragmatic issues the municipality was facing, and Husseini called in one of the city's chief architects and planners, Alaa Shahin. Around 30-years-old, with a quiet smile, he seemed reserved at first, but when asked about the water system, began to animatedly describe the situation. "One of the most crucial problems we have—actually a crisis, not a problem—is to deliver sufficient water to the people, especially in the summertime. So, we invested in one of the most sophisticated water network systems available. We can electronically monitor distribution and control the network remotely to maximize efficiency. Nonetheless, without water going into the network, we can't get our people enough".

Shahin referenced a World Bank study that suggested the average daily water supply per capita in the region should be around 150 litres. "Currently, our average is 50. The Israeli settlers have built their own system with the military and a private company, and they get at least ten times, if not more, than our people". According to Shahin, sufficient water aquifers were available to provide an adequate supply to Palestinians—one to the east of Hebron, and one to the west. But Israeli authorities had limited drilling in Area C, so those aquifers could not be exploited fully.

As our visit wound down, Shahin turned the conversation in a more introspective direction, recounting how he had just started studying architecture before Hebron was separated into two parts. "I feel that I lost my past", he said, putting down some of the papers he had in his hands. "I have not been allowed to go to my grandfather's house in H2 for 15 years. I lost the connection to them. The city is more than just buildings and streets. The city is also a social structure. If we do not renew connections in that structure, and make people understand their history, then the city dies".

Khalil Tufakji,
(Palestinian mapmaker East Jerusalem)

Jerusalem is a defining urban centre for any investigation into territorial conflict in Palestine and Israel, and in many ways it has become the core of the tangled knot around which so many political negotiations and geographic narratives have been spun. We began with a meeting with Khalil Tufakji, the PA's chief mapmaker, at his office in the Orient House, an official base of operations for Palestinian leadership in East Jerusalem. Tufakji had played a seminal, if not quiet, role in the political struggle between Israeli and Palestinian interests since the early 1990s.

Since 1983, Tufakji's office had led efforts to independently monitor settlement construction throughout the West Bank, producing some of the first maps that documented the occupation of land and mechanisms used by the Israeli government and Jewish settlers to seize control. He had also collected historical maps and conducted regular surveys, in order to contest claims of ownership and find loopholes in the complex legal arguments that Israeli authorities employed to justify land seizure. Tufakji's map-making was also motivated by a hope provide a solid geographic underpinning to the future institutions that would govern a Palestinian state, with East Jerusalem as its capital.

When we arrived, there were no draftsmen hunched over ink-stained desks, but rather a series of fluorescent-lit rooms and several computer workstations. Tufakji shook our hands firmly, before launching into an analysis of what drove both his, and Israel's, obsession with charting the land. "Israel is implementing many strategies to avoid a Palestinian majority, with the eventual goal of minimizing the population to a mere 12 percent of the country. One strategy is to change the demographics of established communities through the annexation of Palestinian areas. We see this most dramatically in East Jerusalem, where in 1972, Israel decided to minimize the number of Palestinians to about one-fifth of the total. But in reality the population has grown to 35 percent".

Tufakji highlighted that new research suggested that by 2040 this portion could increase to 55 percent. "So Israel is now pursuing measures to take control of Jerusalem". He unrolled a map and pointed to the periphery of the city, where the separation barrier snaked around certain neighbourhoods. "They excluded 125,000 Palestinians from the city with this wall. This made it impossible to maintain an Israeli identity. Under Israeli law, after seven years out of Israel, they will lose their IDs and Israeli residency". Tufakji explained that after 1967, Israel instituted a complex system of citizenship, residency permits, and ID cards to govern over a politically vague and demographically toxic population throughout their newly won territories.

"My identity as a Palestinian living in Jerusalem is not clear. I am an Israeli resident but not a citizen. In Palestine, I am not fully Palestinian because I do not have a passport. I am also not Jordanian. So I am left with few choices. I could accept Israeli citizenship to obtain a passport, but this would mean I abandon the Palestinian nation, which someday will receive statehood". Tufakji was not grappling with this problem alone. As of 2008, 93 percent of the 260,800 Palestinians in Jerusalem had decided not to become Israeli citizens. While eligible to vote in local elections, pay taxes, and receive social services from the Israeli state, numerous studies had found that their rights were often denied, rendering them at best second-class citizens. Returning to the map, Tufakji brushed his hand westward. "Israeli tactics, primarily with the wall and settlement construction, will make the future metropolitan map of Jerusalem completely different than that of today. The new Jerusalem will be comprised of three fingers of major settlement blocs, potentially growing to cover 10 percent of the West Bank. They are slowly claiming all open land in order to minimize the possibilities of Palestinian expansion". He sighed and rolled the map closed. "We have to map everything in order to know what we are facing. There are facts on the ground that we must understand on paper. I'm trying to publish a book about my recent findings, but the Israelis have closed my office three times".

Maya Guttmann
(Israeli Committee Against Home Demolitions, Jerusalem)

We soon had to leave for our next appointment at the central offices of the Israeli Committee Against Home Demolitions, also known as ICAHD—one of the groups that relied on Tufakji's map making. Founded in 1997 by a mix of secular and religious Israelis, the activist organization sought to influence policy and public opinion in Israel against the occupation of Palestine. We met Maya Guttmann at ICAHD's downtown Jerusalem headquarters. She invited us to get in her small sedan for a driving tour of several neighbourhoods. As we drove eastward, she pulled the car onto the shoulder of Highway 1 and pointed out across the expansive and scrubby territory that stretched beneath the road.

It was one of the three fingers that Tufakji had shown us. "The area right here, known as E1, lies between Jerusalem and the settlement of Ma'ale Adumim". Guttmann said it formed the last connection between Jerusalem and the West Bank, and there were plans to build a settlement. "In 2000, Ehud Barak expropriated the area and annexed it to Ma'ale Adumim, which means it is now legal to commence construction. Due to international pressure, they are yet to begin, but there is a police station, they have started to build access roads, and over there is a billboard advertising homes in the future settlement. There's a lot of talk about a two-state solution, but if E1 is settled by Israelis, perhaps that conversation becomes a lot less useful".

As we continued driving, Guttmann explained a central and complicating aspect to the settlements. "It's tempting to see the settlers all as ideologues happy to be participating in huge human rights abuse. It makes it easier to think about kicking them off the land, though that's getting to be a huge logistical impossibility the more they build. But settlements like Ma'ale Adumim—established in 1979 and home to 45,000 people—are considered by most Israelis to be another suburb of Jerusalem. I had a friend who grew up there, and she told me that she didn't know it was a settlement until she was 18 years-old". Exiting the highway, Guttmann continued; "I recently found out there are people living in settlements that don't want live there, but can't afford to leave. A friend's family lives in a settlement but feels very disconnected. Their child is being brainwashed in the local school, and they don't want to be part of what is happening. But if they sell their house, they could never afford to buy elsewhere in Israel. We have a housing shortage, and the government makes it very cheap for families to live in settlements, especially immigrants with no idea where the real border is. Everything is designed to make them feel safe and part of Israel. They can't see the wall and they have their own roads. It's mass manipulation through landscaping".

Guttmann explained that understanding the housing pressures of contemporary Israel was crucial to understanding the ongoing displacement of Palestinians. ICAHD sought to pierce the veneer of an acceptable occupation, espoused by Israeli courts and media outlets, which kept mainstream Israeli society on side. At the same time, the organization was addressing one of the direct manifestations of the occupation: home demolitions. We spent the next two hours driving through several neighbourhoods of East Jerusalem, looking at some of the Palestinian homes that were demolished by Israel in recent years, as well as homes that ICAHD had helped to rebuild. The organization has calculated that since 1967, Israel has demolished around 48,000 Arab homes across Jerusalem, the West Bank, and the Gaza Strip. While many of these demolitions were cited by Israeli authorities as either collateral damage due to military operations, or as punitive punishment for terrorist activity, a large portion of the home destructions were for 'administrative' reasons, stemming from interpretations of land and building rights. The majority of demolitions in East Jerusalem were administrative, ostensibly justified by complex legal arguments that knit together aspects of Ottoman, British Mandate, and modern Israeli laws. Guttmann stressed that the demolitions were motivated, quite transparently, by a desire to either annex or control more land.

Meeting Jawad Siyam,
(Director Wadi Hilweh Information
Center of East Jerusalem)

In the late afternoon, she dropped us off in the neighbourhood of Silwan, less than a ten-minute walk east from Jerusalem's Old City. We had scheduled a meeting with Jawad Siyam, the Director of the Wadi Hilweh Information Centre, and a rebellious leader among the many residents of East Jerusalem fighting against home seizures and demolitions. When we met Siyam in his family's small, single-story house, he welcomed us with a raspy voice and led us through the cluttered living room to the even more cluttered patio, crammed with political newspapers, pamphlets, and children's books. He offered us a coffee and opened a new packet of cigarettes, one that he would nearly finish by the end of the conversation.

"I was under house arrest for several months earlier this year. This was for an alleged assault, which I did not do, but I found it ironic that I was punished to stay in my house when the government and settlers want us to leave. If I, a Palestinian resident of East Jerusalem, leave my house for too long, whether that's living abroad, going on a trip, or sometimes just being outside of the house for a few hours, settlers will move in and argue in court that according to the Absentee Law, derived from a British Mandate law, they can claim my house as their own".

Speaking broadly about his neighbourhood, he explained, "there are 320 Jewish settlers living in Silwan. They are trying to create a new settlement called City of David, which is apparently on the ruins of King David's former city. There's still a lot of debate about whether the ruins beneath us are what they think they are, but let's say King David was indeed here 3,000 years ago. If that gives the Jews the right to be here, then it should entitle many other people to return to the land of their ancestors. Shall we once again consider Germany to be a part of Italy? And Spain a part of Morocco? I can prove pretty well that my family has lived on this land for the last 900 hundred years".

We asked how land seizures could be accepted in a city that was governed democratically. Siyam responded cynically, describing how "the settlers and their private company, Elad, which manages the archaeology, housing, and tourist development here, get a lot of support from the municipality and state. We protest, but they fight us through the police and the historic preservation authority. They are digging tunnels, damaging our houses and schools, in an effort to prove that they own both our land and history". Across the street from his house, Siyam showed us what appeared to be a major excavation project next to a cluster of dilapidated Palestinian homes. The timing of our arrival was perfect, as the gate to the site opened and a group of a dozen Orthodox Jewish children, led by a young woman and trailed by a man, exited and began walking down the street. An Israeli flag fluttered above the fence, and we walked over to peer into the gaping hole in the earth, filled with drilling equipment, shovels, and dusty rocks. "They take our land if we are using it in a way they say is illegal, or if it is empty", Siyam said bitterly. "We are forbidden from fixing things like pipes, and it is nearly impossible for us to get permits that allow us to construct new homes or build higher. But here, they fast track this speculative archaeological digging".

Bethlehem. © Daniel Schwartz

STATE CONTROL — Hebron (above), Israel (below) @ Daniel Schwartz — 242

Siyam watched the children walk up the hill, before speaking quietly, but forcefully. "When I leave my house, I don't know whether I will return. Dying doesn't scare me anymore, because I could get shot walking down the street. But my family pays the price. They would lose this house if I were not around to claim it. A few years ago, the special units used to come and search my house and the community centre daily. The police threatened to demolish my house if I didn't close the centre. They have written many articles about me in Israeli newspapers comparing me to the devil, but they should be thanking me for taking 460 children off the streets. Instead of throwing stones, these children are now making music and art".

The sun had started to set, so we said goodnight to Siyam, who returned to his house. Walking back to our hotel, we passed the newly opened visitors centre of the King David ruins he had told us about, designed by the Canadian-Israeli architect, Moshe Safdie. The excavated site, located several meters beneath street-level, was filled with an American tour group walking over metal grates perched above stone ruins. Tacky lights, placed in among the ruins themselves, came on and began to cast undulating shades of blue, red, purple, and yellow. It was as if archaeologists had inadvertently revealed a massive, dry jacuzzi under modern-day Jerusalem.

Epilogue
A Long Journey 2011-2018

We finished this research in spring 2018 with a ETHZ Studio trip in the place it had begun, albeit with a dizzying array of voices and experiences competing for space in our heads. The Tel Aviv we had seen seven years ago did not feel the same. Arriving at the central bus station, we transferred to a local bus and headed back to Jaffa. Walking in the southern-most neighbourhood of Ajami, which was still predominantly Arab Christian, we observed traces of the diverse communities of sailors, merchants, and farmers who had populated the area for thousands of years. But a half-century of urban transformation had begun to erase much of this past.

We headed back through the historical centre of Jaffa, appreciating the beautiful stonework of the Ottoman-era buildings. It reminded us of Nablus, although here in Jaffa the buildings were filled with boutique shops and luxury realtor signage, and they had not been riddled with the pockmarks of recent artillery fire. This reminded us of our walk-through Balata, whose original residents had fled these very streets in 1948. The built forms around us were largely the same, but as Alaa Shahin in Hebron would have said, Jaffa was a different city now, because it had a different social structure.

We discussed whether the residents of Balata could, or should, ever come back to this exact piece of land. Whether political questions, such as the right of return, could be divorced from an endlessly complex and confounding spatial problem. Literally thousands of years of settlement had led to competing claims of ownership that could be argued with competing legal systems, environmental evidence, and even cultural mythologies. In the last century, it was as if a deep reservoir had been tapped, springing forth a new type of victimhood that fostered ever more victims. And as an exhausted Khaldun had remarked, "we Palestinians try to forget sometimes about where we came from, but then from time to time, Israelis come and remind us who we are".

We had read a similar sentiment in Israeli newspapers, in reference to the latest Palestinian terror attacks, but we wondered if that created a false equivalency. The cliché binary of Palestinian versus Israeli suffering no longer existed in our minds as an abstract political moral dilemma, but was firmly situated in the scale and magnitude of a distinct territory and the disparate magnitude of suffering felt within it. By now we had traced a route back through the Old City of Jaffa to Charles Clore Park, where Els Verbakel had taken us on our first night in 2011. It was an intentionally cyclical ending point for our journey.

● 1 — Figures from UNRWA https://www.unrwa.org/where-we-work/jordan. ● 2 — Israeli Seizure of Land and Housing in Palestine (2005).● 3 — Additional territory conquered by Israel during the 6 Day War included the Sinai Desert (Egypt) and the Golan Heights (Syria).● 4 — BADIL, Survey of Palestinian Refugees and Internally Displaced Persons 2008-2009 (2009) 37. ● 5 — UNRWA, UNRWA in Figures (Fact Sheet), 30 June 2010. ● 6 — Ethan Bronner and Isabel Kershner, 'In 2 Big West Bank Settlements, a Sign of Hope for a Deal' in The New York Times, 26 July 2009. ● 7 — See Zvi Efrat, The Israeli Project: Building and Architecture 1948-1973 (2004). ● 8 — See Hemda Agid-Ben Yehuda and Yehudit Auerbach, 'Attitudes to an Existence Conflict: Allon and Peres on the Palestinian Issue, 1967-1988' (1991) 35 The Journal of Conflict Resolution 519. 9 See Foundation for Middle East Peace, Israeli Settlements: An Obstacle to a Two-State Peace 1947-2012 (2013). ● 9 — ibid. ● 10 — Mel Frykberg, 'Bringing Hope and History to Balata Camp Youth', The Electronic Intifada, 6 July 2011, accessed at: http://electronicintifada.net/content/bringing-hope-and-history-balata-camp-youth/10146. ● 11 — 15 Amos Hrel. 'Shin Bet: Palestinian Truce Main Cause for Reduced Terror' in Ha'aretz, 2 January 2006. ● 12 — See Vita Bekker, 'Israeli Security Fence Decried as Annexation' in The National, 29 December 2010. ● 13 — See Ofir Feuerstein, Ghost Town: Israel's Separation Policy and Forced Eviction of Palestinians from the Centre of Hebron (2007).

Hebron. © Daniel Schwartz

Undocumented: The architecture of migrant detention. A Graphic Story

An undocumented women seeks shelter while fleeing domestic violence, a mother attempts to enroll her non-status child in primary school, a failed refugee claimant goes to get food bank, and overstayed visitor walks into a medical clinic. For undocumented people in a city, simply carrying out one's daily life is a challenge to borders that everyday threaten detention and deportation.

We live in an era of unprecedented human migration. Mass migration (or mass displacement) is both a process and a condition, driven by global capitalism, neo-colonialism, war and imperialism, and environmental destruction. Borders, material and immaterial ones, are proliferating around and between us.

As the world has become borderless to "flows" of capital, the movement of migrant bodies is restricted as never before. And so, millions of migrants live precarious lives a precarious labourers, as refugees and as undocumented people.

Migrants' journeys are commonly portrayed as linear progressions from home to host nations, but in reality they are replete with interruptions and discontinuities, occupying spaces of hiding, waiting, diversion, escape, settlement, and return – spaces which are largely invisible to the public. Among those are spaces used for mass detentions and deportations.

In these pages you will find an incomplete view into the world of migrant detention in Canada, explored at scales descending from physical landscapes to the human body. This illustrated documentary is an ongoing project developed through reading, listening, organizing, writing, drawing, and imagining. The stories are borrowed from the lived experiences of anonymous individuals.

by
Tings Chak

BETWEEN 2006 and 2013, over 100,000 people were jailed in Canada, without charge or trial, and with no end in sight. This includes children, who are detained or separated indefinitely from their caregivers. Migrants are detained primarily because they are undocumented. Likewise, these sites of detention bare little trace—drawings and photos are classified; access is extremely limited.

STATE CONTROL

In 2013, 13,000 people were deported from Canada,

8,838 people were detained,

289 of them were children,

adding to the nearly 100,000 migrants who have been detained and deported since 2006.

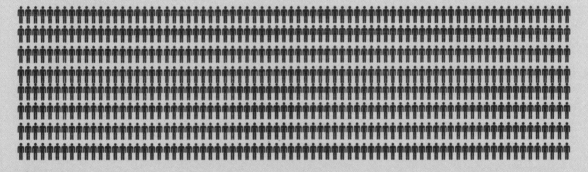

Immigration detention is the fastest growing incarceration sector in an already booming prison construction industry. Despite this, the sites, buildings, and people involved remain largely invisible, just as the apparatus that manages and controls the flow of human bodies is designed to be.

How do we make visible the sites and stories of detention, bring them into conversations about our built environment, and frame immigration detention as an architectural problem? Embedded in the politics of visibility, architecture has as much to do with the built reality as it does with representation.

Employing conventional architectural tools of representation, the following images document a physical reality in lieu of drawings and photographs, interrupted by the silenced voices of individuals who, while detained and denied presence in our built environment, continue to engage in daily forms of resistance.

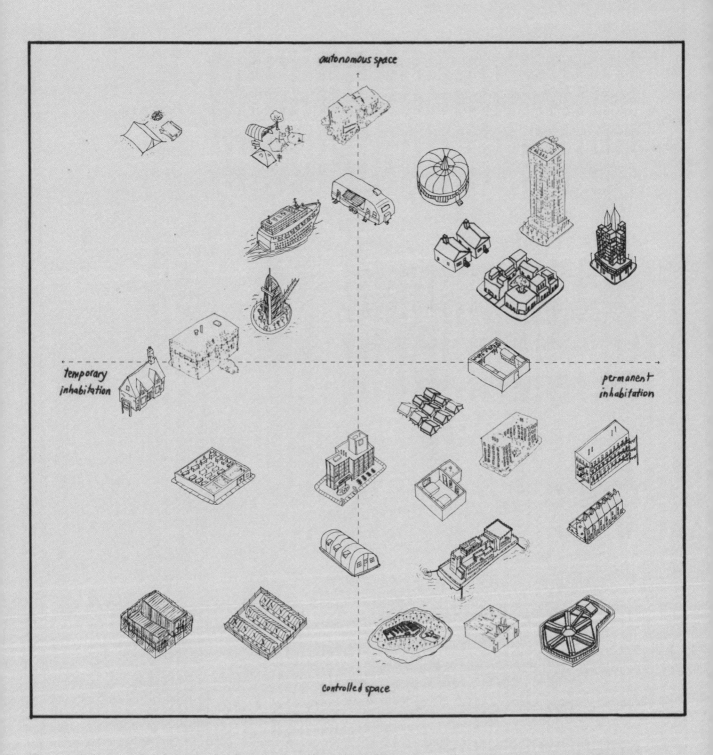

Spaces of incarceration just may be the mass (ware)housing solution of our time, where those who are deemed undesirable and dangerous are caged. In a securitized world, the gated community mirrors the detention centre, the micro-condominium isn't so different from the cell, they are sites of exclusion and seclusion. Sometimes it's difficult to tell who is being protected from whom.

STATE CONTROL

So how do we remove the elements of distinction,
challenge the integrity of the wall,
how do we make the borders disappear?

Mass incarceration is a modern idea.
We can unlearn and re-imagine,
and design a world without prisons.

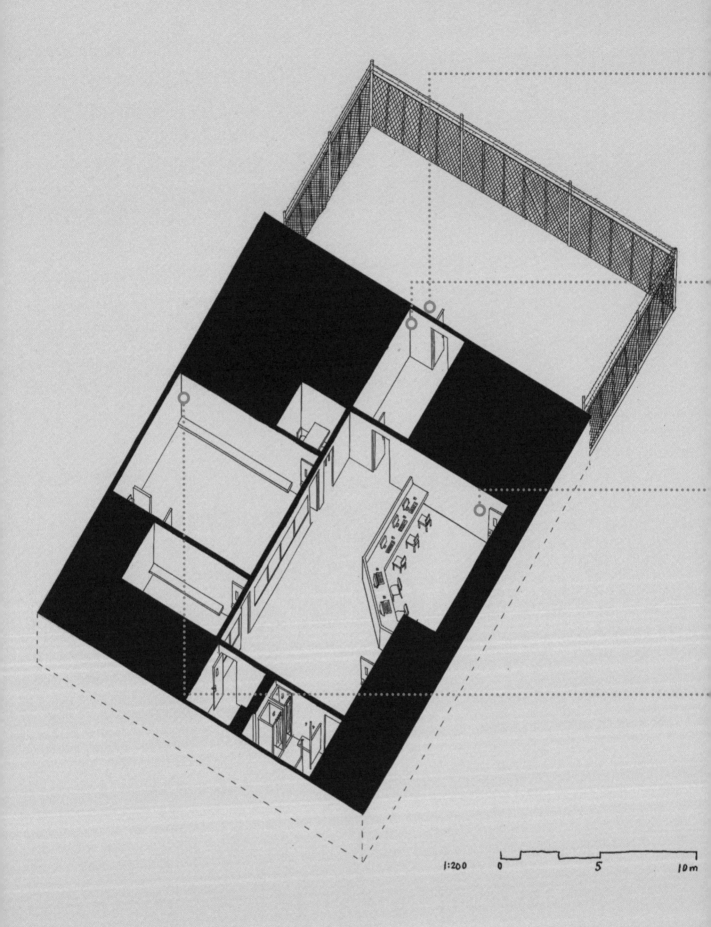

STATE CONTROL

250

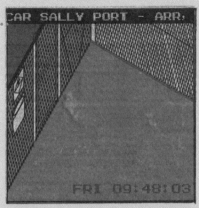
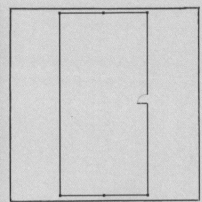

MINIMUM SIZE: 7.3 X 8.5 M = 62.1 M²
WALLS: GALVANIZED STEEL SECURITY
BARBED WIRE STRAND
FLOORS: ASPHALT CONCRETE
CEILING: DETENTION CEILING
DOORS: HOLLOW METAL W/VISION PAN
GLAZING: N/A
PLUMBING: N/A
HVAC: N/A
LIGHTING: SURFACE MOUNTED FLUORE
SECURITY: ELECTRONIC ACCESS FOR (
SURVEILLANCE
COMMUNICATIONS: INTERCOM AT SECU
NOTE: ENCLOSED, NEXT TO INTAKE - (

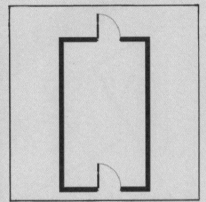

MINIMUM SIZE: 3.7 X 6.1 M = 22.6 (
WALLS: REINFORCED CONCRETE BLO(
FLOORS: SEALED CONCRETE
CEILING: EXTERIOR GRADE GYPSUM
DOORS: HOLLOW METAL
GLAZING: N/A
PLUMBING: FLOOR DRAIN
HVAC: TYPICAL W/EXHAUST
LIGHTING: SURFACE MOUNTED FLUOR
SECURITY: ELECTRONIC ACCESS CONT
SURVEILLANCE
COMMUNICATIONS: INTERCOM AT PASS

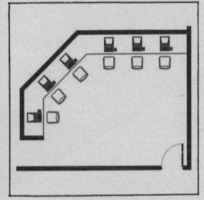

MINIMUM SIZE: 7.3 X 6.0 M = 45.6 M
WALLS: REINFORCED MASONRY
FLOORS: SEALED CONCRETE
CEILING: GYPSUM BOARD
DOORS: N/A
GLAZING: N/A
PLUMBING: N/A
HVAC: TYPICAL W/EXHAUST
LIGHTING: RECESSED FLUORESCENT
SECURITY: VIDEO SURVEILLANCE
COMMUNICATIONS: VOICE/DATA FOR PR

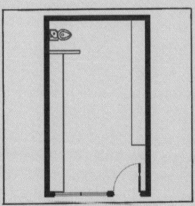

MINIMUM SIZE: 7.3 X 8.5 M = 62.1 M
WALLS: REINFORCED CONCRETE BLO(
FLOORS: SEALED CONCRETE
CEILING: DETENTION CEILING
DOORS: HOLLOW METAL
GLAZING: BULLET RESISTANT
PLUMBING: DETENTION TOILET/SINK (
HVAC: TYPICAL W/EXHAUST
LIGHTING: RECESSED FLUORESCENT
SECURITY: ELECTRONIC ACCESS FOR (
SURVEILLANCE
COMMUNICATIONS: N/A
NOTE: TEMPORARY CONFINEMENT UP

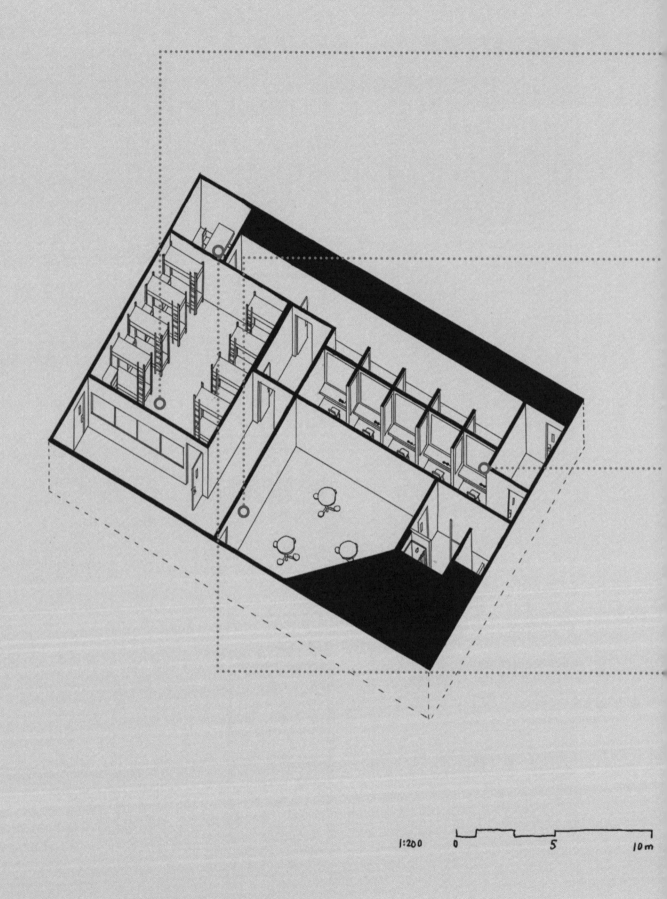

STATE CONTROL 252

DORMITORY — SAT 08:01:10

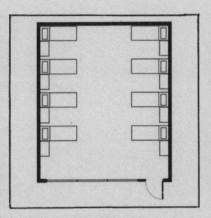

DIMENSION: 7.3 X 8.5 M = 62.1 M²
WALLS: REINFORCED CONCRETE BLO(
FLOORS: SEALED CONCRETE
CEILING: DETENTION CEILING
DOORS: HOLLOW METAL W/VISION PA
GLAZING: 7/16" GLASS CLAD POLYCA
PLUMBING: FLOOR DRAIN
HVAC: TYPICAL W/EXHAUST
LIGHTING: RECESSED FLUORESCENT
SECURITY: ELECTRONIC ACCESS CONT
SURVEILLANCE: ABILITY FOR LOCK I
COMMUNICATIONS: N/A
NOTE: CAPACITY OF 16 IN DOUBLE B
PER DETAINEE

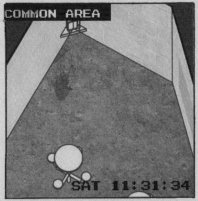
COMMON AREA — SAT 11:31:34

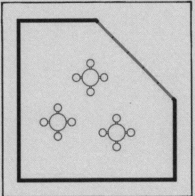

DIMENSION: 8.5 X 8.5 M = 72.3 M²
WALLS: REINFORCED CONCRETE BLO(
FLOORS: SEALED CONCRETE
CEILING: GYPSUM BOARD
DOORS: HOLLOW METAL W/VISION PA
GLAZING: 7/16" GLASS CLAD POLYCA
PLUMBING: FLOOR DRAIN
HVAC: TYPICAL W/EXHAUST
LIGHTING: RECESSED FLUORESCENT
SECURITY: ELECTRONIC ACCESS CONT
SURVEILLANCE
COMMUNICATIONS: N/A
NOTE: COMMON AREA W/COLOUR TEL
OPTIONAL: PRAYER AND LIBRARY ARE

VISITATION — SAT 14:15:48

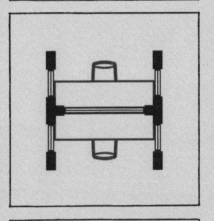

MINIMUM SIZE: 1.9 X 1.9 M = 3.6 M²
WALLS: REINFORCED CONCRETE BLO
FLOORS: SEALED CONCRETE
CEILING: GYPSUM BOARD
DOORS: N/A
GLAZING: 7/16" GLASS CLAD POLYCA
PLUMBING: N/A
HVAC: TYPICAL W/EXHAUST
LIGHTING: RECESSED FLUORESCENT
SECURITY: VIDEO SURVEILLANCE
COMMUNICATIONS: 32" ARMOURED COF
NOTE: 30 MIN. NON-CONTACT VISITA
ACCOMMODATE 10 PERCENT OF DETA

COUNSEL VISITATION — SAT 14:16:17

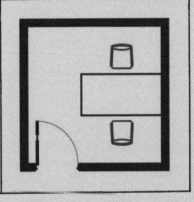

MINIMUM SIZE: 3.0 X 3.0 M = 9.0 M
WALLS: REINFORCED CONCRETE BLOC
FLOORS: SEALED CONCRETE
CEILING: GYPSUM BOARD
DOORS: HOLLOW METAL W/VISION PA
GLAZING: N/A
PLUMBING: N/A
HVAC: TYPICAL W/EXHAUST
LIGHTING: RECESSED FLUORESCENT
SECURITY: VIDEO SURVEILLANCE
COMMUNICATIONS: N/A
NOTE: ATTORNEY VISITING ROOM

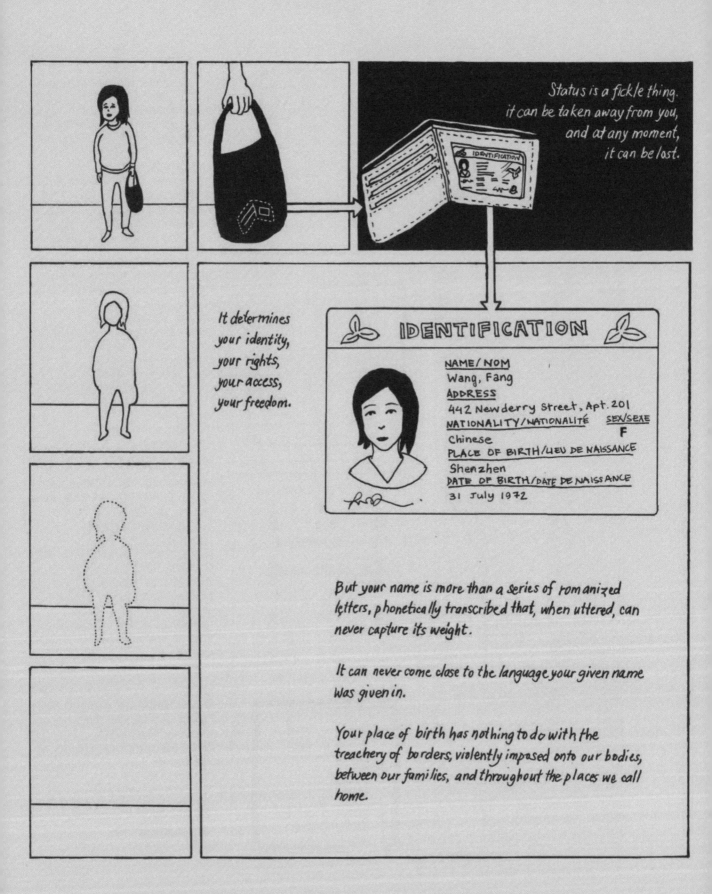

There is an immigration detainee on hunger strike for over sixty days in protest of indefinite detention. Held for 28 months in a maximum security prison without charge or trial, he said, "I missed three of my son's birthdays, I missed three anniversaries with my wife... I cannot see myself here being detained indefinitely and thinking about them. That will drive me crazy. So I have to keep it out of sight and out of mind. How inhumane is that?"

"I am a father and I am a husband."

"Should I even be allowed to feel like this?"

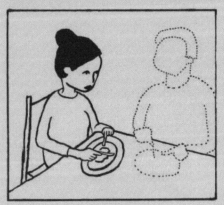

STATE CONTROL

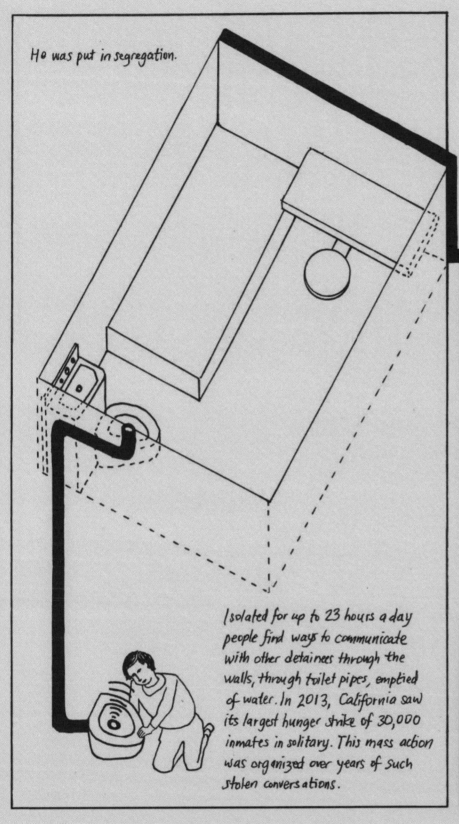

He was put in segregation.

Isolated for up to 23 hours a day people find ways to communicate with other detainees through the walls, through toilet pipes, emptied of water. In 2013, California saw its largest hunger strike of 30,000 inmates in solitary. This mass action was organized over years of such stolen conversations.

According to Corrections Canada, solitary confinement is euphemistically called "administrative segregation," used to ensure the "safety of all inmates, staff, and visitors," rather than for punitive reasons. In the control of bodies, architecture manages risk, so that the system never has to confront the aggregated power of inmates.

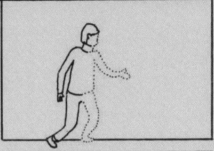

Prisoners held in prolonged segregation speak about the feeling of merging with the walls...

07H: WAKE UP

22H: LIGHTS OUT

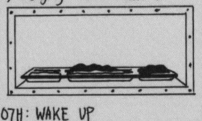

where the distinction between an individual's body and self becomes indistinguishable

from the individual cell itself.

STATE CONTROL

The penitentiary was born of a modern desire for more efficient punishment, likewise modern housing was defined by functionalism. Existenzminimum (subsistence dwelling) became a design sensibility that sought the highest comfort through the most efficient means. Since then, the logic of the minimum has permeated the design of our world. The bare minimum becomes regulation. It is standardized, measured in time, dollars, material, and energy.

minimum energy *minimum home*

PRISON MULT. OCCUPANCY
A = 3.7M²/PERSON
V = 7.3M³/PERSON
NATURAL LIGHT = 0.015M²/PERSON
OR NO OPENING LARGER THAN 0.13M

PRISON DORMITORY
A = 2.0M²/PERSON
V = 3.5M³/PERSON
NATURAL LIGHT = 0.015M²/PERSON
OR NO OPENING LARGER THAN 0.13M.

PRISON SINGLE OCCUPANCY
A = 4.6M²/PERSON
V = 9.0M³/PERSON
NATURAL LIGHT = 0.015M²/PERSON
OR NO OPENING LARGER THAN 0.13M

PRISON SHARED BUNK
A = 2.5M²/PERSON
V = 4.9M³/PERSON
NATURAL LIGHT = 0.015M²/PERSON
OR NO OPENING LARGER THAN 0.13M

EMERGENCY SHELTER
A = 3.5M²/PERSON
V = 3.4M³/PERSON

EMERGENCY CAMP
A = 3.5M²/PERSON
V = 0.17M³/PERSON

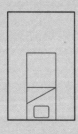 

HOSPITAL SINGLE ROOM
A = 8.1M²/PERSON
V = 15.8M³/PERSON
NATURAL LIGHT = 0.81M²/PERSON

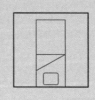 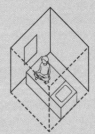

HOSPITAL CUBICLE
A = 6.1M²/PERSON
V = 11.9M³/PERSON
NATURAL LIGHT = 0.61M²/PERSON

STATE CONTROL

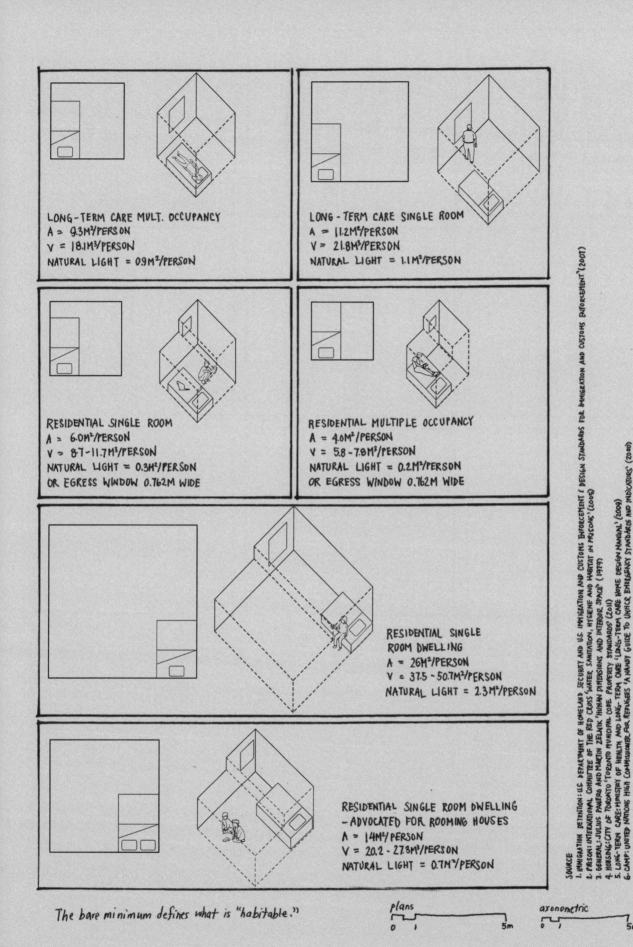

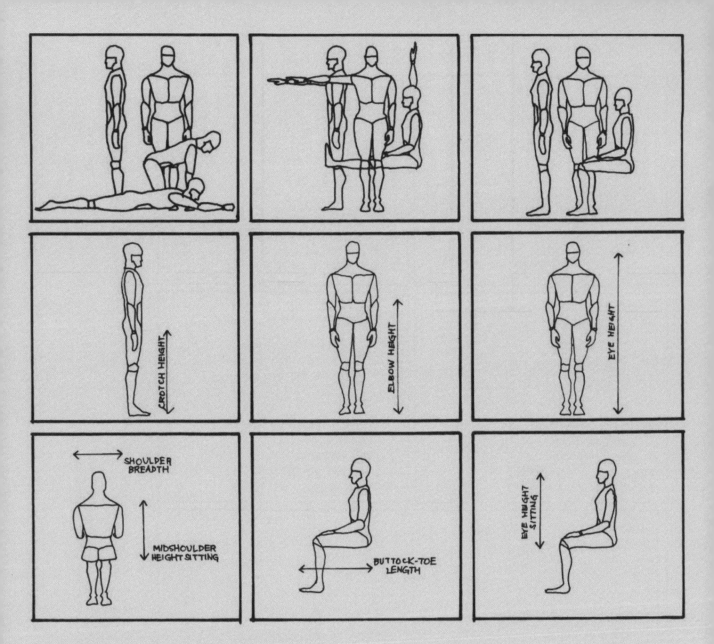

Accordingly, the modern cell is based on the idea of the modern individual, the minimum social unit to which everything is scaled. From the automobile to the micro-condominium, the secure housing unit to the hospital cubicle, our bodies are standardized and our needs, quantified.

The minimum habitable space for an incarcerated individual is measured.

   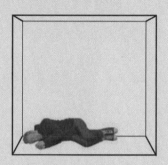

2 square metres of floor area

and 3.5 cubic metre of air space.

In this volume, the contents of your life are caged. But not every human action can be programmed or predicted. Our bodies always find ways to carve out space, to refocus our attention from the geometry to the lived experience, from the container to the contained.

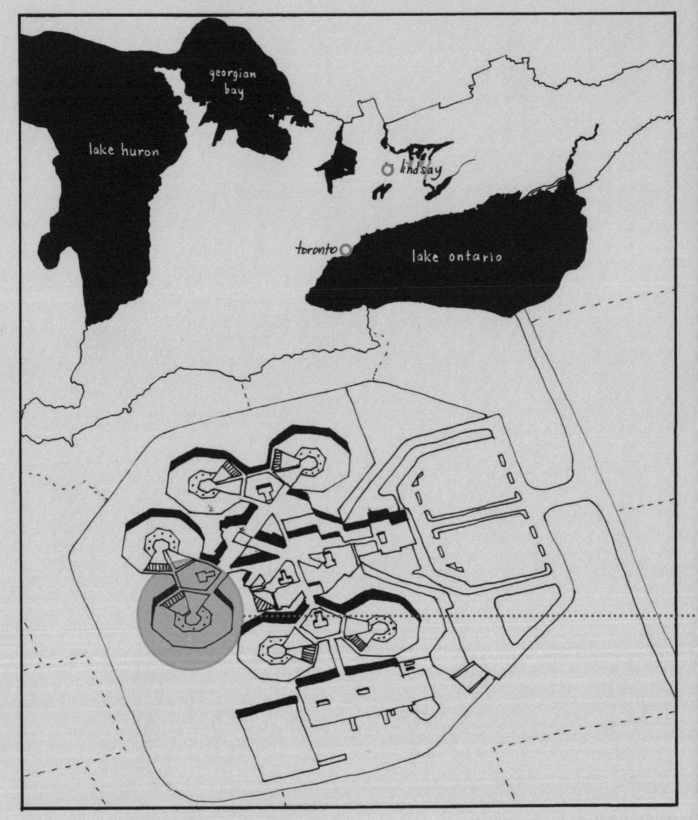

On September 17th, 2013, 191 detainees in Central East Correctional Centre in Lindsay, Ontario took the largest known collective action among immigration detainees.

STATE CONTROL

One of the detainees who was on hunger strike for over 60 days said, "Whatever it takes, we will do it."

PARANGOLÉ

ISSUE N°1 2021 MOTHERLAND

Editor-in-chief

Alfredo Brillembourg

Guest editors

Synne Bergby and Ida Zeline Lien

English edition

268 pages, 168 photos, 60 illustrations;
28 x 20 cm   ISBN 978-3-7757-5030-1

©2021 for the reproduced articles by

Nishat Awan, Naseem Badiey, Synne Bergby, Bjørn Enge Bertelsen, Charlot Boonekamp, Alfredo Brillembourg, Karen Büscher, Marielly Casanova, Tings Chak, Teddy Cruz, Christian Doll, Fonna Forman, Bjørnar Haveland, Manuel Herz, Alexis Kalagas, Irit Katz, Caroline Wanjiku Kihato, Are John Knudsen, Milena Gomez Kopp, Jonas König, Loren B. Landau, Ida Zeline Lien, Wooldy Edson Louidor, Aya Musmar, Lucas Oesch, Xavier Ribas, Juan Francisco Saldarriaga, Daniel Schwartz, Mandisi Di Sindo, Kai Vöckler, Michael Waldrep.

©2021 for the reproduced photographs by

Iwan Baan, Naseem Badiey, Synne Bergby, Bjørn Enge Bertelsen, Lorena Branks, Alfredo Brillembourg, Tamas Buynovszky, Karen Büscher, George Castellanos, Andre Cypriano, Christian Doll, Dràpen i Havet, Estudio Teddy Cruz + Fonna Forman, Bjørnar Haveland, Irit Katz, Jonas Koenig, Paul Kranzler, Milena Gomez Kopp, Ida Zeline Lien, Jona Maier, Lucas Oesch, Klearjos Papanicolau, Sergey Ponomarev, Ronald Rael, Jan Ras, Xavier Ribas, Daniel Schwartz, Mandisi Di Sindo, Marco Tiberio, Ververidis Vasilis / Shutterstock.com, Donovan Wiley.

©2021 for the reproduced illustrations by

Tahira Al-Raisi, Marwa al-Sabouni, Facundo Arboit, Tings Chak, Estudio Teddy Cruz + Fonna Forman, Bjørnar Haveland, Tan Ke, Nidal Majeed, Manuel Herz Architects, Juan Francisco Saldarriaga, Irhana Šehović, Ebru Sen, Urban-Think Tank, Xinfei Zhao, Zhuoying Wang, Ziwei Liu.

©2021 for the reproduced projects and exhibits by

Border Materialities design studio, EOOS, Bouchra Khalili, Fondazione Nicola Trussardi, Urban-Think Tank

Acknowledgements

Maria Burasovskaya, Micola Brambilla, Massimiliano Gioni, Charles Hailey, Markus Heibo, Marwa al-Sabouni.

Disclaimer

Parangolé has contacted copyright holders of the images presented. If you claim ownership over images used and have not been properly identified, please contact us and we will be sure to make a formal acknowledgement in a future issue.

We hope you will support and stock Parangolé.

Distributed worldwide by

Hatje Cantz Verlag GmbH
Mommsenstr. 27
10629 Berlin
Germany

Produced and published by

Gran Horizonte Media GmbH
c/o Barandun AG
Mühlebachstr. 25
P.O. Box 757
CH-8024 Zurich
Switzerland

Printed in Czech Republic by

Graspo CZ Inc.